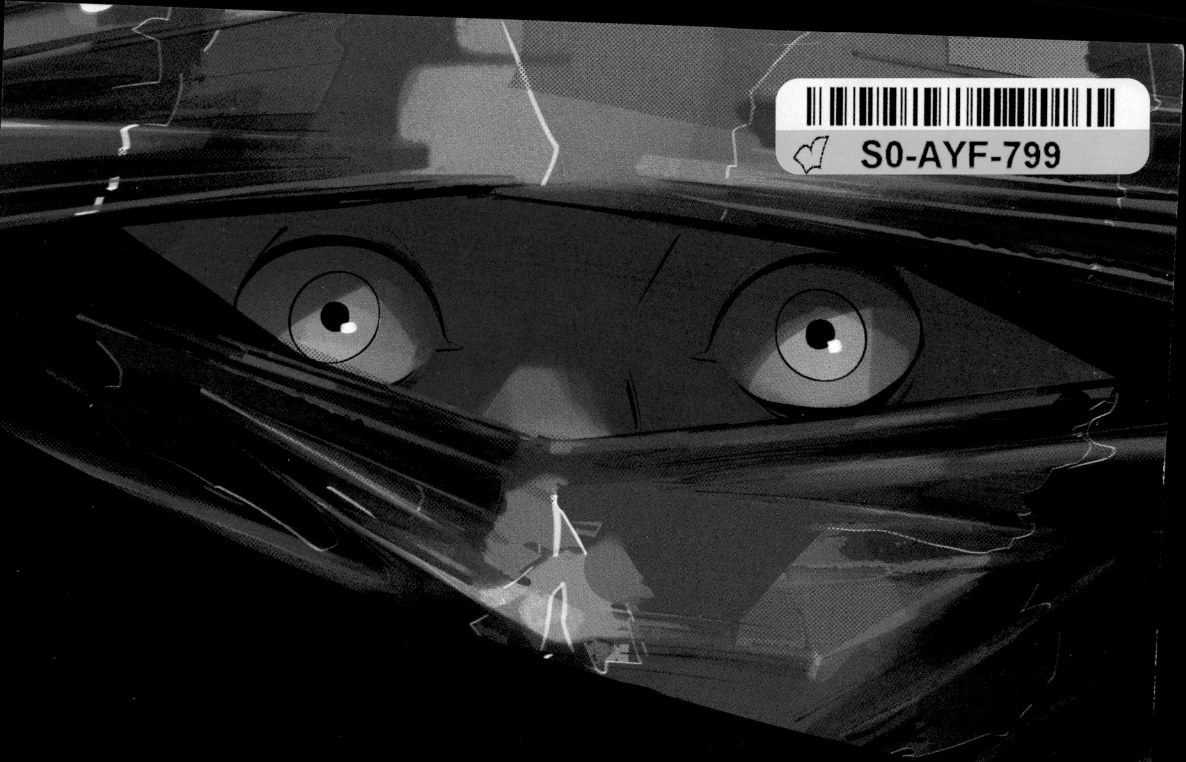

SHOPLIFTERS WILL BE LIQUIDATED™

PATRICK KINDLON

STEFANO SIMONE

HASSAN OTSMANE-ELHAOU

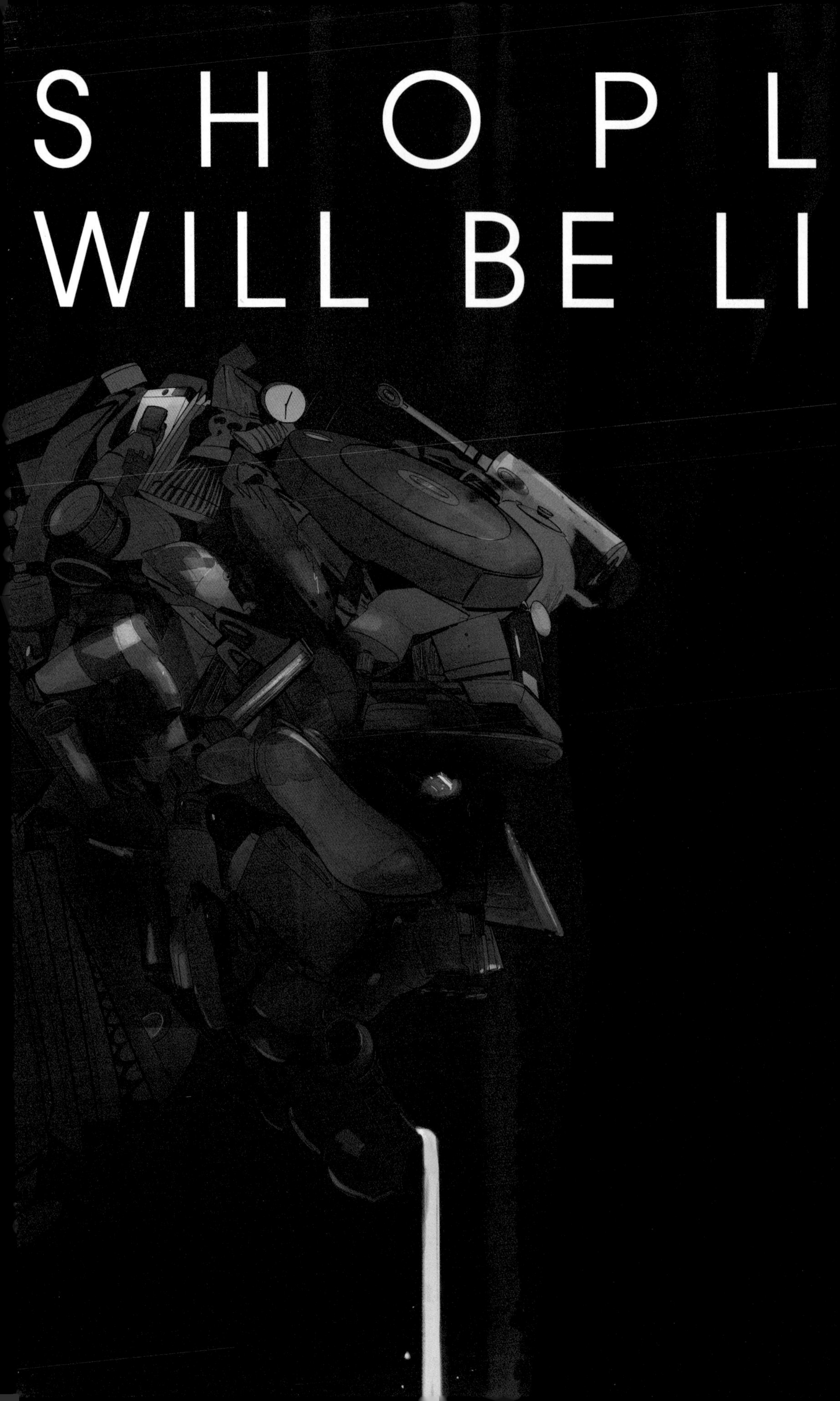
S H O P L
WILL BE LI

IFTERS™
QUIDATED

PATRICK KINDLON co-creator & writer

STEFANO SIMONE co-creator, artist & colorist

HASSAN OTSMANE-ELHAOU letterer

STEFANO SIMONE front & original series covers

ANTONIO FUSO variant cover

CHARLES PRITCHETT logo designer

COREY BREEN book designer

MIKE MARTS editor

AFTERSHOCK™

MIKE MARTS - Editor-in-Chief • JOE PRUETT - Publisher/CCO • LEE KRAMER - President • JON KRAMER - Chief Executive Officer
STEVE ROTTERDAM - SVP, Sales & Marketing • DAN SHIRES - VP, Film & Television UK • CHRISTINA HARRINGTON - Managing Editor
MARC HAMMOND - Sr. Retail Sales Development Manager • RUTHANN THOMPSON - Sr. Retailer Relations Manager • KATHERINE JAMISON - Marketing Manager
BLAKE STOCKER - Director of Finance • AARON MARION - Publicist • LISA MOODY - Finance • RYAN CARROLL - Development Coordinator
JAWAD QURESHI - Technology Advisor/Strategist • CHARLES PRITCHETT - Comics Production • COREY BREEN - Collections Production
TEDDY LEO - Editorial Assistant • STEPHANIE CASEBIER & SARAH PRUETT - Publishing Assistants

AfterShock Logo Design by COMICRAFT
Publicity: contact AARON MARION (aaron@publichausagency.com) & RYAN CROY (ryan@publichausagency.com) at PUBLICHAUS
Special thanks to: ATOM! FREEMAN, IRA KURGAN, MARINE KSADZHIKYAN, & ANTONIA LIANOS

First Printing: September 2020. 10 9 8 7 6 5 4 3 2 1

AFTERSHOCKCOMICS.COM Follow us on social media

HELLO, SHOPPERS!

Hope this finds you well. 2020 has offered some challenges to brick and mortar businesses, and many of you might be tempted to use mail-order. We here at Caucasus Brands understand your concerns. But we assure you our antiseptic, tidy, *safe* retail outlets are still the best possible shopping experience.

And to get you in the door, we're offering our everyday discount prices on AGGRESSIVE SATIRE, EXPRESSIVE CARTOONING and ROLLICKING FUN.

Savvy shoppers take note: we've bundled those items in the trade paperback collection you hold in your hands! Truly there is no better conduit of DARK COMEDY, ACTION and CHARACTER EXPLORATION than the paper device you are currently eyeballing! And for such a reasonable price, it seems practically *criminal* to pass it up!

It can't be overstated that in this time of great political and social change we all need some constants in our lives. Caucasus is that constant. That reliable friend who sells you everything you need, at consistently deep discounts, who would never betray your patronage or undervalue your role in the well-oiled machine that is our corporate family.

Caucasus is the brother-in-law who hires you when you get out of prison. Caucasus is the aunt who lets you live in her basement until you get back on your feet. The mom who dips into her retirement to finance your ill-advised new business venture! Our dedication to your shopping dollar is truly thicker than water.

Proud to be servicing you. Today, tomorrow and for all your time on Earth.

Everyday low prices. Everyday high spirits. *That's the Caucasus promise.*

PATRICK KINDLON
Co-Creator SHOPLIFTERS WILL BE LIQUIDATED
Co-VP of Paper Novelties, Caucasus Brands Unlimited
July 2020

1

WORKPLACE INJURY

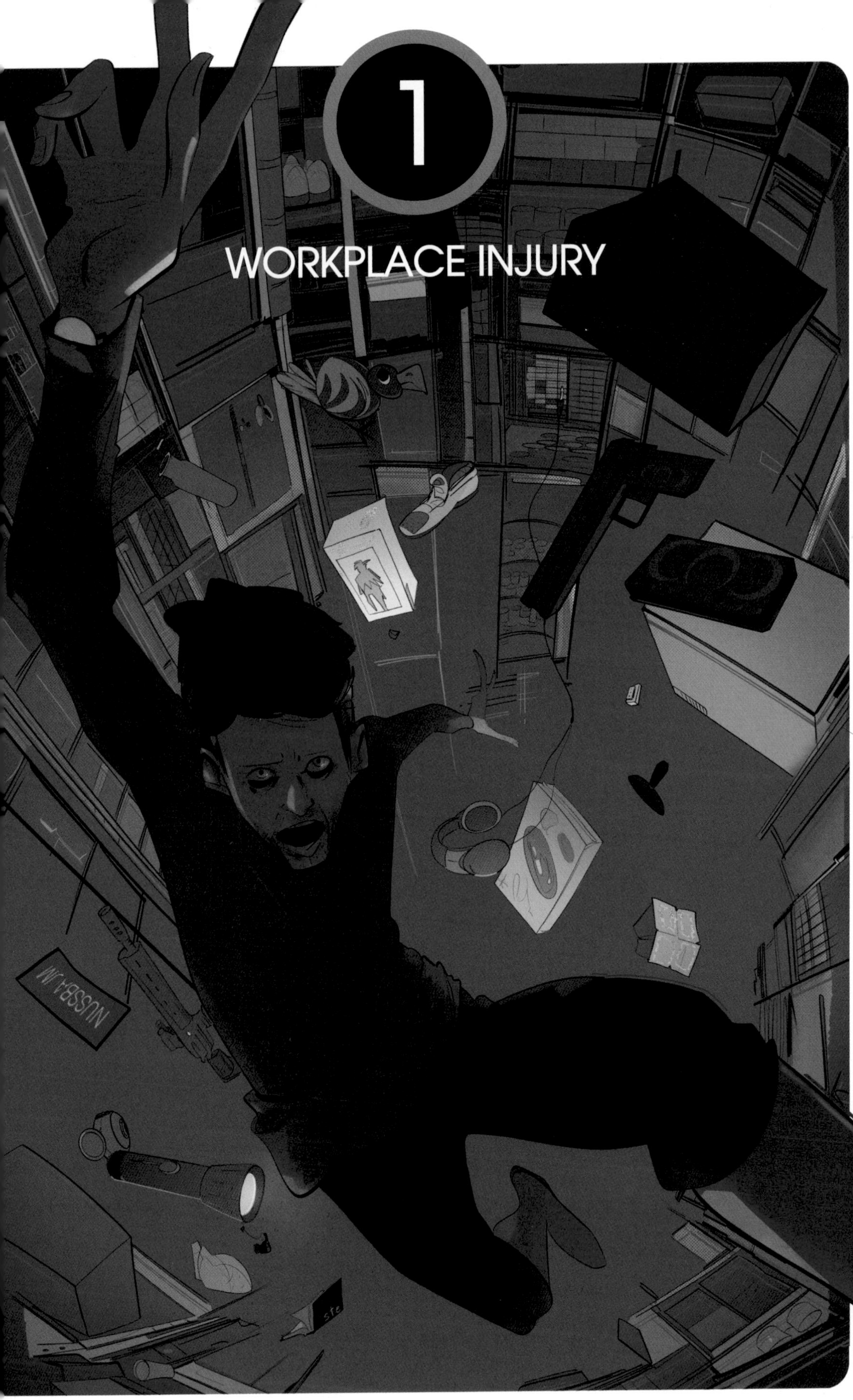

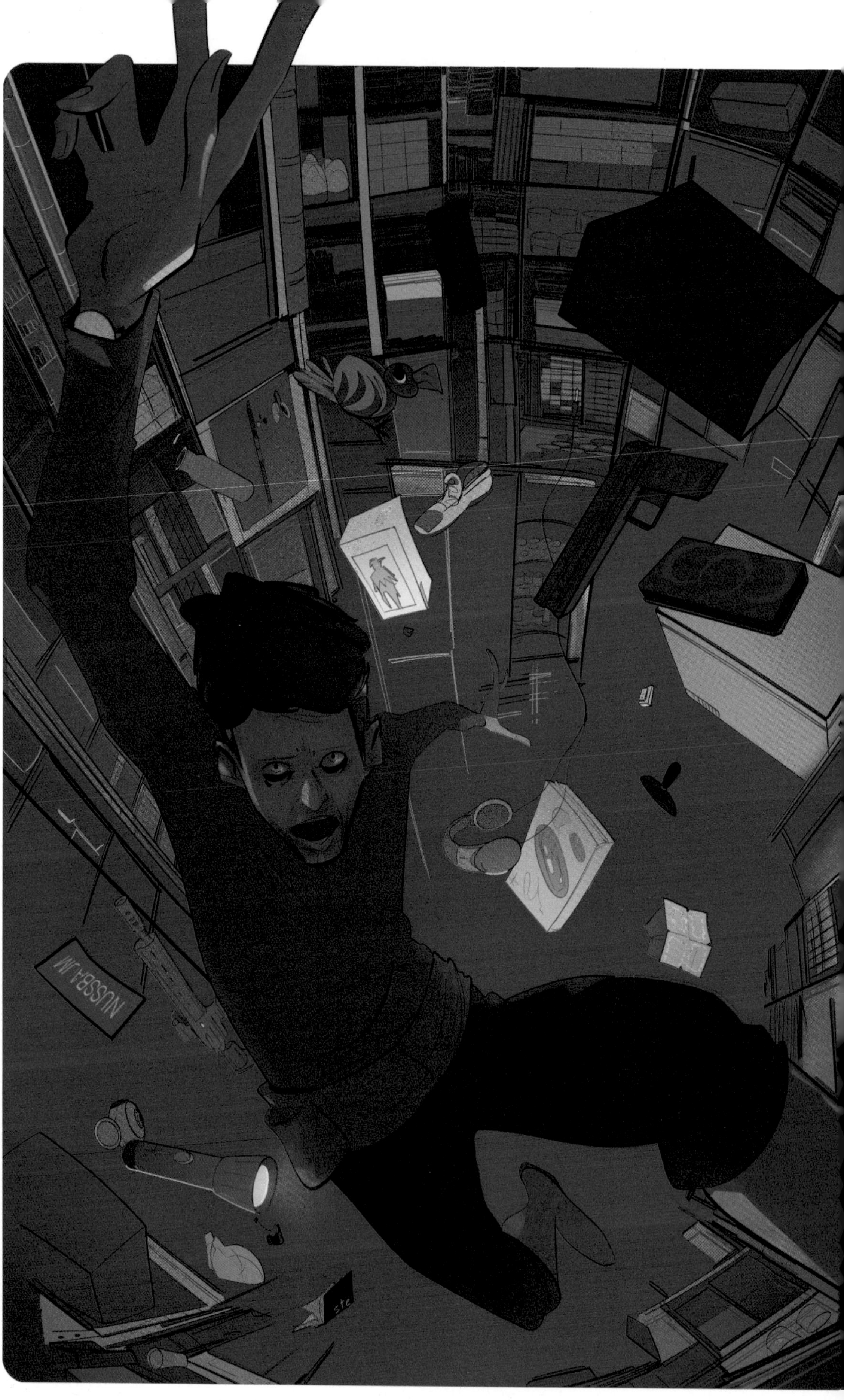
NUSSBAUM

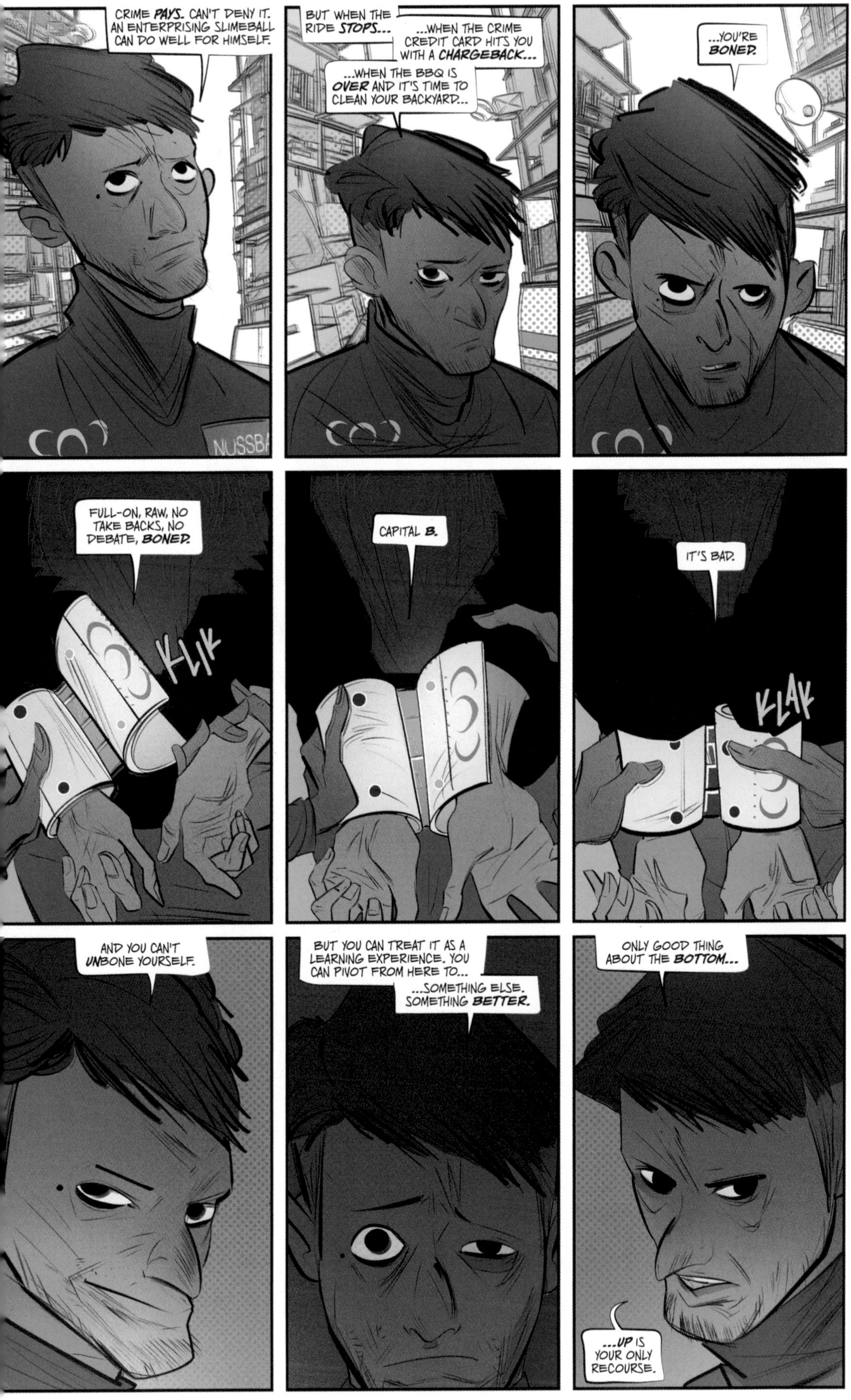

CRIME PAYS. CAN'T DENY IT. AN ENTERPRISING SLIMEBALL CAN DO WELL FOR HIMSELF.
NUSSBA
BUT WHEN THE RIDE STOPS...
...WHEN THE CRIME CREDIT CARD HITS YOU WITH A CHARGEBACK...
...WHEN THE BBQ IS OVER AND IT'S TIME TO CLEAN YOUR BACKYARD...
...YOU'RE BONED.
FULL-ON, RAW, NO TAKE BACKS, NO DEBATE, BONED.
KLIK
CAPITAL B.
IT'S BAD.
KLAK
AND YOU CAN'T UNBONE YOURSELF.
BUT YOU CAN TREAT IT AS A LEARNING EXPERIENCE. YOU CAN PIVOT FROM HERE TO...
...SOMETHING ELSE. SOMETHING BETTER.
ONLY GOOD THING ABOUT THE BOTTOM...
...UP IS YOUR ONLY RECOURSE.

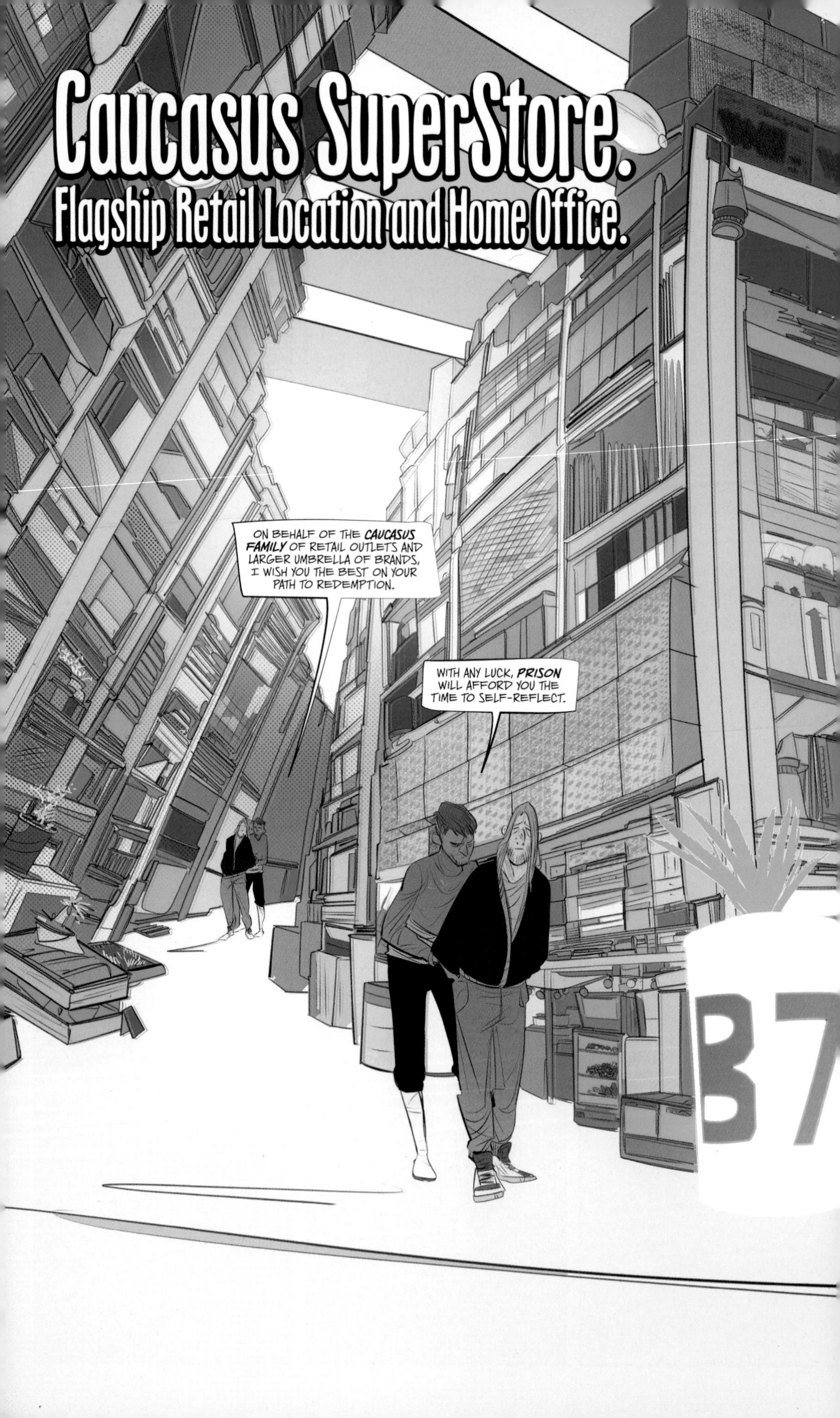
Caucasus SuperStore.
Flagship Retail Location and Home Office.
ON BEHALF OF THE CAUCASUS FAMILY OF RETAIL OUTLETS AND LARGER UMBRELLA OF BRANDS, I WISH YOU THE BEST ON YOUR PATH TO REDEMPTION.
WITH ANY LUCK, PRISON WILL AFFORD YOU THE TIME TO SELF-REFLECT.
B7

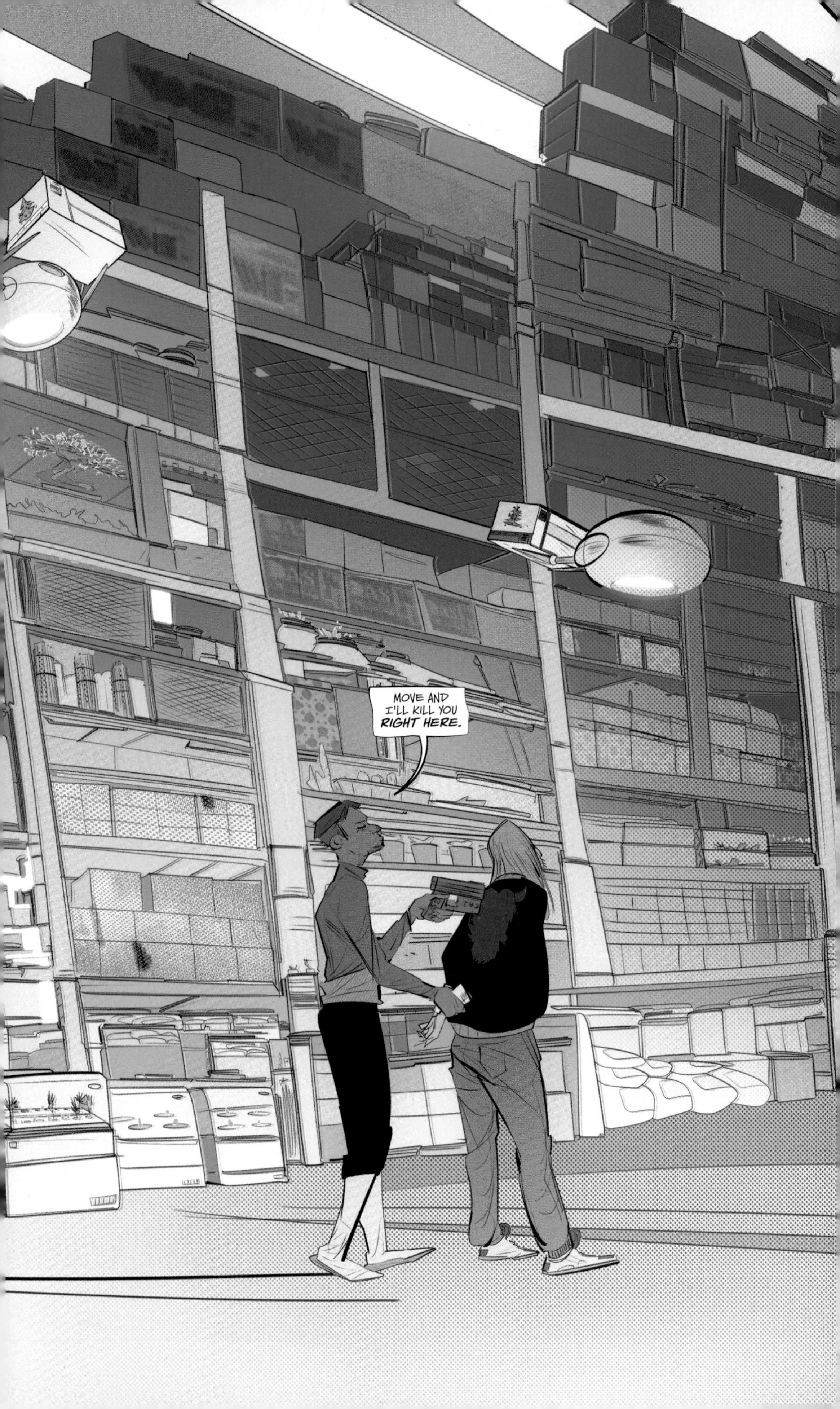
MOVE AND I'LL KILL YOU RIGHT HERE.

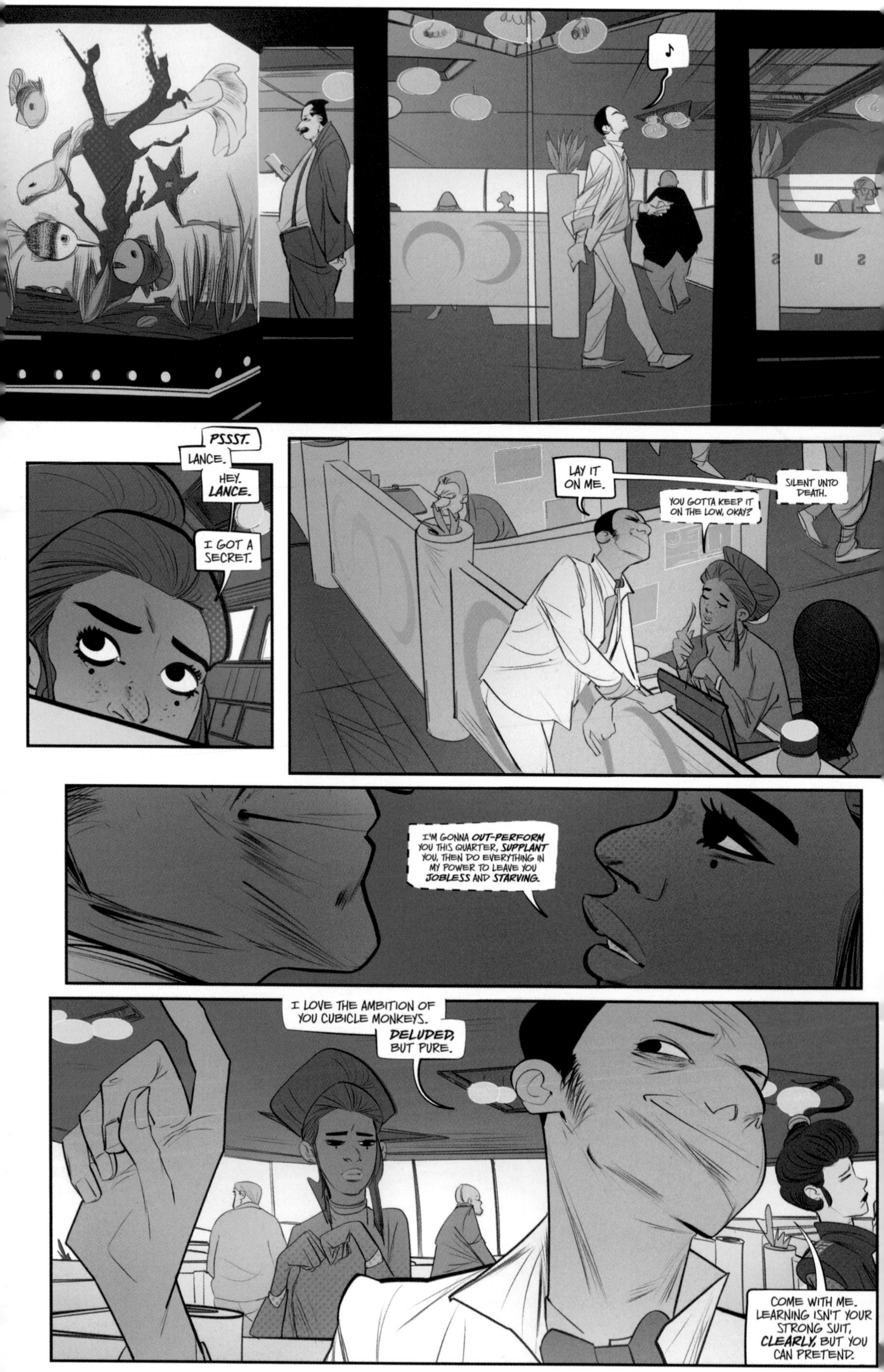
♪
PSSST.
LANCE.
HEY. LANCE.
I GOT A SECRET.
LAY IT ON ME.
SILENT UNTO DEATH.
YOU GOTTA KEEP IT ON THE LOW, OKAY?
I'M GONNA OUT-PERFORM YOU THIS QUARTER, SUPPLANT YOU, THEN DO EVERYTHING IN MY POWER TO LEAVE YOU JOBLESS AND STARVING.
I LOVE THE AMBITION OF YOU CUBICLE MONKEYS.
DELUDED, BUT PURE.
COME WITH ME. LEARNING ISN'T YOUR STRONG SUIT, CLEARLY, BUT YOU CAN PRETEND.

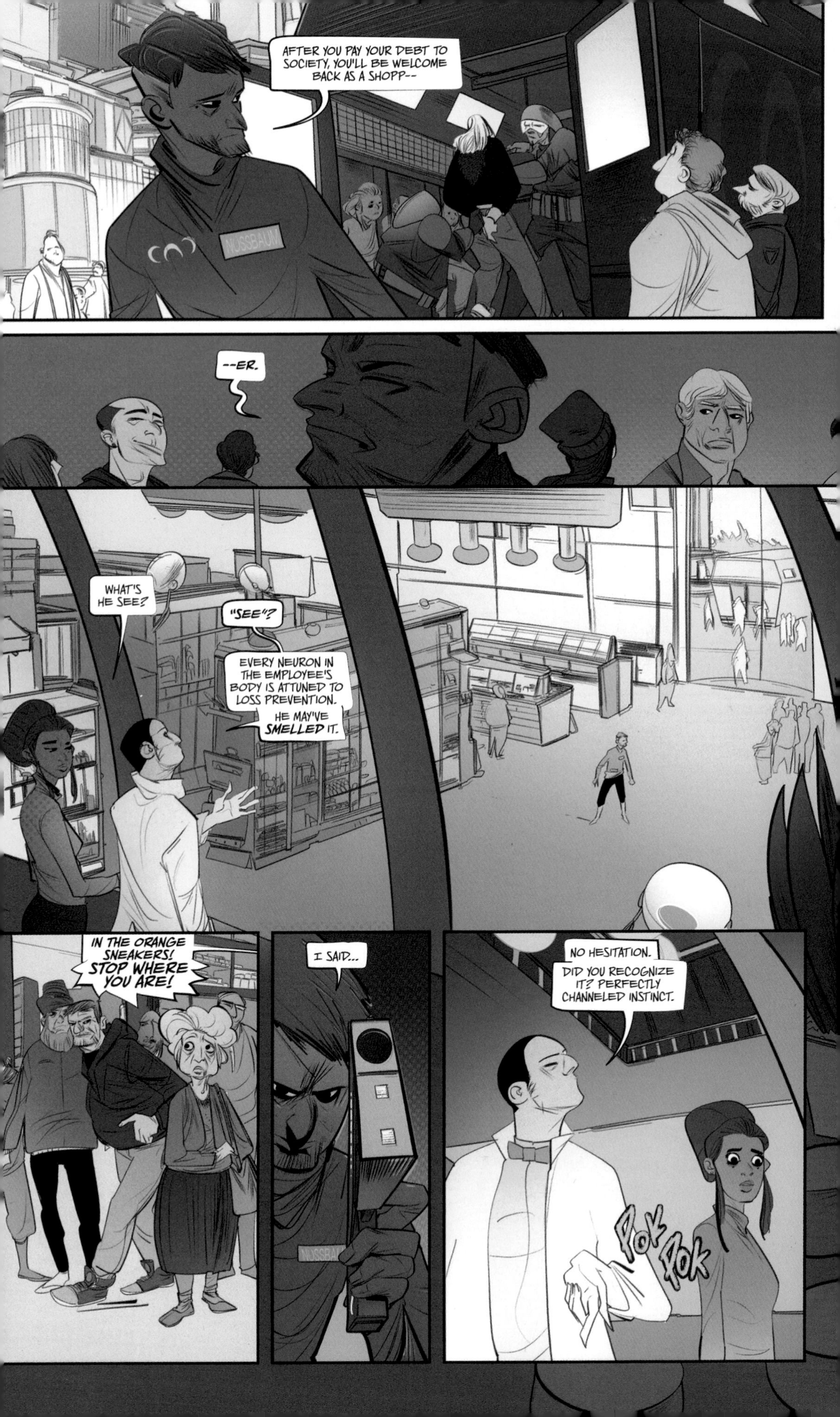
AFTER YOU PAY YOUR DEBT TO SOCIETY, YOU'LL BE WELCOME BACK AS A SHOPP--
NOSSBAUM
--ER.
WHAT'S HE SEE?
"SEE"?
EVERY NEURON IN THE EMPLOYEE'S BODY IS ATTUNED TO LOSS PREVENTION.
HE MAY'VE SMELLED IT.
IN THE ORANGE SNEAKERS! STOP WHERE YOU ARE!
I SAID...
NO HESITATION.
DID YOU RECOGNIZE IT? PERFECTLY CHANNELED INSTINCT.
POK POK

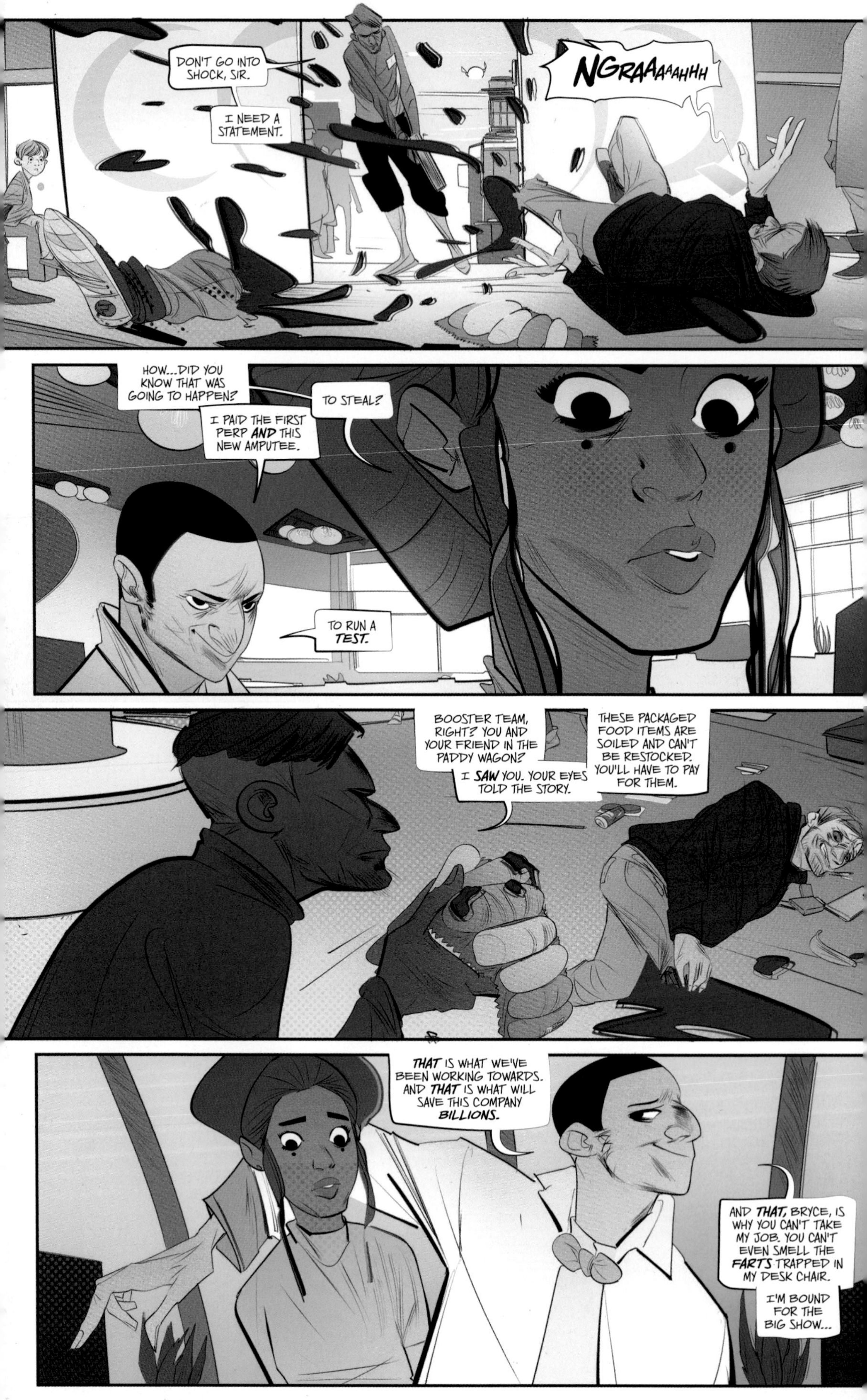
DON'T GO INTO SHOCK, SIR.
I NEED A STATEMENT.
NGRAAAAAHHH
HOW...DID YOU KNOW THAT WAS GOING TO HAPPEN?
TO STEAL?
I PAID THE FIRST PERP AND THIS NEW AMPUTEE.
TO RUN A TEST.
BOOSTER TEAM, RIGHT? YOU AND YOUR FRIEND IN THE PADDY WAGON?
I SAW YOU. YOUR EYES TOLD THE STORY.
THESE PACKAGED FOOD ITEMS ARE SOILED AND CAN'T BE RESTOCKED. YOU'LL HAVE TO PAY FOR THEM.
THAT IS WHAT WE'VE BEEN WORKING TOWARDS. AND THAT IS WHAT WILL SAVE THIS COMPANY BILLIONS.
AND THAT, BRYCE, IS WHY YOU CAN'T TAKE MY JOB. YOU CAN'T EVEN SMELL THE FARTS TRAPPED IN MY DESK CHAIR.
I'M BOUND FOR THE BIG SHOW...

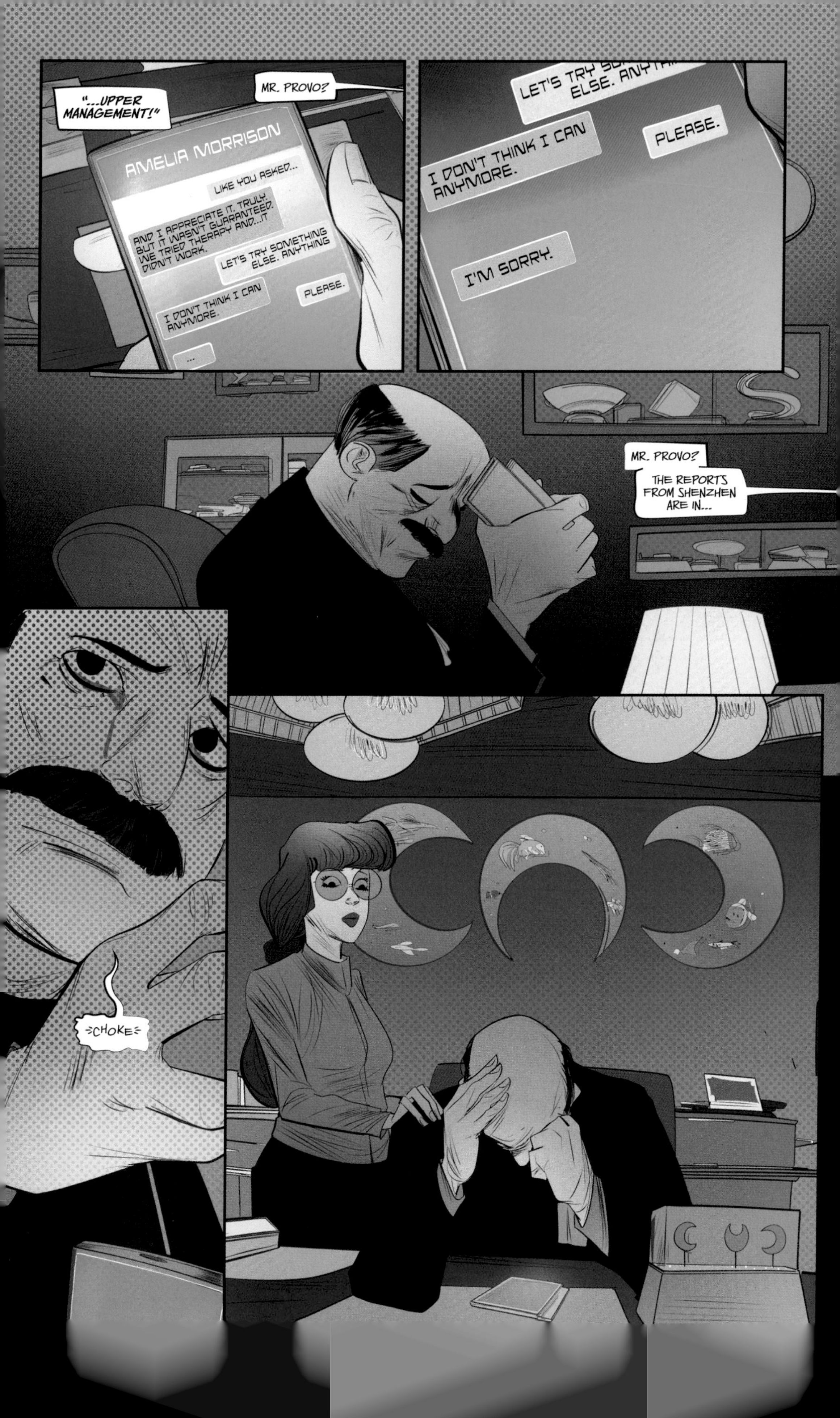
"...UPPER MANAGEMENT!"
MR. PROVO?
AMELIA MORRISON
LIKE YOU ASKED...
AND I APPRECIATE IT. TRULY. BUT IT WASN'T GUARANTEED. WE TRIED THERAPY AND...IT DIDN'T WORK.
LET'S TRY SOMETHING ELSE. ANYTHING
I DON'T THINK I CAN ANYMORE.
PLEASE.
...
I DON'T THINK I CAN ANYMORE.
PLEASE.
I'M SORRY.
MR. PROVO?
THE REPORTS FROM SHENZHEN ARE IN...
CHOKE

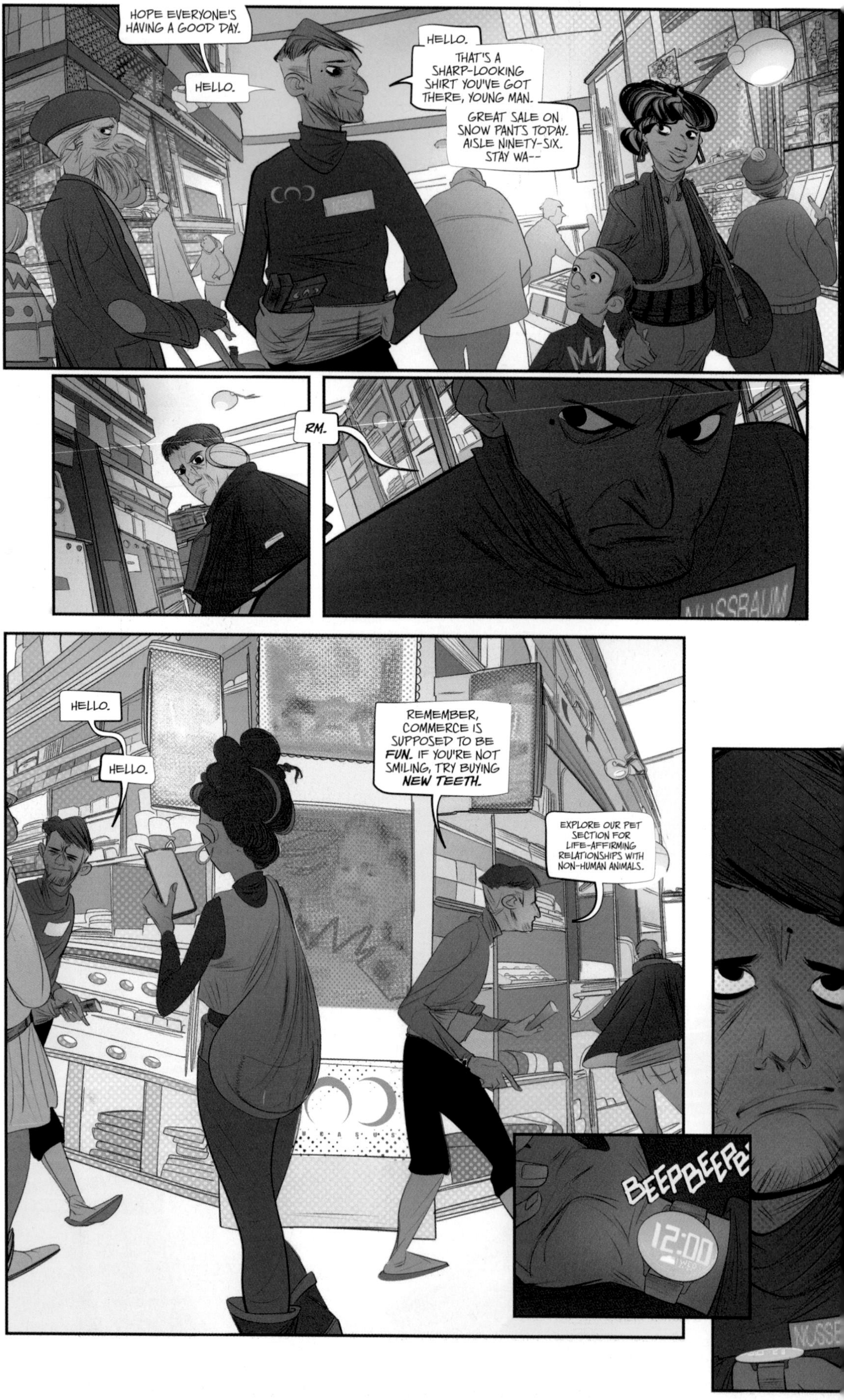
HOPE EVERYONE'S HAVING A GOOD DAY.
HELLO.
HELLO.
THAT'S A SHARP-LOOKING SHIRT YOU'VE GOT THERE, YOUNG MAN.
GREAT SALE ON SNOW PANTS TODAY. AISLE NINETY-SIX. STAY WA--
RM.
NUSSBAUM
HELLO.
HELLO.
REMEMBER, COMMERCE IS SUPPOSED TO BE FUN. IF YOU'RE NOT SMILING, TRY BUYING NEW TEETH.
EXPLORE OUR PET SECTION FOR LIFE-AFFIRMING RELATIONSHIPS WITH NON-HUMAN ANIMALS.
BEEPBEEPBE
12:00

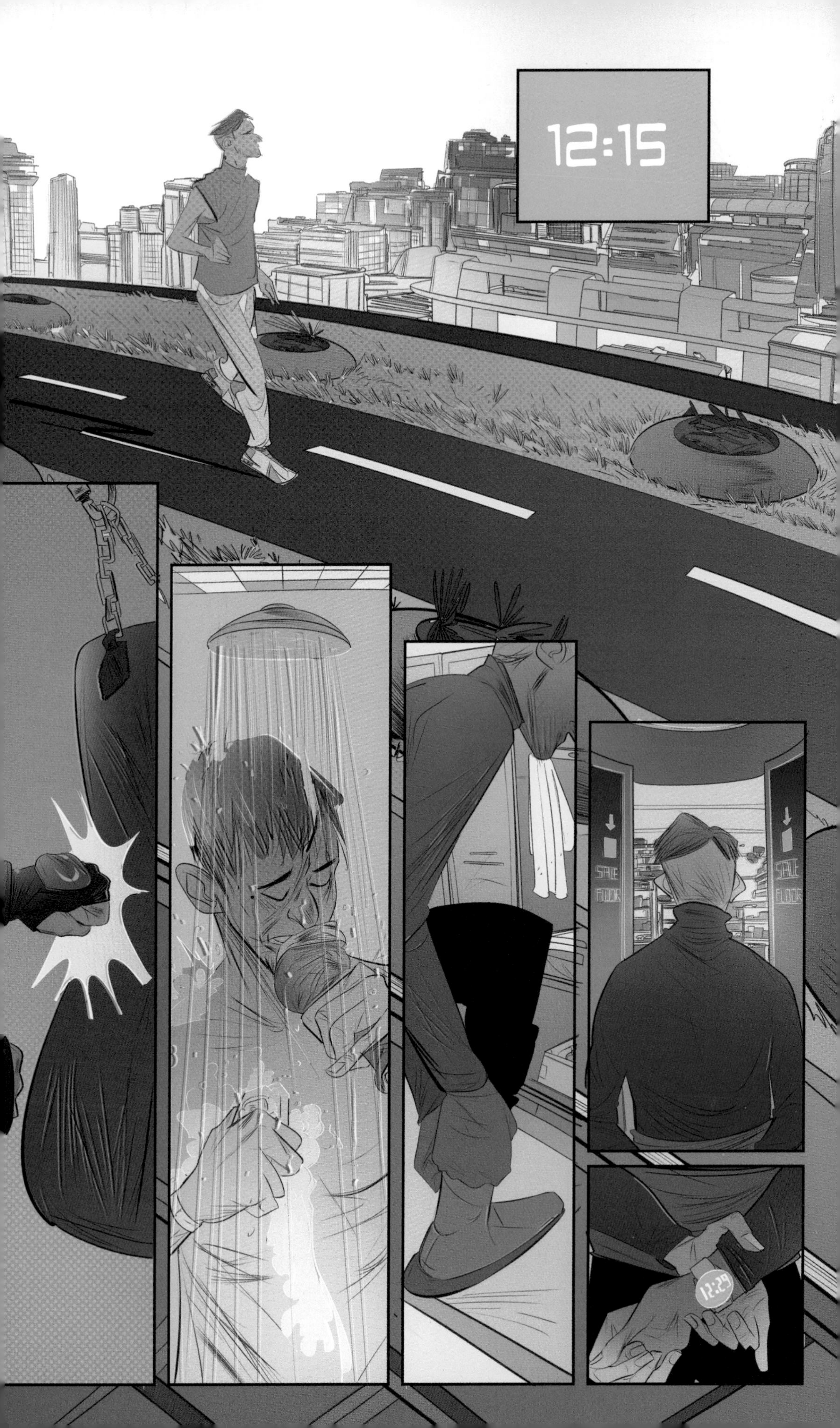

12:15
SAFE FLOOR
SAFE FLOOR
12:29

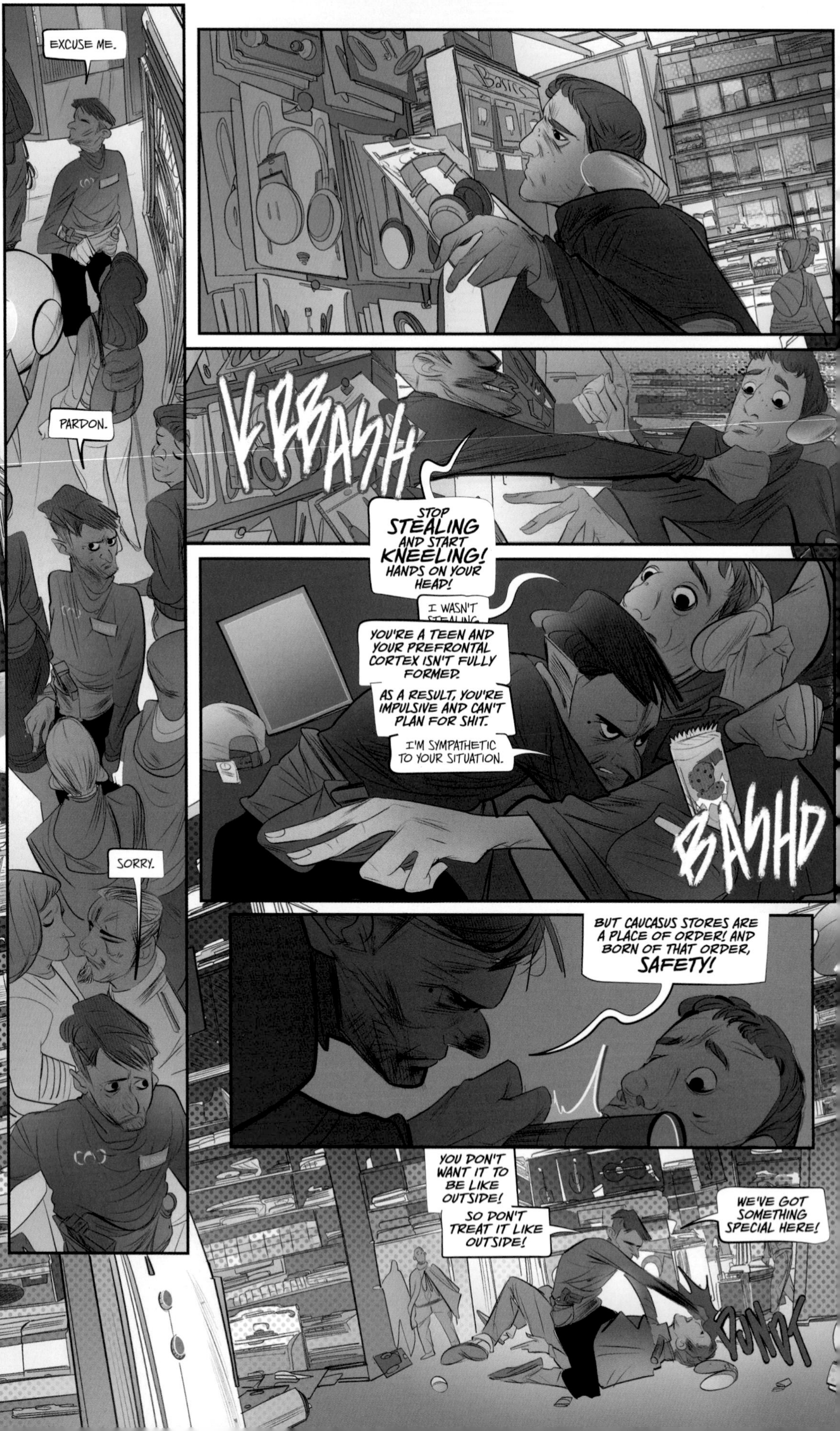

EXCUSE ME.
PARDON.
SORRY.
KRBASH
STOP STEALING AND START KNEELING! HANDS ON YOUR HEAD!
I WASN'T
YOU'RE A TEEN AND YOUR PREFRONTAL CORTEX ISN'T FULLY FORMED.
AS A RESULT, YOU'RE IMPULSIVE AND CAN'T PLAN FOR SHIT.
I'M SYMPATHETIC TO YOUR SITUATION.
BASHD
BUT CAUCASUS STORES ARE A PLACE OF ORDER! AND BORN OF THAT ORDER, SAFETY!
YOU DON'T WANT IT TO BE LIKE OUTSIDE!
SO DON'T TREAT IT LIKE OUTSIDE!
WE'VE GOT SOMETHING SPECIAL HERE!

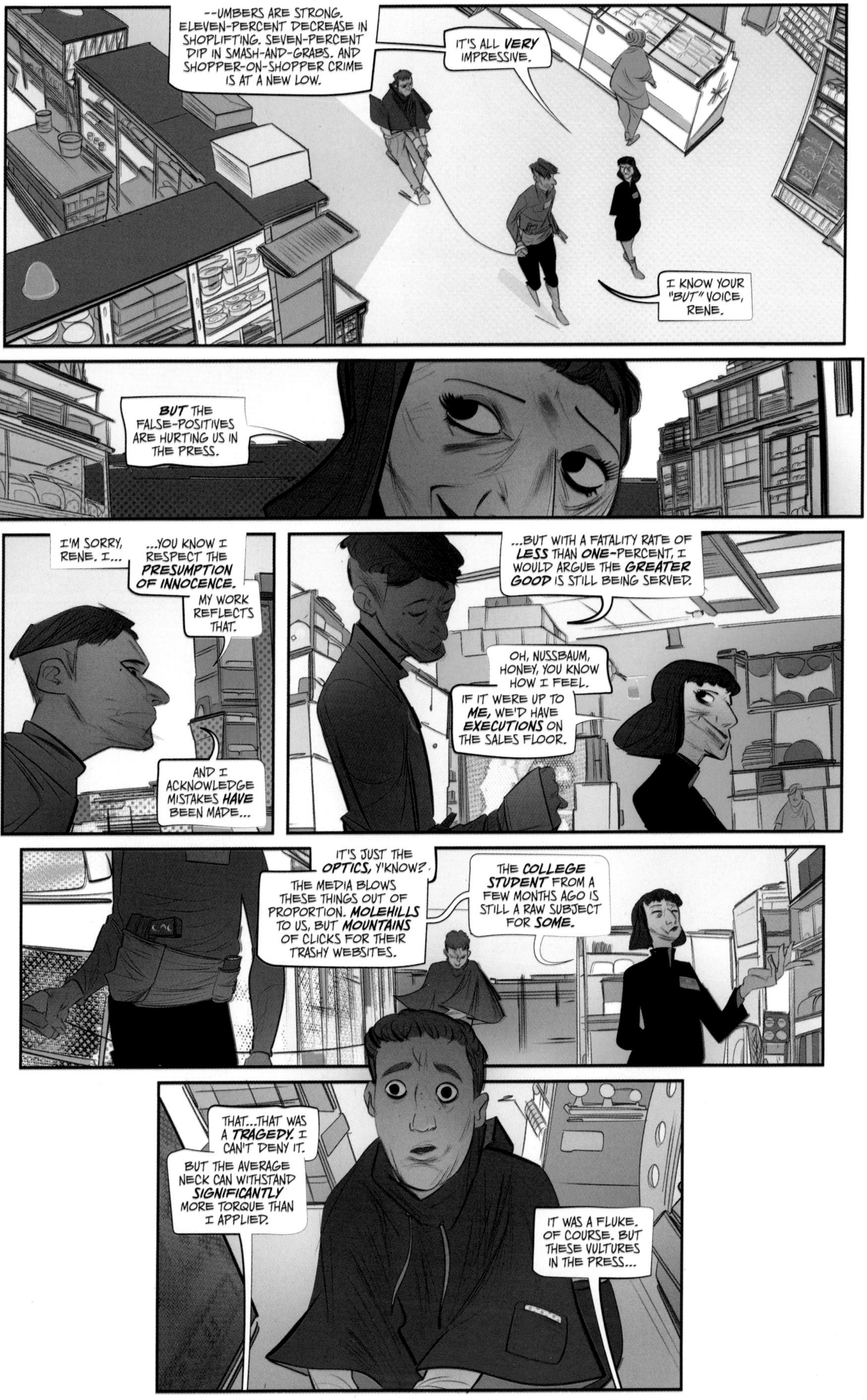
--UMBERS ARE STRONG. ELEVEN-PERCENT DECREASE IN SHOPLIFTING. SEVEN-PERCENT DIP IN SMASH-AND-GRABS. AND SHOPPER-ON-SHOPPER CRIME IS AT A NEW LOW.
IT'S ALL VERY IMPRESSIVE.
I KNOW YOUR "BUT" VOICE, RENE.
BUT THE FALSE-POSITIVES ARE HURTING US IN THE PRESS.
I'M SORRY, RENE. I...
...YOU KNOW I RESPECT THE PRESUMPTION OF INNOCENCE.
MY WORK REFLECTS THAT.
AND I ACKNOWLEDGE MISTAKES HAVE BEEN MADE...
...BUT WITH A FATALITY RATE OF LESS THAN ONE-PERCENT, I WOULD ARGUE THE GREATER GOOD IS STILL BEING SERVED.
OH, NUSSBAUM, HONEY, YOU KNOW HOW I FEEL.
IF IT WERE UP TO ME, WE'D HAVE EXECUTIONS ON THE SALES FLOOR.
IT'S JUST THE OPTICS, Y'KNOW?
THE MEDIA BLOWS THESE THINGS OUT OF PROPORTION. MOLEHILLS TO US, BUT MOUNTAINS OF CLICKS FOR THEIR TRASHY WEBSITES.
THE COLLEGE STUDENT FROM A FEW MONTHS AGO IS STILL A RAW SUBJECT FOR SOME.
THAT...THAT WAS A TRAGEDY. I CAN'T DENY IT.
BUT THE AVERAGE NECK CAN WITHSTAND SIGNIFICANTLY MORE TORQUE THAN I APPLIED.
IT WAS A FLUKE. OF COURSE. BUT THESE VULTURES IN THE PRESS...

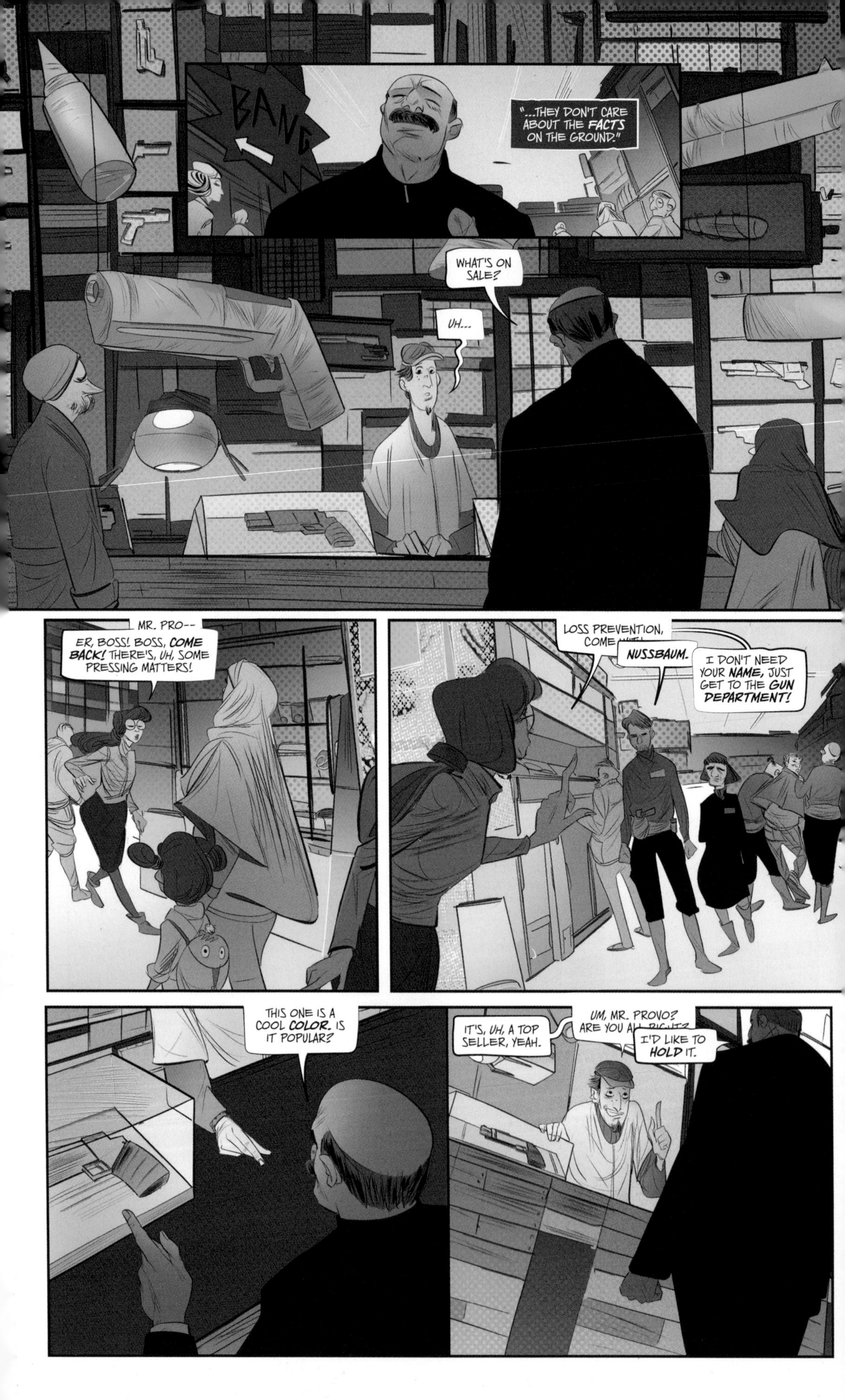

BANG
"...THEY DON'T CARE ABOUT THE FACTS ON THE GROUND."
WHAT'S ON SALE?
UH...
MR. PRO--
ER, BOSS! BOSS, COME BACK! THERE'S, UH, SOME PRESSING MATTERS!
LOSS PREVENTION, COME
NUSSBAUM.
I DON'T NEED YOUR NAME, JUST GET TO THE GUN DEPARTMENT!
THIS ONE IS A COOL COLOR. IS IT POPULAR?
IT'S, UH, A TOP SELLER, YEAH.
UM, MR. PROVO? ARE YOU
I'D LIKE TO HOLD IT.

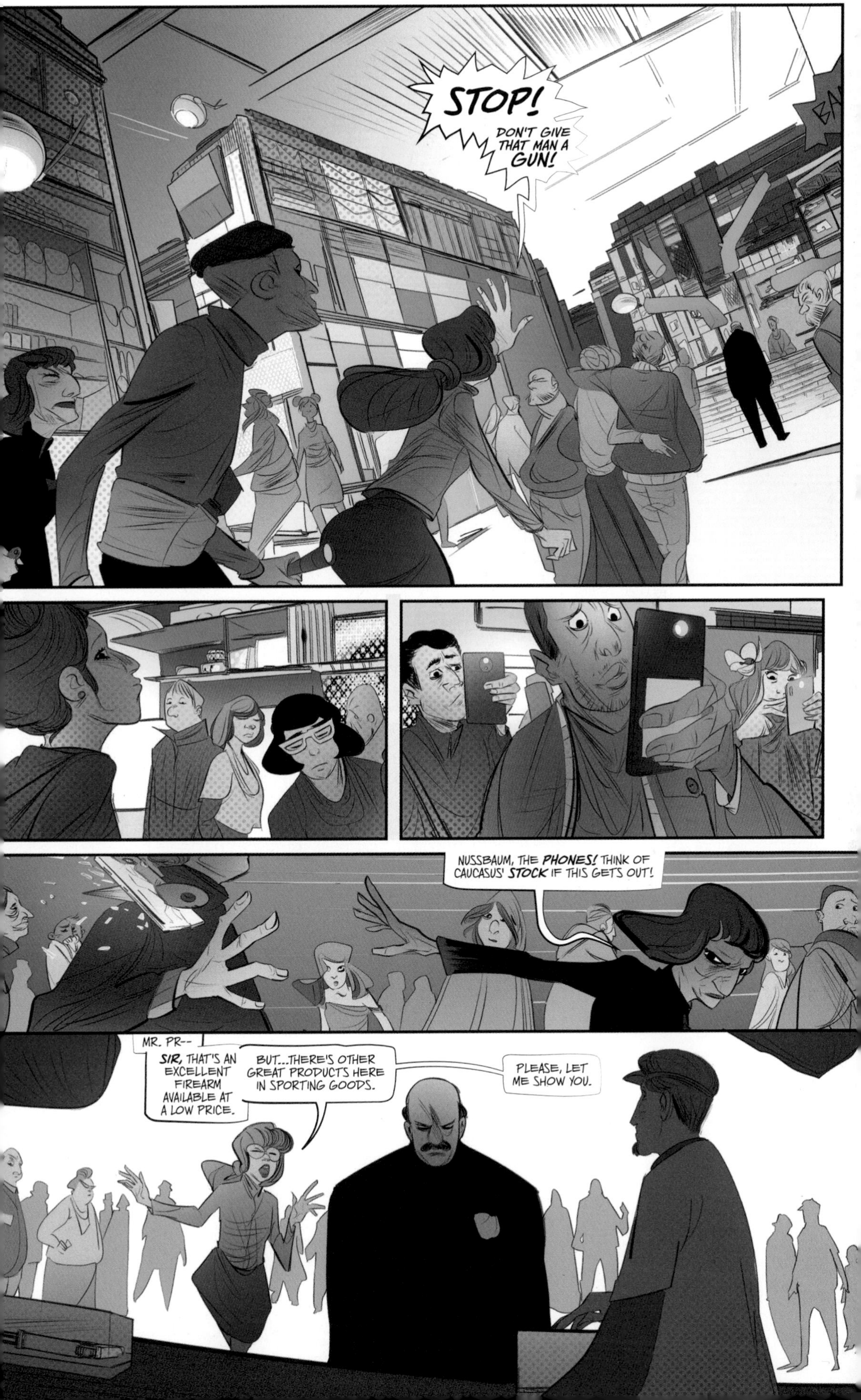

STOP!
DON'T GIVE THAT MAN A GUN!
BA
NUSSBAUM, THE PHONES! THINK OF CAUCASUS' STOCK IF THIS GETS OUT!
MR. PR--
SIR, THAT'S AN EXCELLENT FIREARM AVAILABLE AT A LOW PRICE.
BUT...THERE'S OTHER GREAT PRODUCTS HERE IN SPORTING GOODS.
PLEASE, LET ME SHOW YOU.

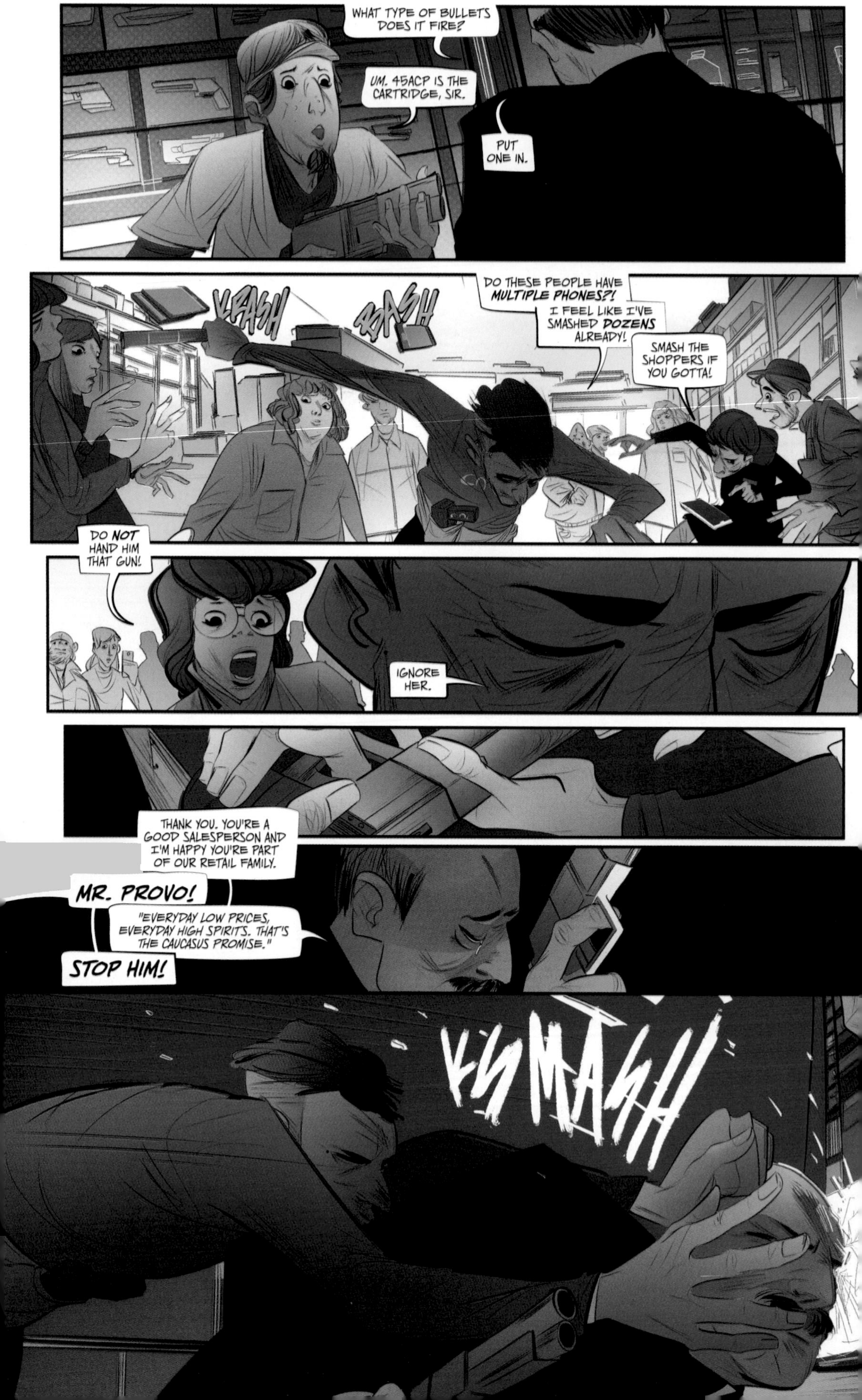
WHAT TYPE OF BULLETS DOES IT FIRE?
UM. 45ACP IS THE CARTRIDGE, SIR.
PUT ONE IN.
KRASH
SMASH
DO THESE PEOPLE HAVE MULTIPLE PHONES?!
I FEEL LIKE I'VE SMASHED DOZENS ALREADY!
SMASH THE SHOPPERS IF YOU GOTTA!
DO NOT HAND HIM THAT GUN!
IGNORE HER.
THANK YOU. YOU'RE A GOOD SALESPERSON AND I'M HAPPY YOU'RE PART OF OUR RETAIL FAMILY.
MR. PROVO!
"EVERYDAY LOW PRICES, EVERYDAY HIGH SPIRITS. THAT'S THE CAUCASUS PROMISE."
STOP HIM!
KSMASH

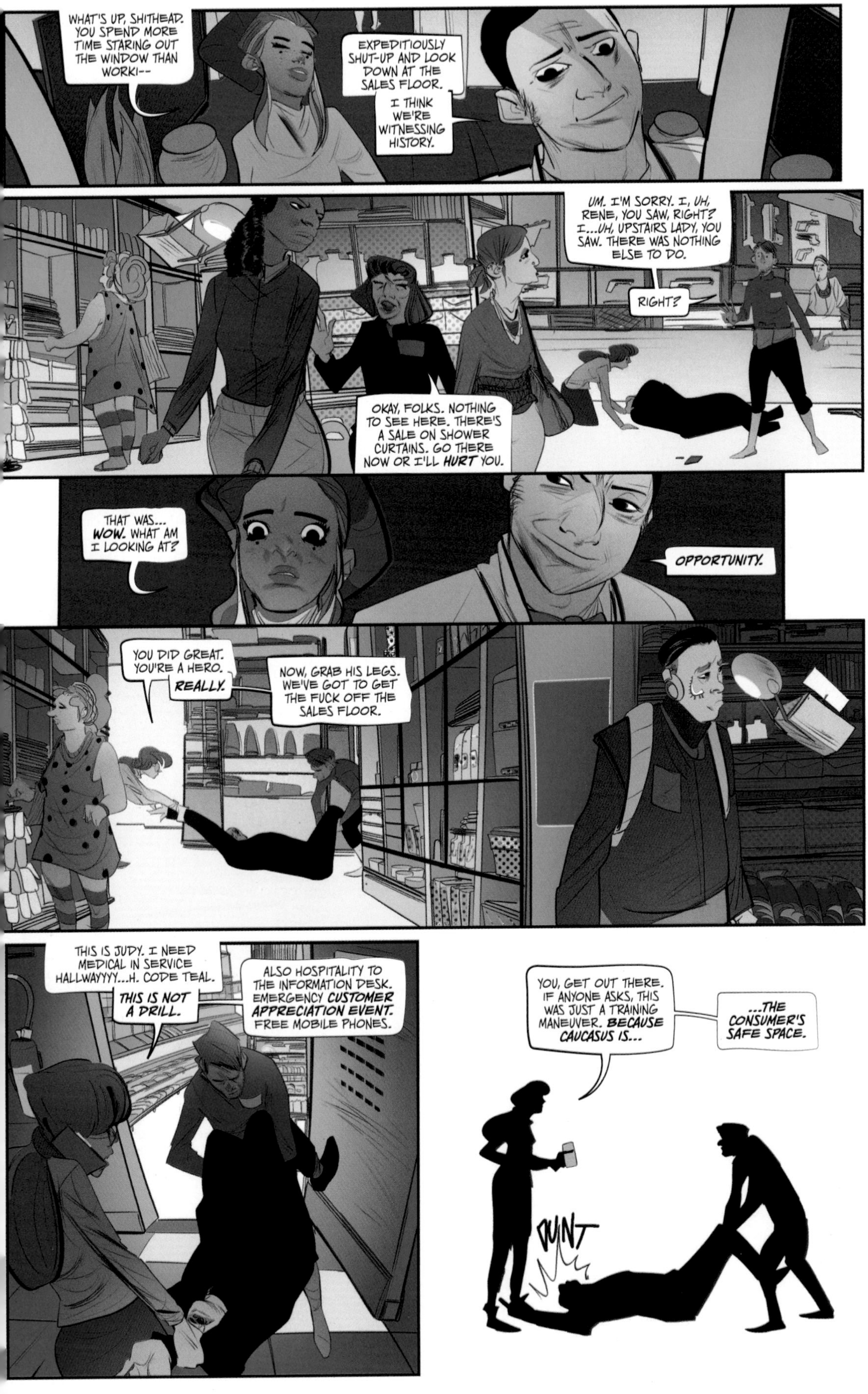
WHAT'S UP, SHITHEAD. YOU SPEND MORE TIME STARING OUT THE WINDOW THAN WORKI--
EXPEDITIOUSLY SHUT-UP AND LOOK DOWN AT THE SALES FLOOR.
I THINK WE'RE WITNESSING HISTORY.
UM. I'M SORRY. I, UH, RENE, YOU SAW, RIGHT? I...UH, UPSTAIRS LADY, YOU SAW. THERE WAS NOTHING ELSE TO DO.
RIGHT?
OKAY, FOLKS. NOTHING TO SEE HERE. THERE'S A SALE ON SHOWER CURTAINS. GO THERE NOW OR I'LL HURT YOU.
THAT WAS... WOW. WHAT AM I LOOKING AT?
OPPORTUNITY.
YOU DID GREAT. YOU'RE A HERO. REALLY.
NOW, GRAB HIS LEGS. WE'VE GOT TO GET THE FUCK OFF THE SALES FLOOR.
THIS IS JUDY. I NEED MEDICAL IN SERVICE HALLWAYYYY...H. CODE TEAL. THIS IS NOT A DRILL.
ALSO HOSPITALITY TO THE INFORMATION DESK. EMERGENCY CUSTOMER APPRECIATION EVENT. FREE MOBILE PHONES.
YOU, GET OUT THERE. IF ANYONE ASKS, THIS WAS JUST A TRAINING MANEUVER. BECAUSE CAUCASUS IS...
...THE CONSUMER'S SAFE SPACE.
DUNT

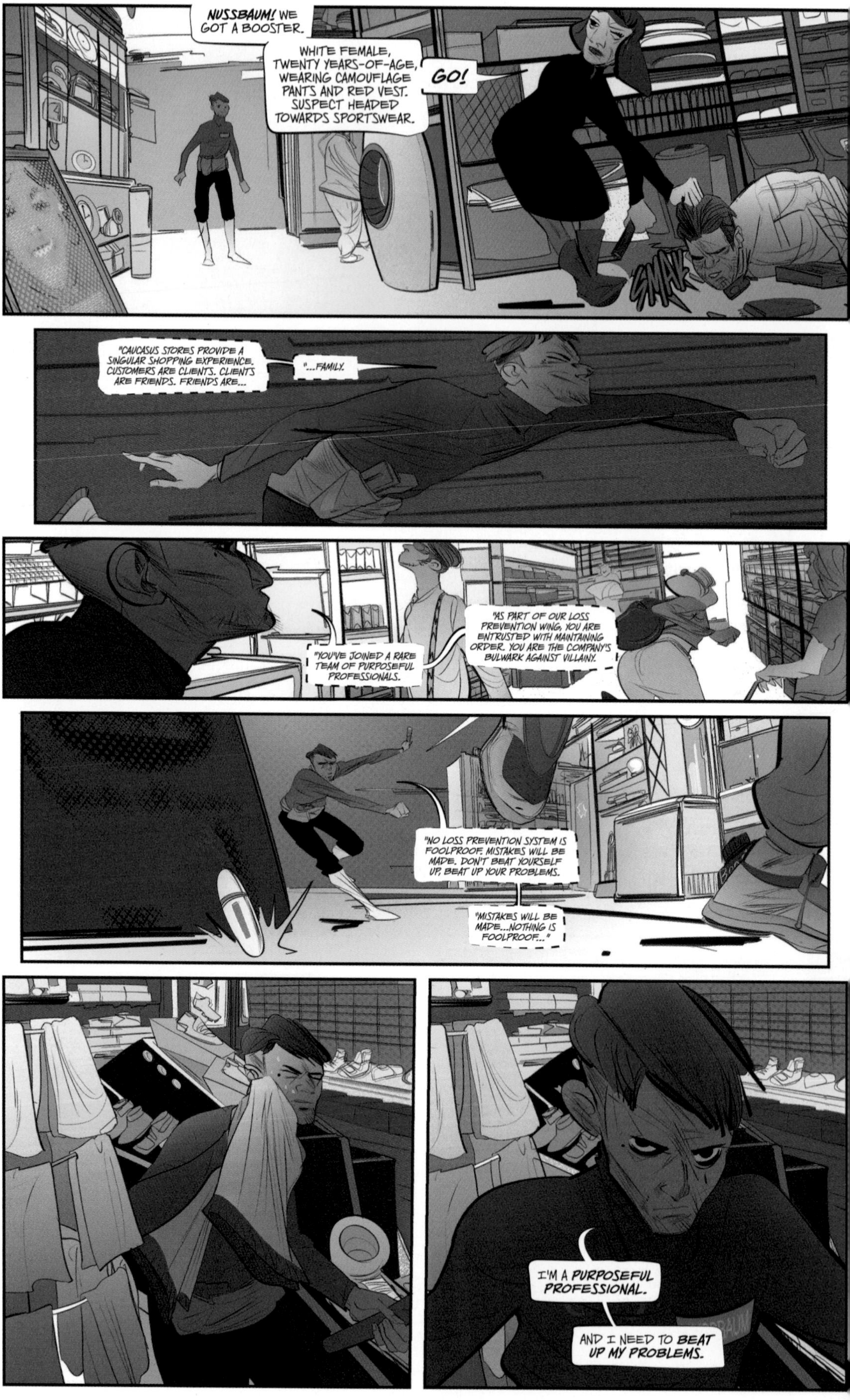
NUSSBAUM! WE GOT A BOOSTER.
WHITE FEMALE, TWENTY YEARS-OF-AGE, WEARING CAMOUFLAGE PANTS AND RED VEST. SUSPECT HEADED TOWARDS SPORTSWEAR.
GO!
"CAUCASUS STORES PROVIDE A SINGULAR SHOPPING EXPERIENCE. CUSTOMERS ARE CLIENTS. CLIENTS ARE FRIENDS. FRIENDS ARE...
"...FAMILY.
"YOU'VE JOINED A RARE TEAM OF PURPOSEFUL PROFESSIONALS.
"AS PART OF OUR LOSS PREVENTION WING, YOU ARE ENTRUSTED WITH MAINTAINING ORDER. YOU ARE THE COMPANY'S BULWARK AGAINST VILLAINY.
"NO LOSS PREVENTION SYSTEM IS FOOLPROOF. MISTAKES WILL BE MADE. DON'T BEAT YOURSELF UP, BEAT UP YOUR PROBLEMS.
"MISTAKES WILL BE MADE...NOTHING IS FOOLPROOF..."
I'M A PURPOSEFUL PROFESSIONAL.
AND I NEED TO BEAT UP MY PROBLEMS.

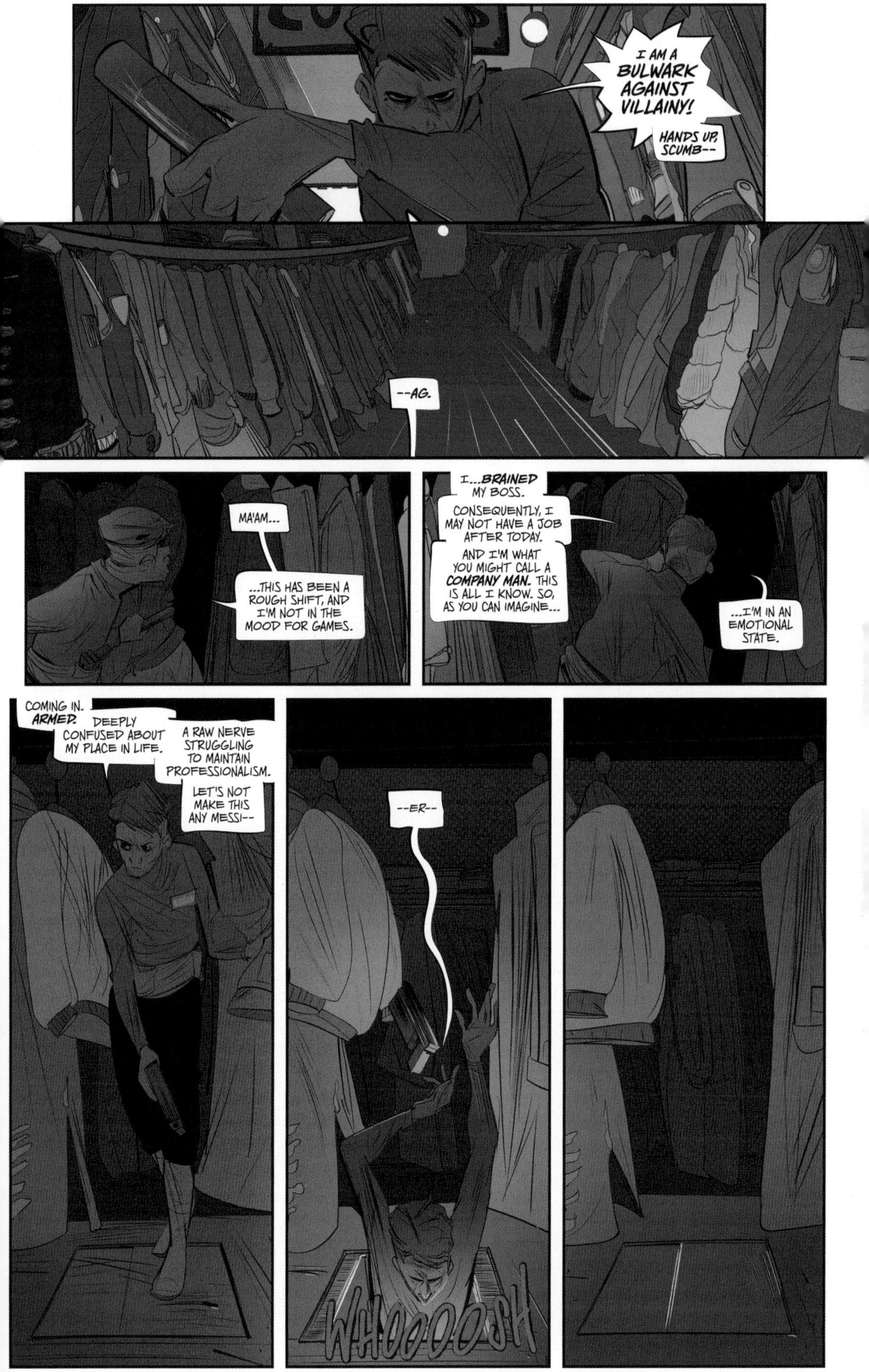
I AM A BULWARK AGAINST VILLAINY!
HANDS UP, SCUMB--
--AG.
MA'AM...
...THIS HAS BEEN A ROUGH SHIFT, AND I'M NOT IN THE MOOD FOR GAMES.
I...BRAINED MY BOSS.
CONSEQUENTLY, I MAY NOT HAVE A JOB AFTER TODAY.
AND I'M WHAT YOU MIGHT CALL A COMPANY MAN. THIS IS ALL I KNOW. SO, AS YOU CAN IMAGINE...
...I'M IN AN EMOTIONAL STATE.
COMING IN. ARMED.
DEEPLY CONFUSED ABOUT MY PLACE IN LIFE.
A RAW NERVE STRUGGLING TO MAINTAIN PROFESSIONALISM.
LET'S NOT MAKE THIS ANY MESSI--
--ER--
WHOOOOSH

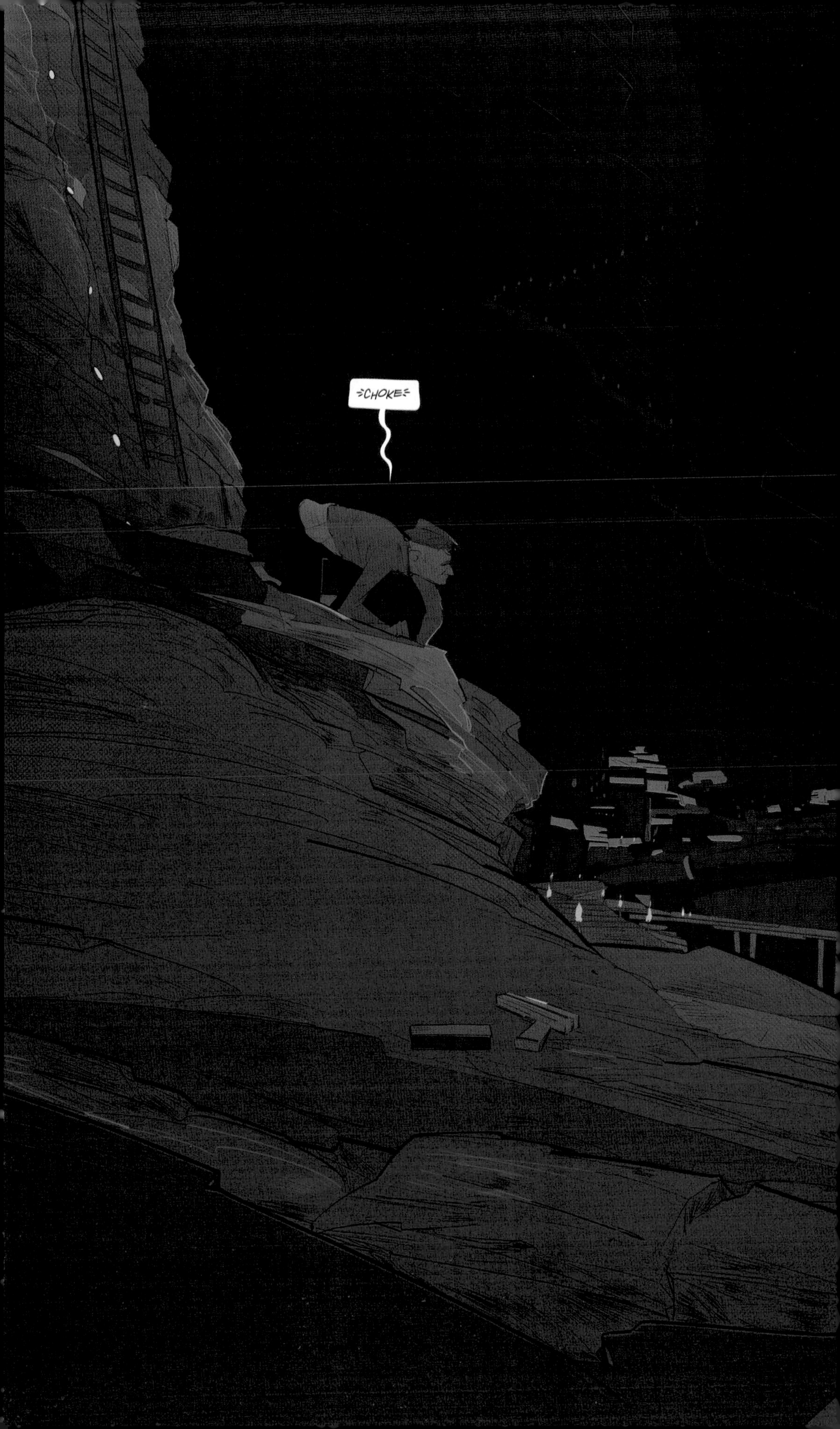
CHOKE

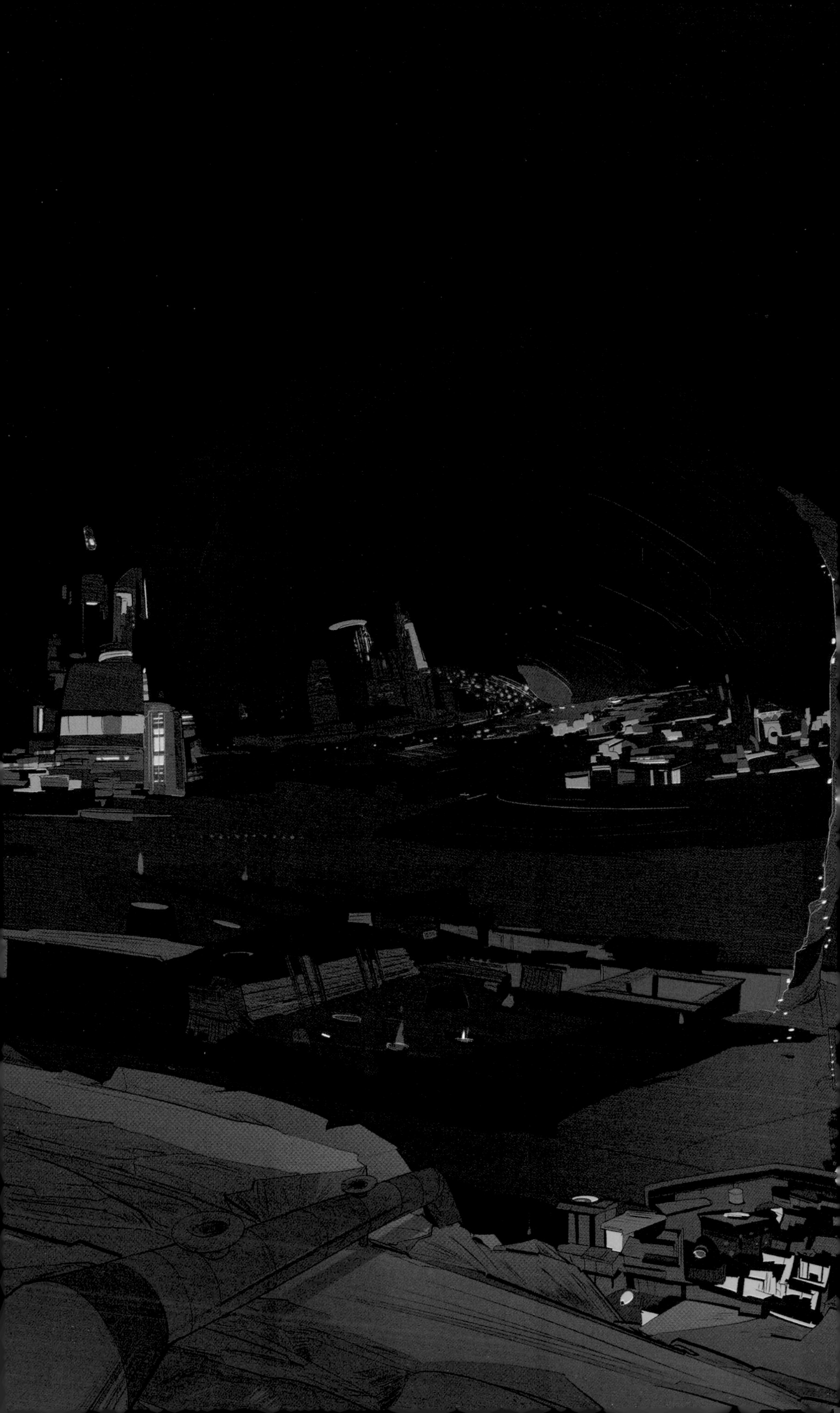

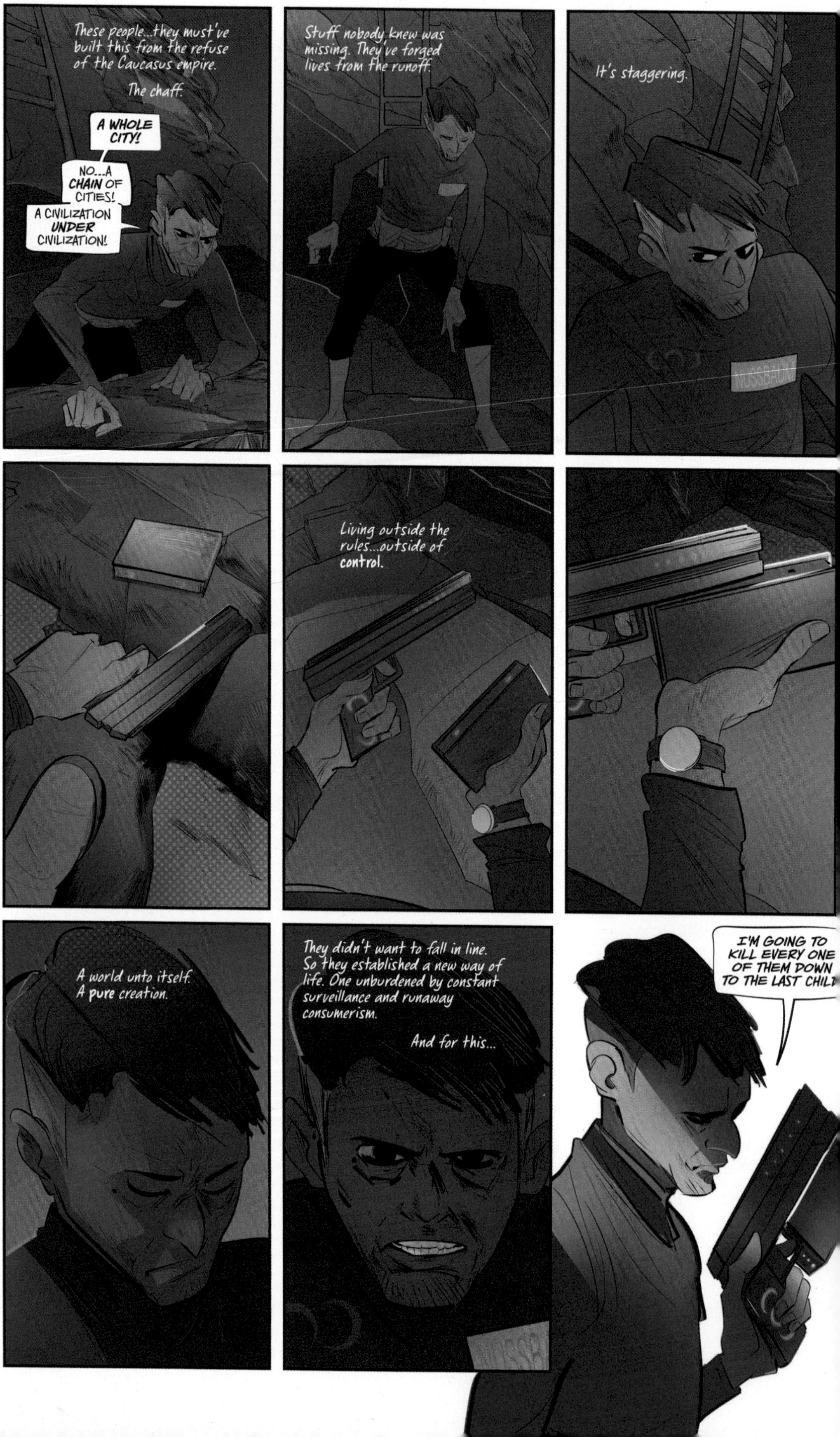
These people...they must've built this from the refuse of the Caucasus empire.
The chaff.
A WHOLE CITY!
NO...A CHAIN OF CITIES!
A CIVILIZATION UNDER CIVILIZATION!
Stuff nobody knew was missing. They've forged lives from the runoff.
It's staggering.
NUSSBAUM
Living outside the rules...outside of control.
A world unto itself. A pure creation.
They didn't want to fall in line. So they established a new way of life. One unburdened by constant surveillance and runaway consumerism.
And for this...
I'M GOING TO KILL EVERY ONE OF THEM DOWN TO THE LAST CHILD

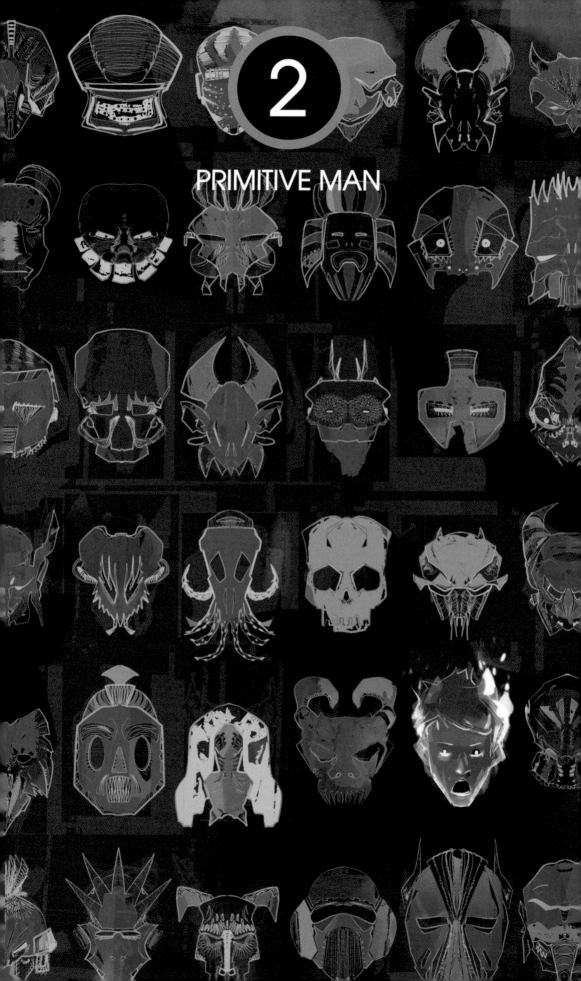

2

PRIMITIVE MAN

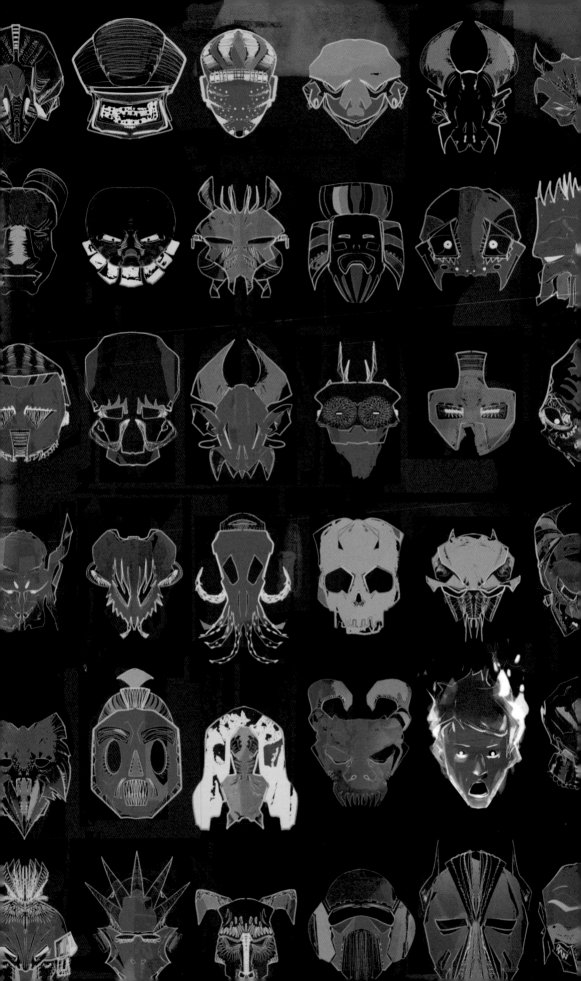

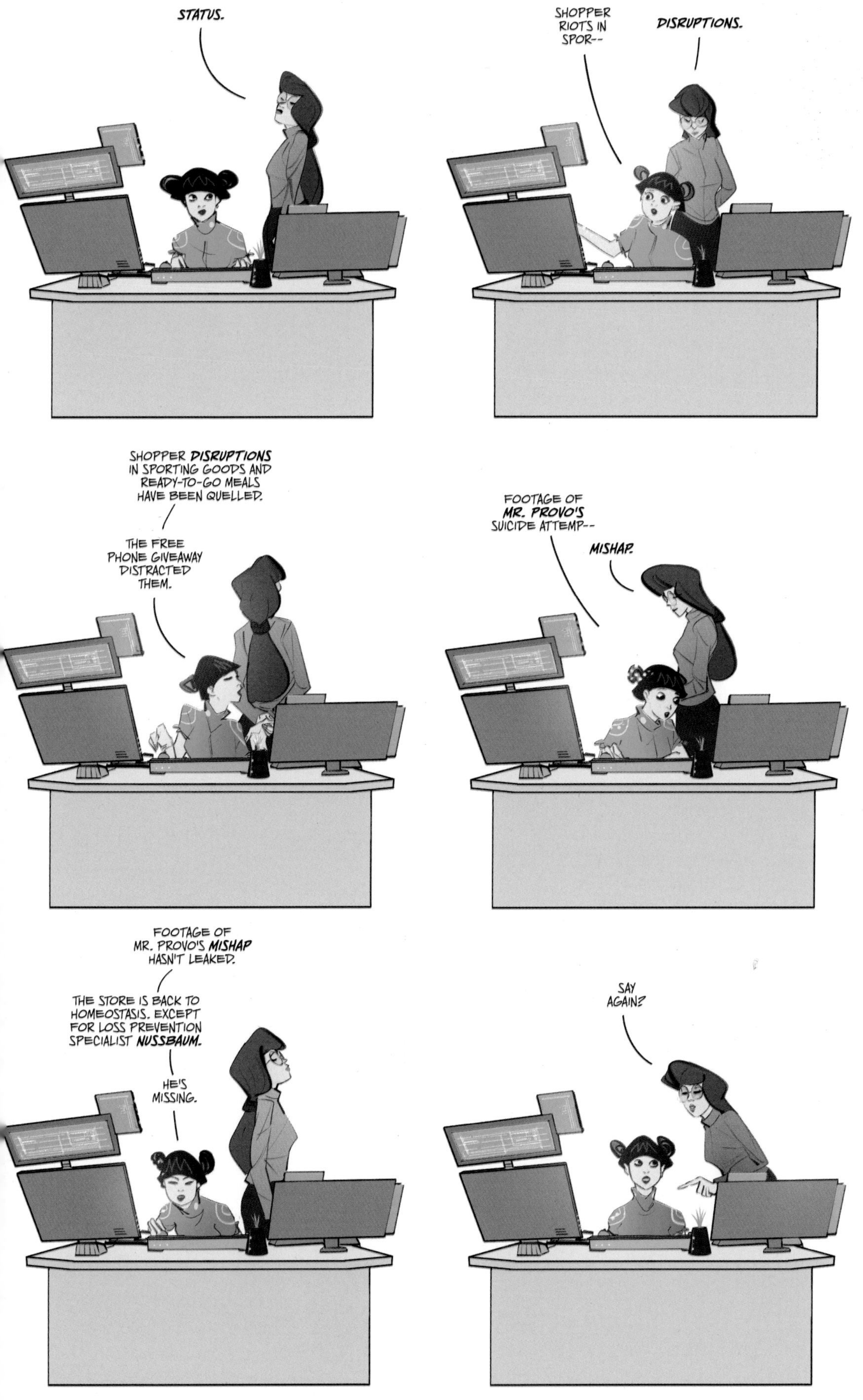
STATUS.
SHOPPER RIOTS IN SPOR--
DISRUPTIONS.
SHOPPER DISRUPTIONS IN SPORTING GOODS AND READY-TO-GO MEALS HAVE BEEN QUELLED.
THE FREE PHONE GIVEAWAY DISTRACTED THEM.
FOOTAGE OF MR. PROVO'S SUICIDE ATTEMP--
MISHAP.
FOOTAGE OF MR. PROVO'S MISHAP HASN'T LEAKED.
THE STORE IS BACK TO HOMEOSTASIS. EXCEPT FOR LOSS PREVENTION SPECIALIST NUSSBAUM.
HE'S MISSING.
SAY AGAIN?

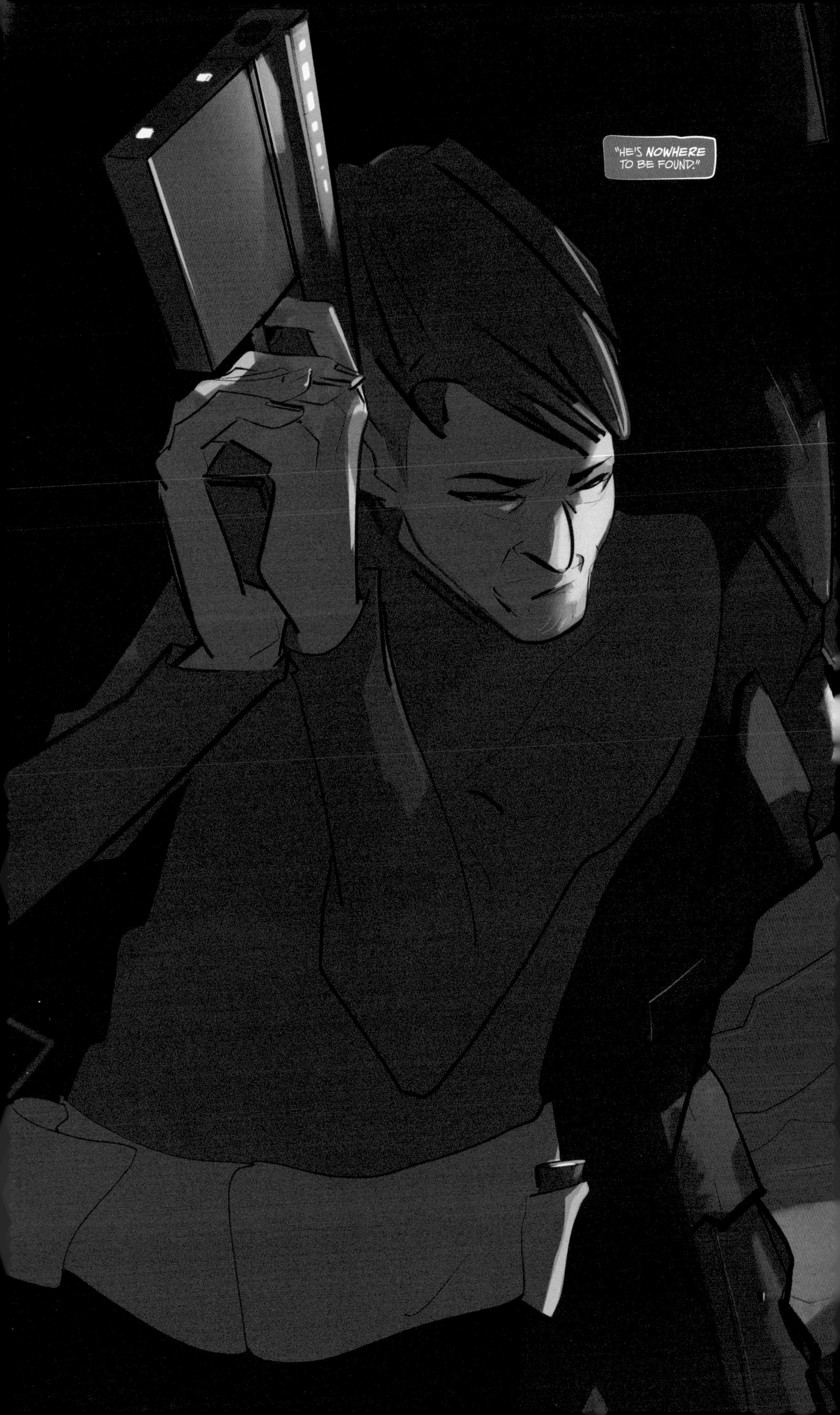
"HE'S NOWHERE TO BE FOUND."

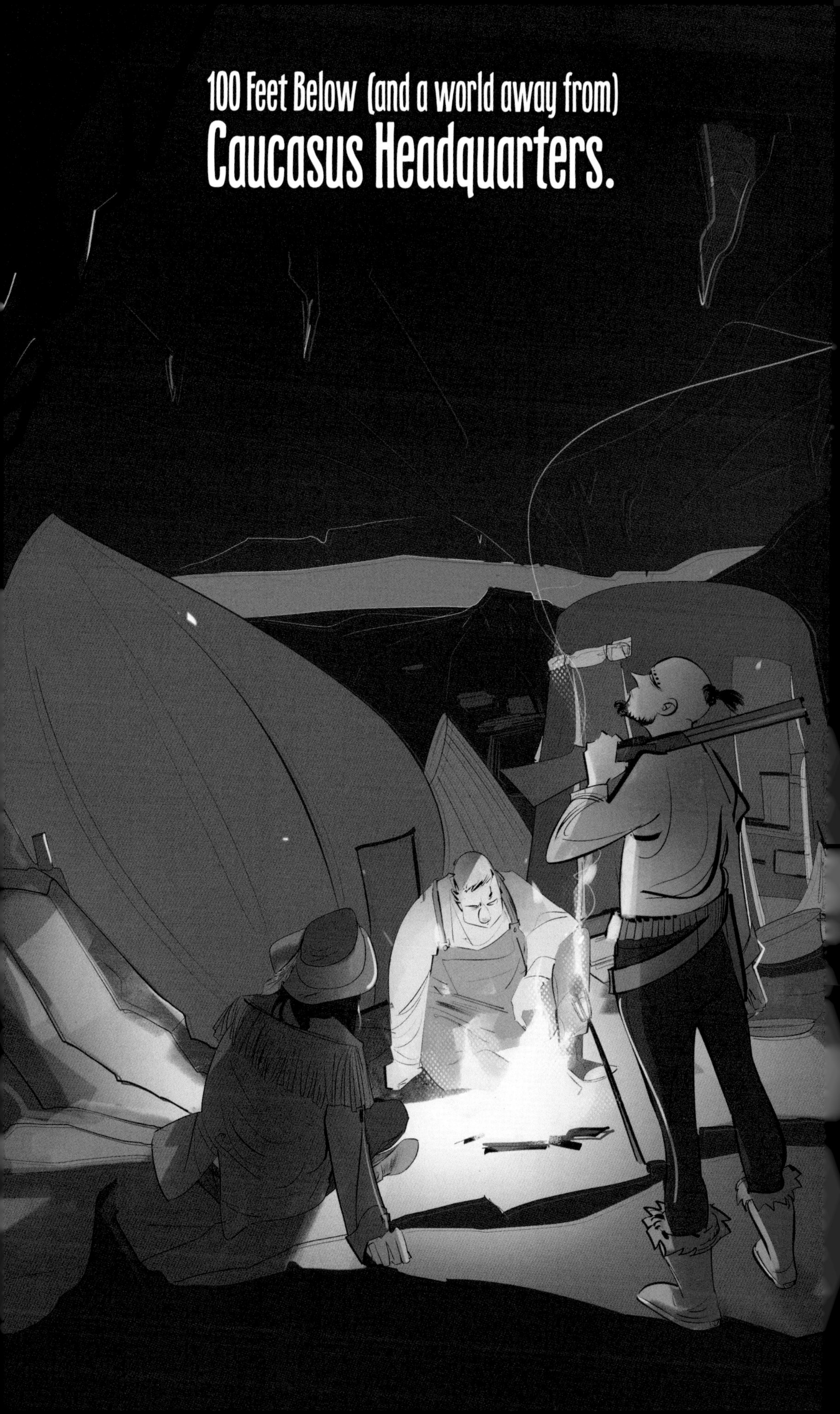
100 Feet Below (and a world away from)
Caucasus Headquarters.

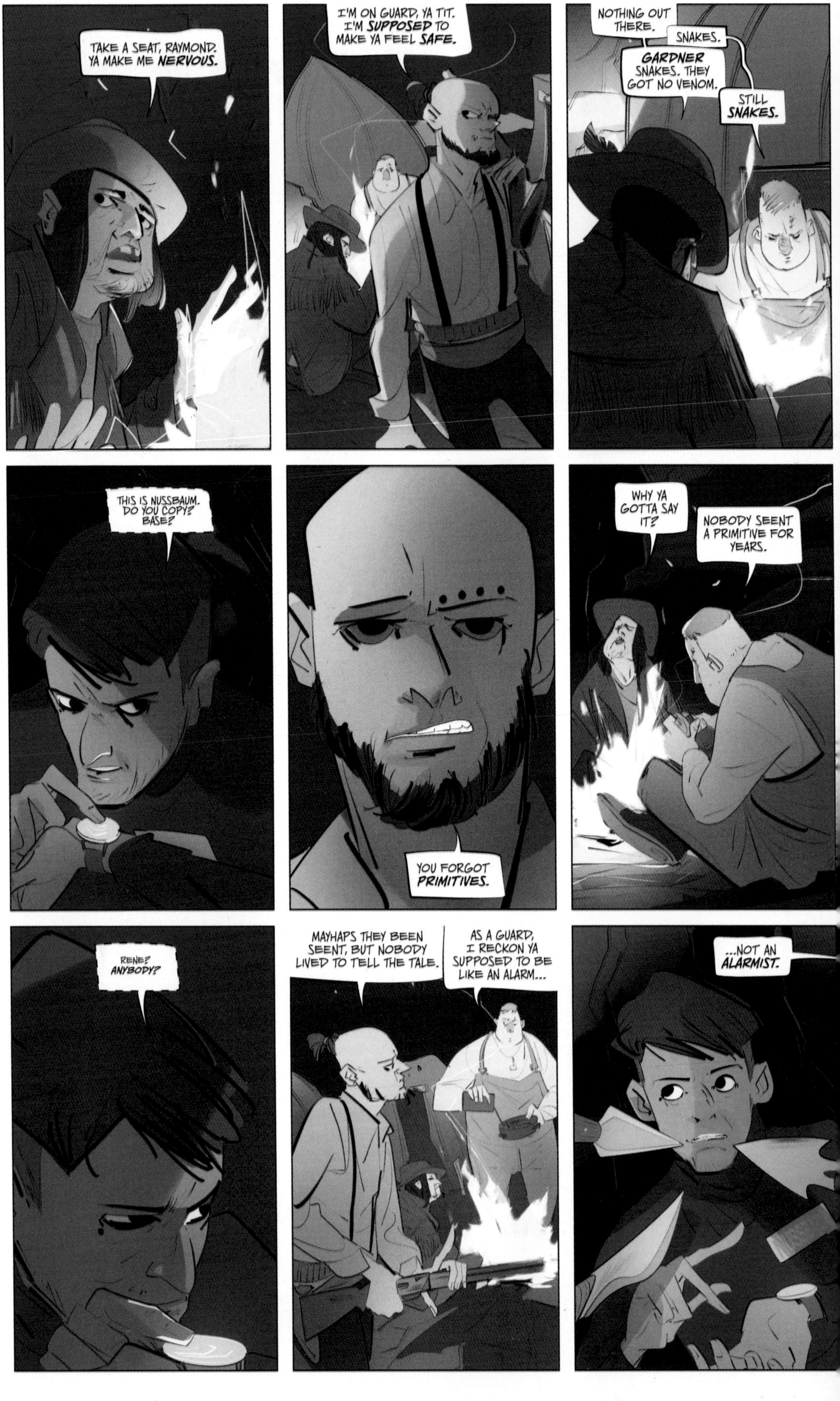
TAKE A SEAT, RAYMOND. YA MAKE ME NERVOUS.
I'M ON GUARD, YA TIT. I'M SUPPOSED TO MAKE YA FEEL SAFE.
NOTHING OUT THERE.
SNAKES.
GARDNER SNAKES. THEY GOT NO VENOM.
STILL SNAKES.
THIS IS NUSSBAUM. DO YOU COPY? BASE?
YOU FORGOT PRIMITIVES.
WHY YA GOTTA SAY IT?
NOBODY SEENT A PRIMITIVE FOR YEARS.
RENE? ANYBODY?
MAYHAPS THEY BEEN SEENT, BUT NOBODY LIVED TO TELL THE TALE.
AS A GUARD, I RECKON YA SUPPOSED TO BE LIKE AN ALARM...
...NOT AN ALARMIST.

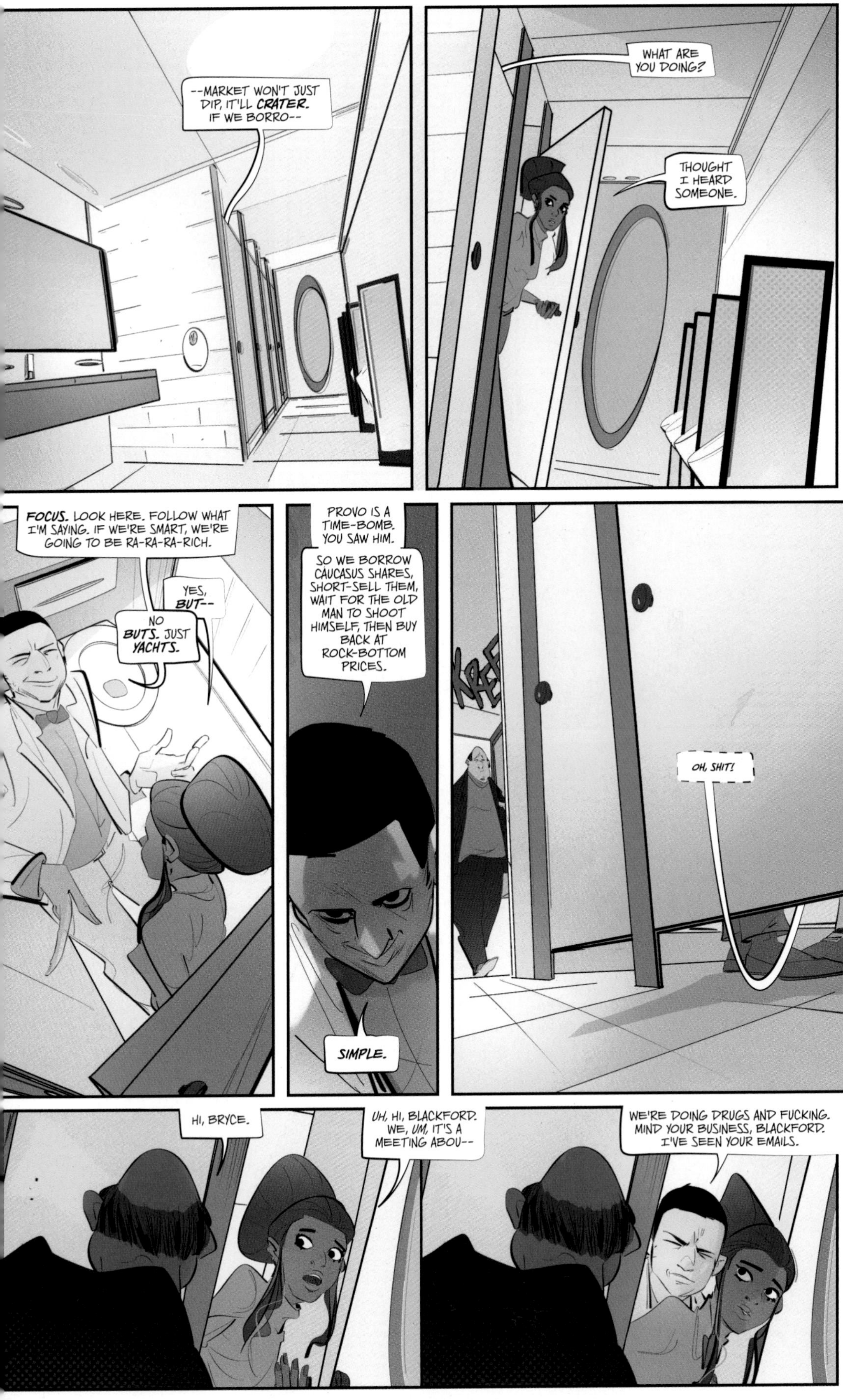
--MARKET WON'T JUST DIP, IT'LL CRATER. IF WE BORRO--
WHAT ARE YOU DOING?
THOUGHT I HEARD SOMEONE.
FOCUS. LOOK HERE. FOLLOW WHAT I'M SAYING. IF WE'RE SMART, WE'RE GOING TO BE RA-RA-RA-RICH.
YES, BUT--
NO BUTS. JUST YACHTS.
PROVO IS A TIME-BOMB. YOU SAW HIM.
SO WE BORROW CAUCASUS SHARES, SHORT-SELL THEM, WAIT FOR THE OLD MAN TO SHOOT HIMSELF, THEN BUY BACK AT ROCK-BOTTOM PRICES.
SIMPLE.
OH, SHIT!
HI, BRYCE.
UH, HI, BLACKFORD. WE, UM, IT'S A MEETING ABOU--
WE'RE DOING DRUGS AND FUCKING. MIND YOUR BUSINESS, BLACKFORD. I'VE SEEN YOUR EMAILS.

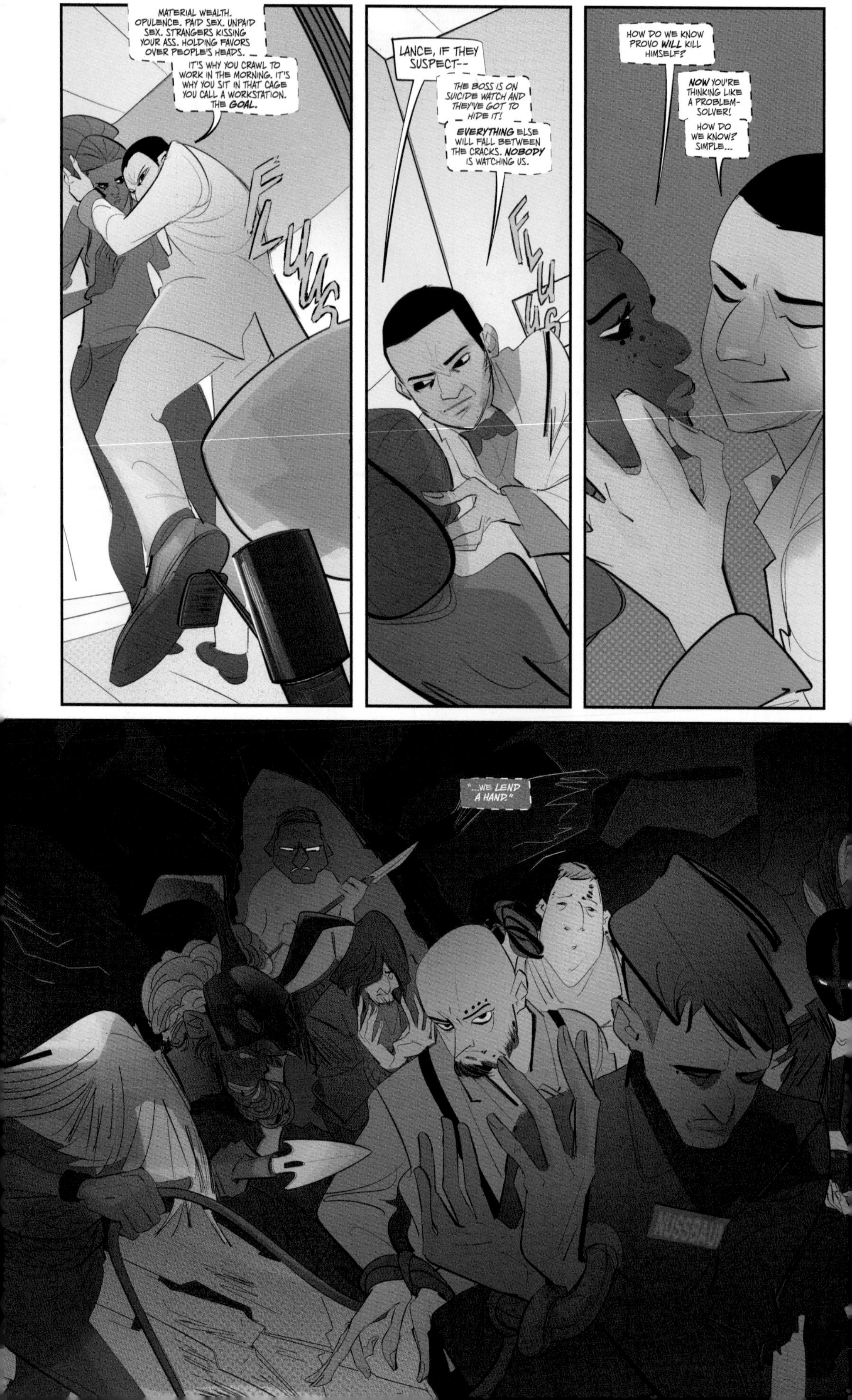
MATERIAL WEALTH. OPULENCE. PAID SEX. UNPAID SEX. STRANGERS KISSING YOUR ASS. HOLDING FAVORS OVER PEOPLE'S HEADS.
IT'S WHY YOU CRAWL TO WORK IN THE MORNING. IT'S WHY YOU SIT IN THAT CAGE YOU CALL A WORKSTATION. THE GOAL.
FLUUSS
LANCE, IF THEY SUSPECT--
THE BOSS IS ON SUICIDE WATCH AND THEY'VE GOT TO HIDE IT!
EVERYTHING ELSE WILL FALL BETWEEN THE CRACKS. NOBODY IS WATCHING US.
FLUUS
HOW DO WE KNOW PROVO WILL KILL HIMSELF?
NOW YOU'RE THINKING LIKE A PROBLEM-SOLVER!
HOW DO WE KNOW? SIMPLE...
"...WE LEND A HAND."
NUSSBAU

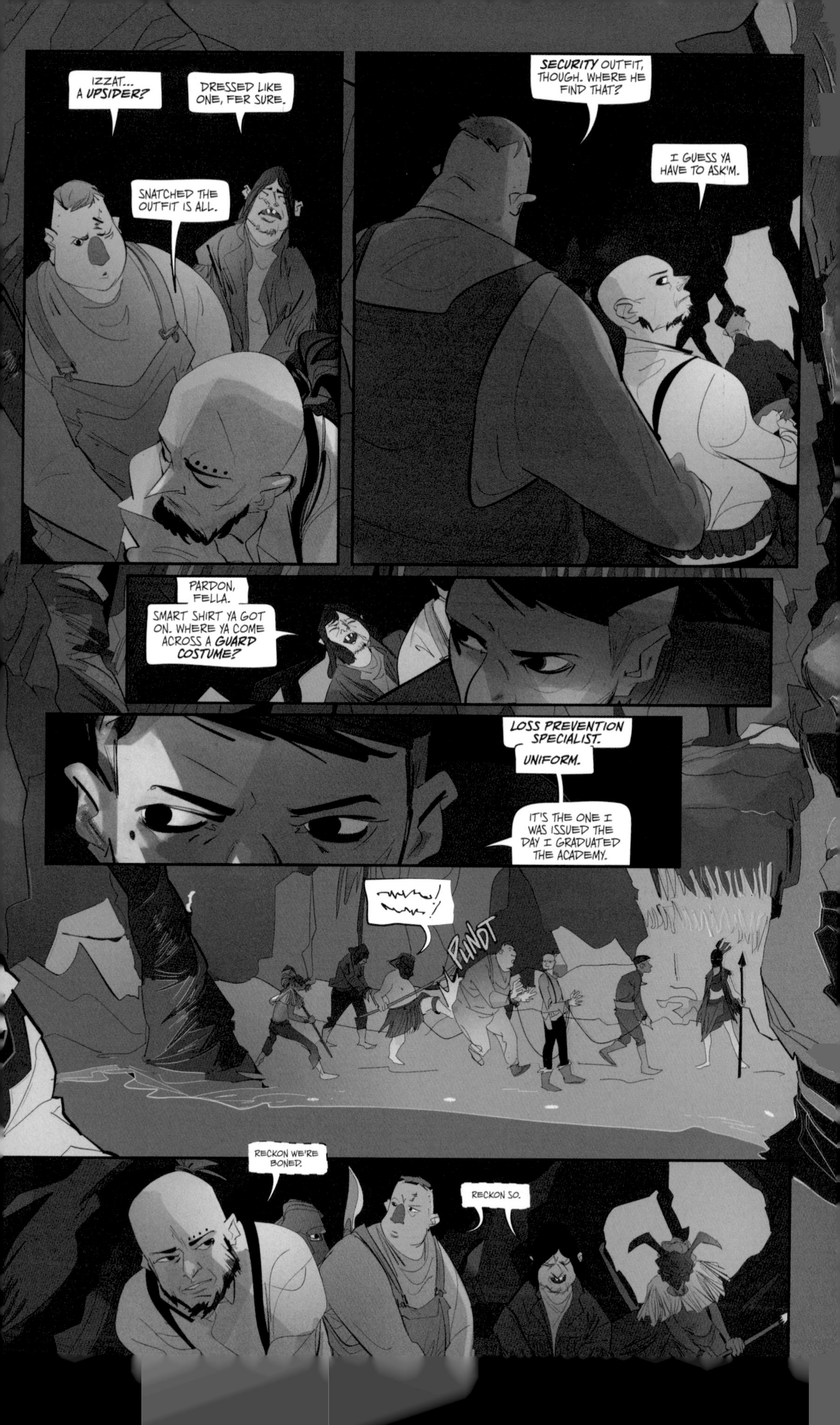

IZZAT... A UPSIDER?
DRESSED LIKE ONE, FER SURE.
SNATCHED THE OUTFIT IS ALL.
SECURITY OUTFIT, THOUGH. WHERE HE FIND THAT?
I GUESS YA HAVE TO ASK'M.
PARDON, FELLA.
SMART SHIRT YA GOT ON. WHERE YA COME ACROSS A GUARD COSTUME?
LOSS PREVENTION SPECIALIST.
UNIFORM.
IT'S THE ONE I WAS ISSUED THE DAY I GRADUATED THE ACADEMY.
PUNDT
RECKON WE'RE BONED.
RECKON SO.

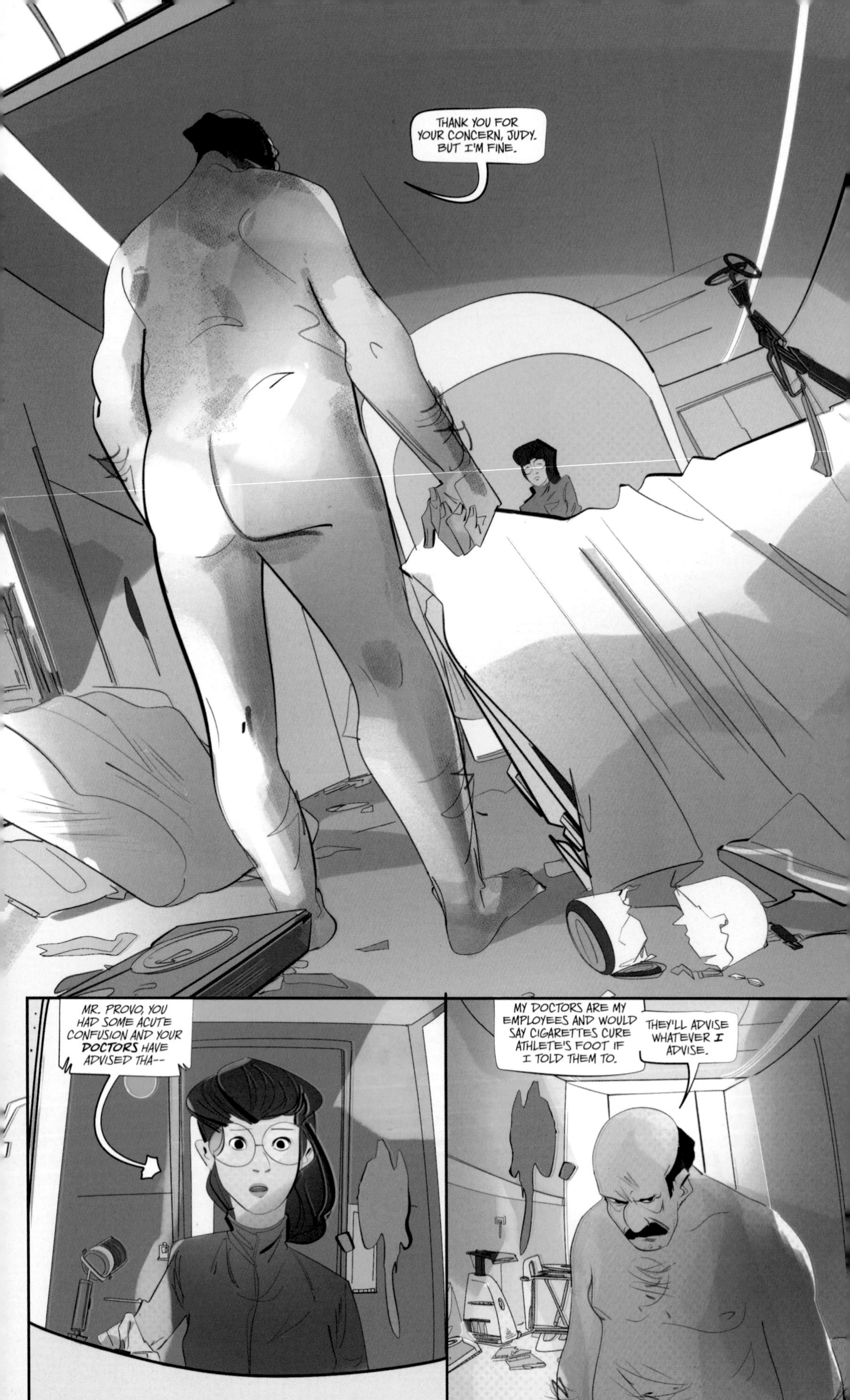
THANK YOU FOR YOUR CONCERN, JUDY. BUT I'M FINE.
MR. PROVO, YOU HAD SOME ACUTE CONFUSION AND YOUR **DOCTORS** HAVE ADVISED THA--
MY DOCTORS ARE MY EMPLOYEES AND WOULD SAY CIGARETTES CURE ATHLETE'S FOOT IF I TOLD THEM TO.
THEY'LL ADVISE WHATEVER *I* ADVISE.

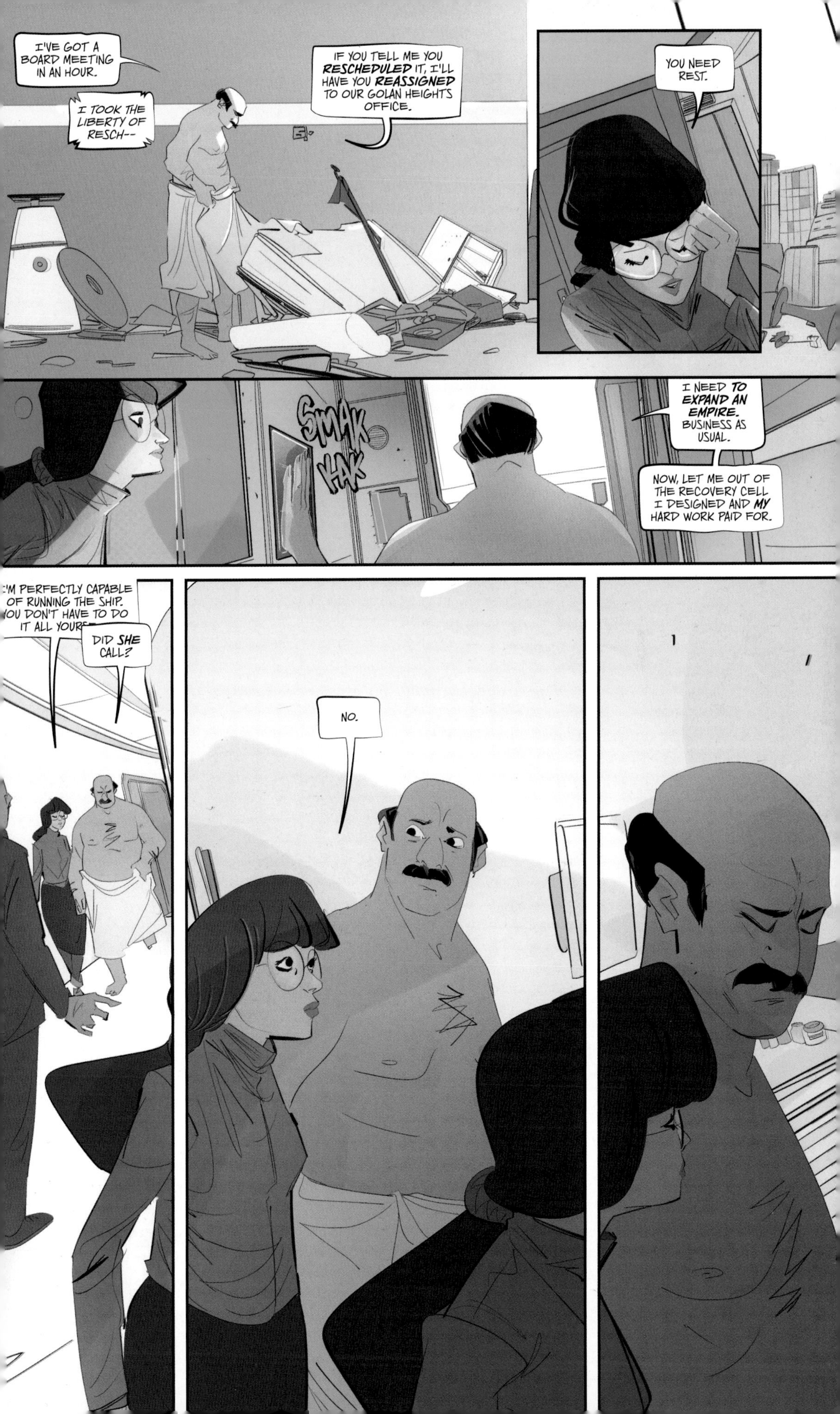
I'VE GOT A BOARD MEETING IN AN HOUR.
I TOOK THE LIBERTY OF RESCH--
IF YOU TELL ME YOU RESCHEDULED IT, I'LL HAVE YOU REASSIGNED TO OUR GOLAN HEIGHTS OFFICE.
YOU NEED REST.
SMAK
KAK
I NEED TO EXPAND AN EMPIRE. BUSINESS AS USUAL.
NOW, LET ME OUT OF THE RECOVERY CELL I DESIGNED AND MY HARD WORK PAID FOR.
I'M PERFECTLY CAPABLE OF RUNNING THE SHIP. YOU DON'T HAVE TO DO IT ALL YOURS--
DID SHE CALL?
NO.

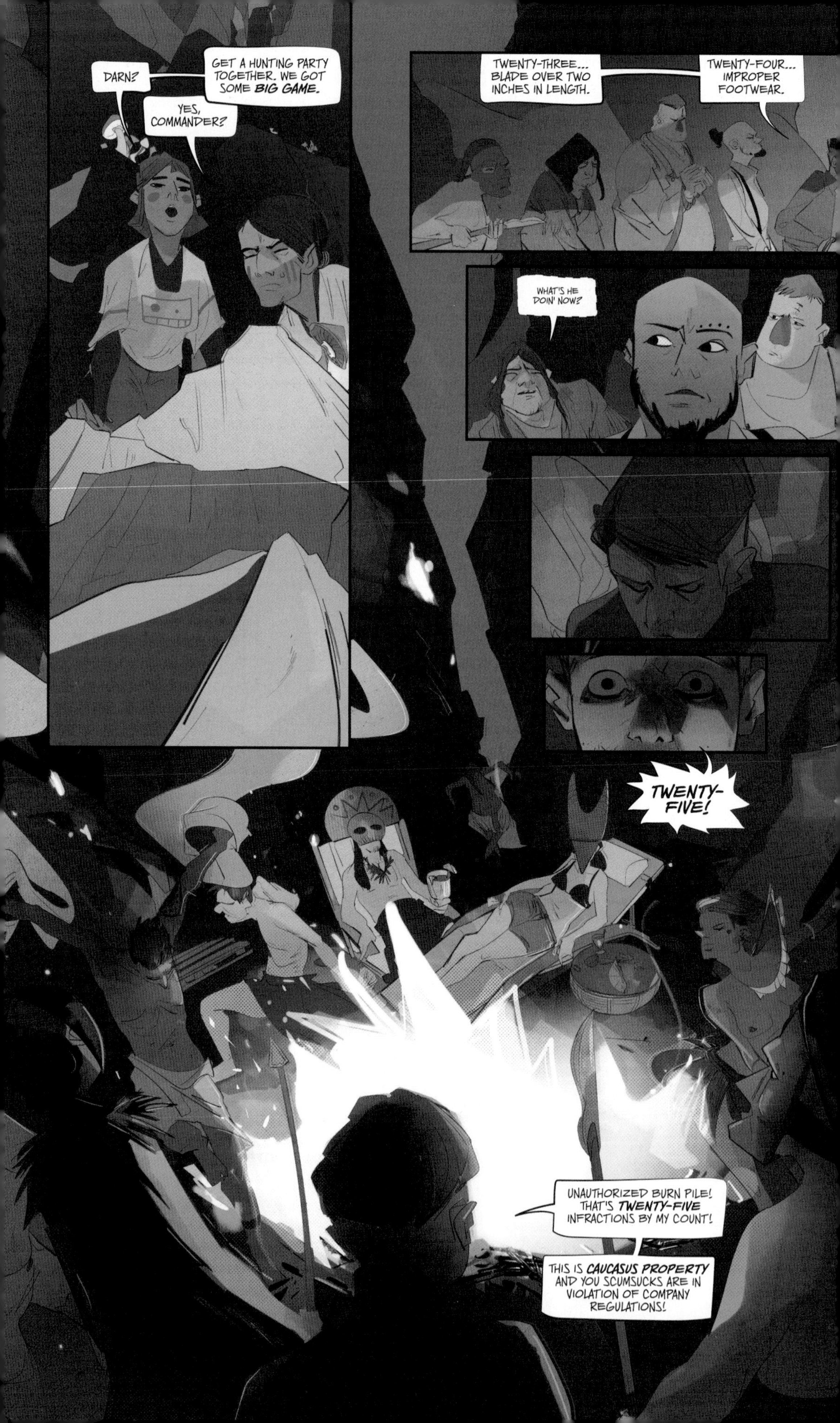
DARN?
GET A HUNTING PARTY TOGETHER. WE GOT SOME BIG GAME.
YES, COMMANDER?
TWENTY-THREE... BLADE OVER TWO INCHES IN LENGTH.
TWENTY-FOUR... IMPROPER FOOTWEAR.
WHAT'S HE DOIN' NOW?
TWENTY-FIVE!
UNAUTHORIZED BURN PILE! THAT'S TWENTY-FIVE INFRACTIONS BY MY COUNT!
THIS IS CAUCASUS PROPERTY AND YOU SCUMSUCKS ARE IN VIOLATION OF COMPANY REGULATIONS!

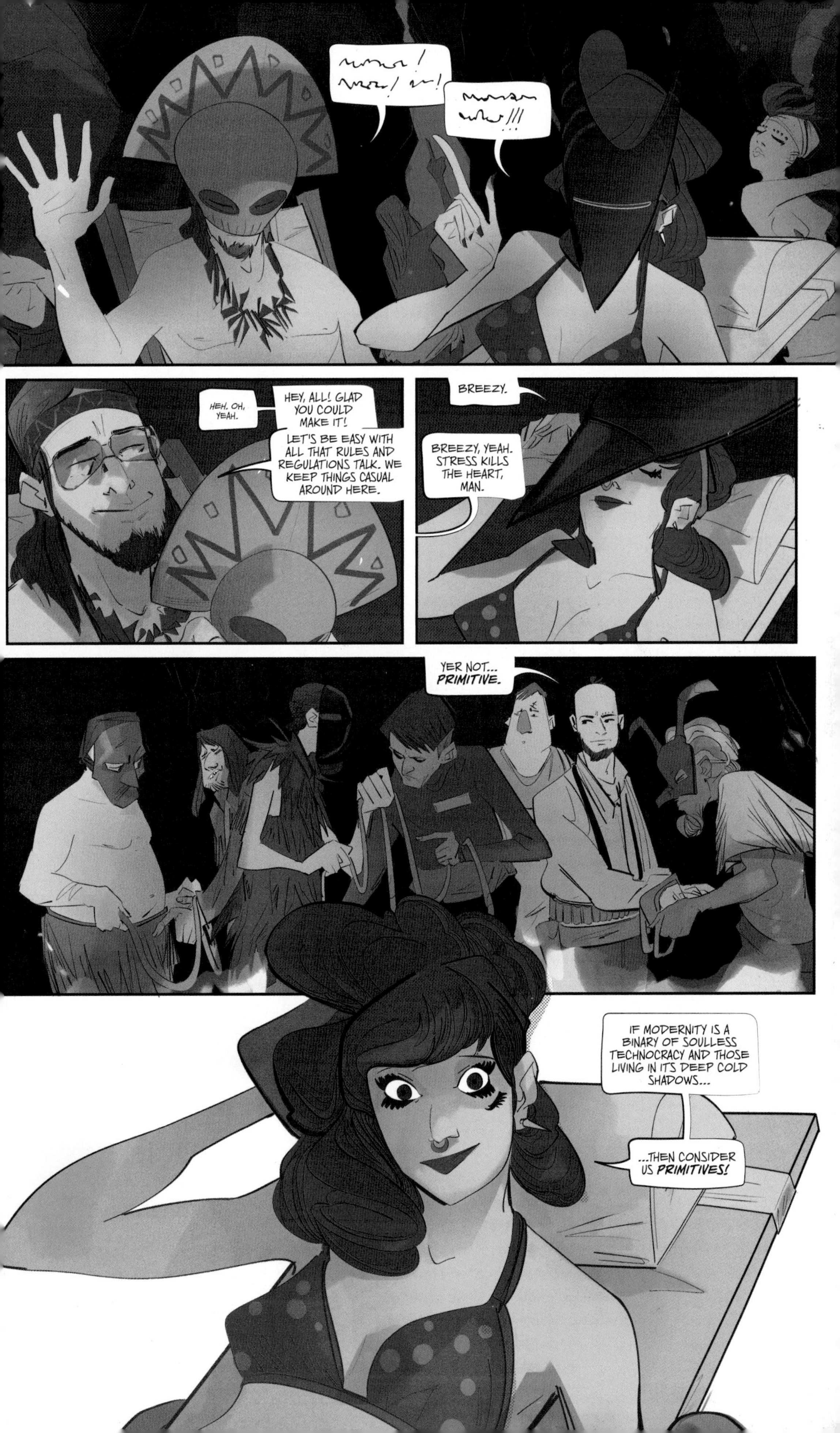
HEH. OH, YEAH.
HEY, ALL! GLAD YOU COULD MAKE IT!
LET'S BE EASY WITH ALL THAT RULES AND REGULATIONS TALK. WE KEEP THINGS CASUAL AROUND HERE.
BREEZY.
BREEZY, YEAH. STRESS KILLS THE HEART, MAN.
YER NOT... PRIMITIVE.
IF MODERNITY IS A BINARY OF SOULLESS TECHNOCRACY AND THOSE LIVING IN ITS DEEP COLD SHADOWS...
...THEN CONSIDER US PRIMITIVES!

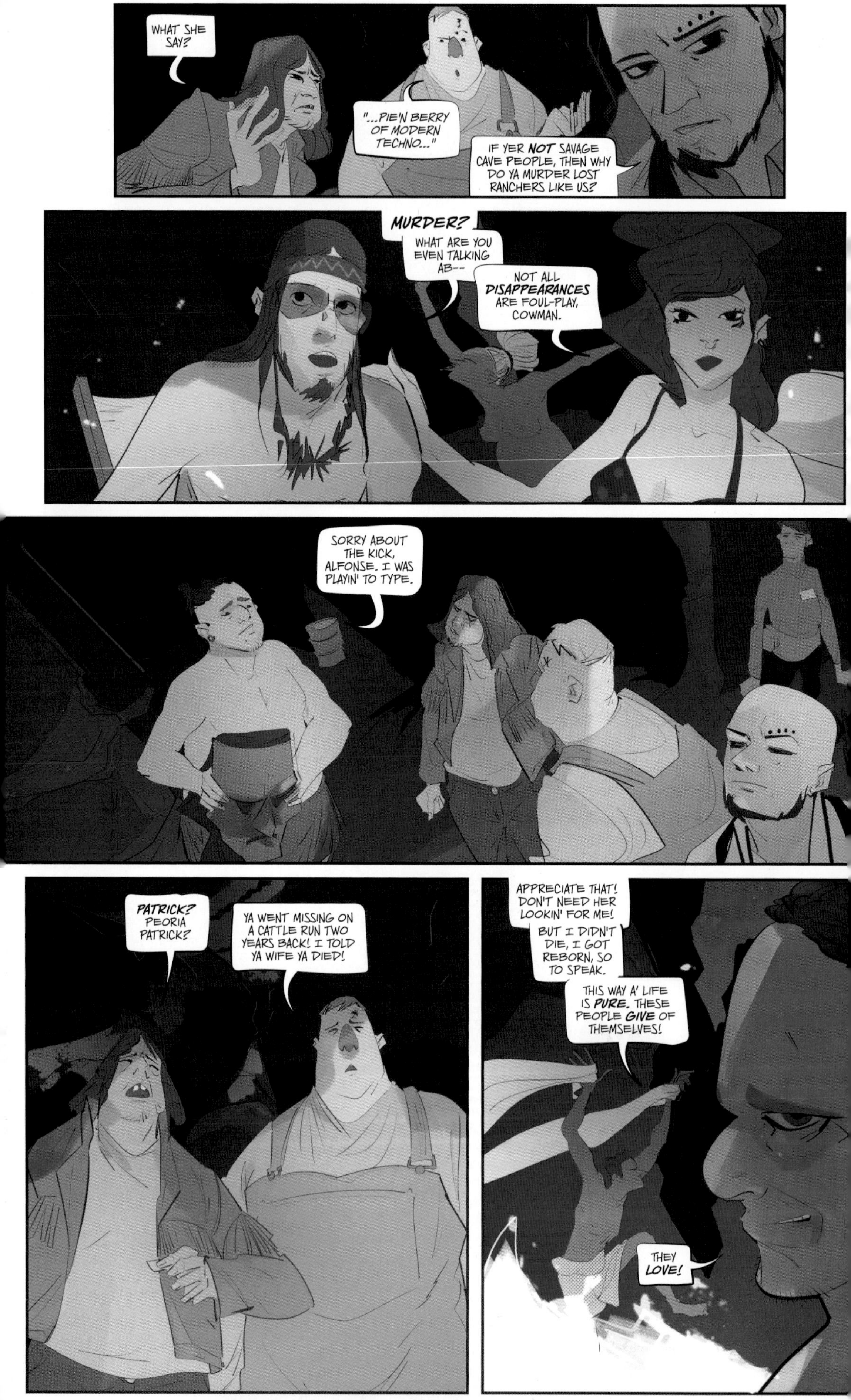
WHAT SHE SAY?
"...PIE'N BERRY OF MODERN TECHNO..."
IF YER NOT SAVAGE CAVE PEOPLE, THEN WHY DO YA MURDER LOST RANCHERS LIKE US?
MURDER?
WHAT ARE YOU EVEN TALKING AB--
NOT ALL DISAPPEARANCES ARE FOUL-PLAY, COWMAN.
SORRY ABOUT THE KICK, ALFONSE. I WAS PLAYIN' TO TYPE.
PATRICK? PEORIA PATRICK?
YA WENT MISSING ON A CATTLE RUN TWO YEARS BACK! I TOLD YA WIFE YA DIED!
APPRECIATE THAT! DON'T NEED HER LOOKIN' FOR ME!
BUT I DIDN'T DIE, I GOT REBORN, SO TO SPEAK.
THIS WAY A' LIFE IS PURE. THESE PEOPLE GIVE OF THEMSELVES!
THEY LOVE!

HOW'D YA FALL IN WITH THESE TYPES?

THERE'S NO *OUTSIDER* TO THESE PEOPLE. JUST FRIENDS IN-WAITING.

AN YA SPEND YER DAYS DOIN' WHAT NOW? DANCIN'?

THEY CREATE ART FOR ITS OWN SAKE. IT'S *BEAUTIFUL* TO WITNESS!

BUT WHAT DO Y'ALL DO FER CASH?

THERE'S NO MONEY HERE. WHAT WOULD THE USE BE? THEY SHARE FREELY WHAT THEY HAVE!

WHAT 'BOUT THE GOVERNORS OVER THERE?

MEREDITH AND GREGGY? FREELY ELECTED! VERY LIMITED POWER!

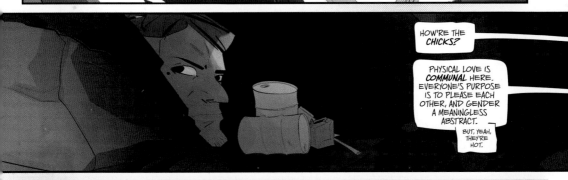

HOW'RE THE *CHICKS?*

PHYSICAL LOVE IS *COMMUNAL* HERE. EVERYONE'S PURPOSE IS TO PLEASE EACH OTHER, AND GENDER A MEANINGLESS ABSTRACT.

BUT, YEAH, THEY'RE HOT.

IT'S PARADISE, BROTHERS. AND I'D BE HONORED IF YOU'D JOIN US.

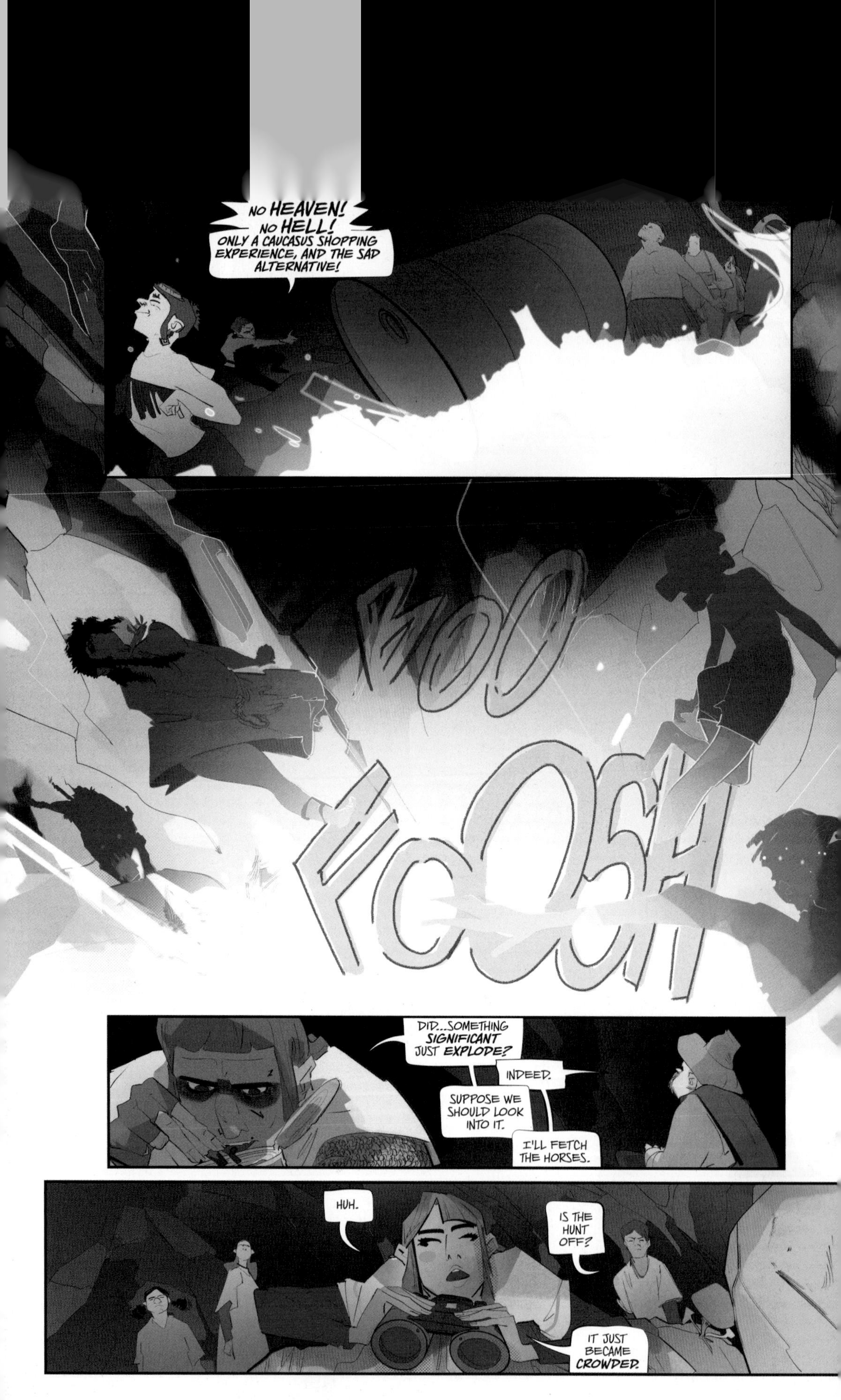
NO HEAVEN! NO HELL! ONLY A CAUCASUS SHOPPING EXPERIENCE, AND THE SAD ALTERNATIVE!
WHOOO
FOOSH
DID...SOMETHING SIGNIFICANT JUST EXPLODE?
INDEED.
SUPPOSE WE SHOULD LOOK INTO IT.
I'LL FETCH THE HORSES.
HUH.
IS THE HUNT OFF?
IT JUST BECAME CROWDED.

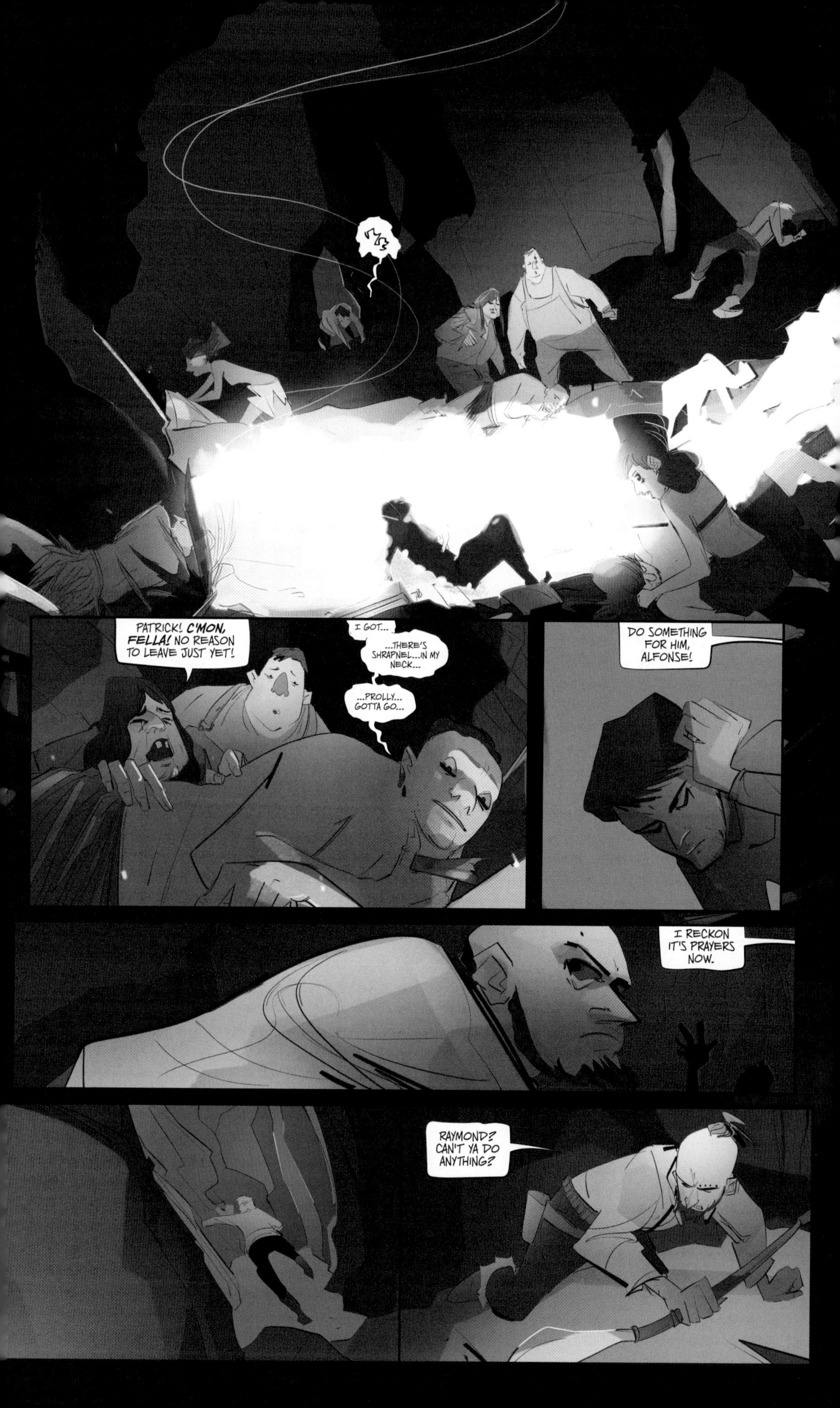
PATRICK! C'MON, FELLA! NO REASON TO LEAVE JUST YET!
I GOT...
...THERE'S SHRAPNEL...IN MY NECK...
...PROLLY... GOTTA GO...
DO SOMETHING FOR HIM, ALFONSE!
I RECKON IT'S PRAYERS NOW.
RAYMOND? CAN'T YA DO ANYTHING?

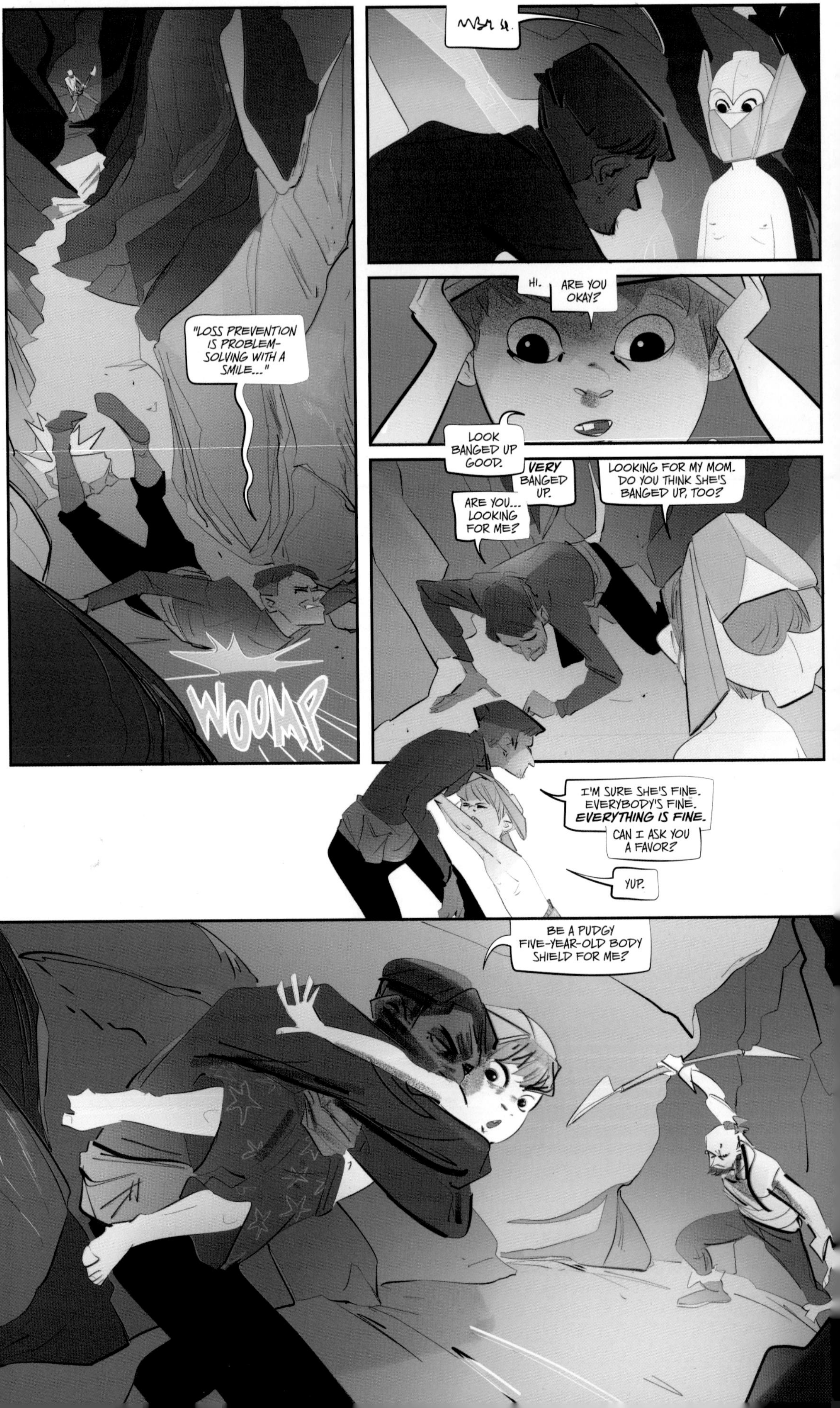
"LOSS PREVENTION IS PROBLEM-SOLVING WITH A SMILE..."
WOOMP
HI.
ARE YOU OKAY?
LOOK BANGED UP GOOD.
VERY BANGED UP.
ARE YOU... LOOKING FOR ME?
LOOKING FOR MY MOM. DO YOU THINK SHE'S BANGED UP, TOO?
I'M SURE SHE'S FINE. EVERYBODY'S FINE. EVERYTHING IS FINE.
CAN I ASK YOU A FAVOR?
YUP.
BE A PUDGY FIVE-YEAR-OLD BODY SHIELD FOR ME?

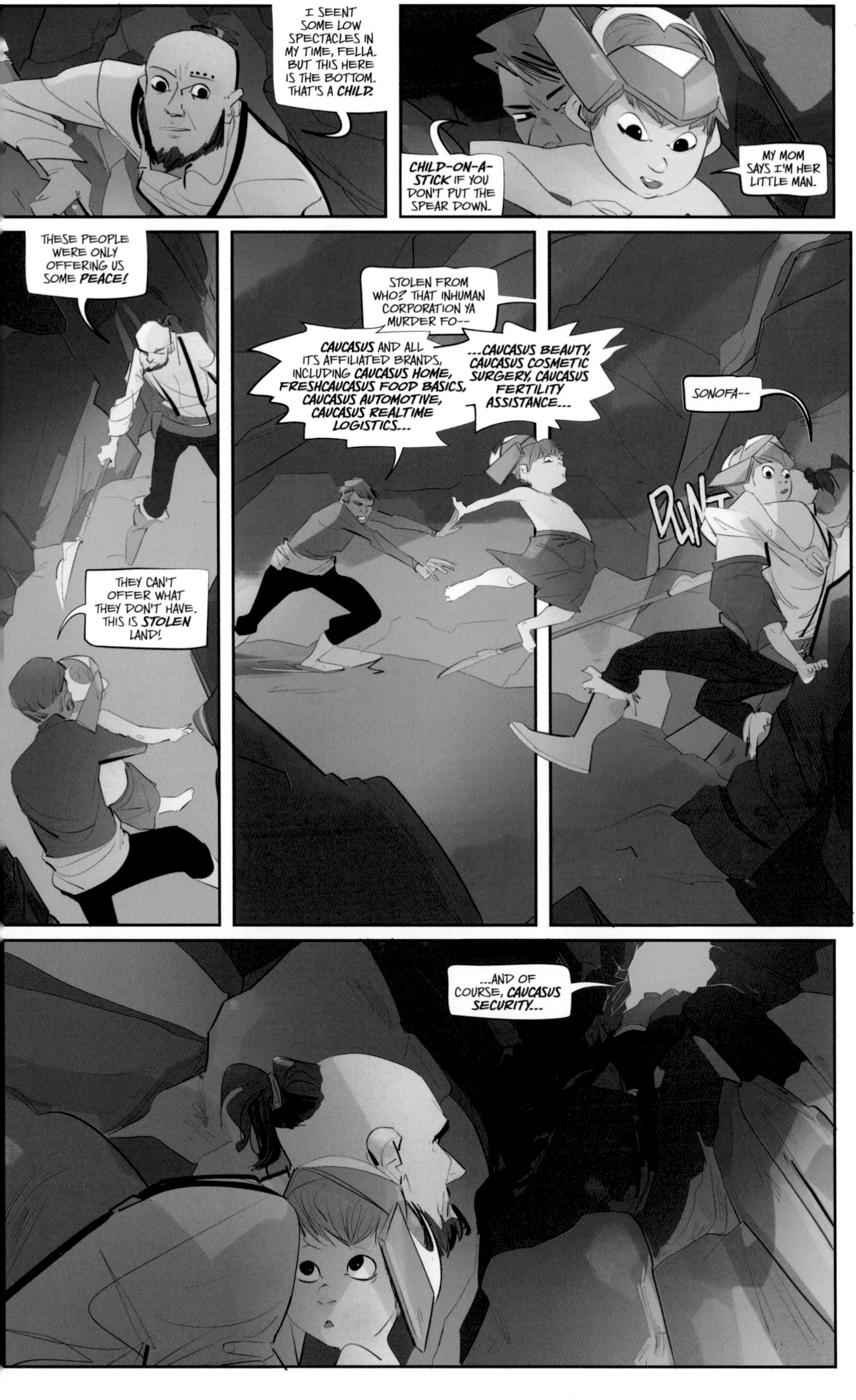
I SEENT SOME LOW SPECTACLES IN MY TIME, FELLA. BUT THIS HERE IS THE BOTTOM. THAT'S A CHILD.
CHILD-ON-A-STICK IF YOU DON'T PUT THE SPEAR DOWN.
MY MOM SAYS I'M HER LITTLE MAN.
THESE PEOPLE WERE ONLY OFFERING US SOME PEACE!
THEY CAN'T OFFER WHAT THEY DON'T HAVE. THIS IS STOLEN LAND!
STOLEN FROM WHO? THAT INHUMAN CORPORATION YA MURDER FO--
CAUCASUS AND ALL ITS AFFILIATED BRANDS, INCLUDING CAUCASUS HOME, FRESHCAUCASUS FOOD BASICS, CAUCASUS AUTOMOTIVE, CAUCASUS REALTIME LOGISTICS...
...CAUCASUS BEAUTY, CAUCASUS COSMETIC SURGERY, CAUCASUS FERTILITY ASSISTANCE...
SONOFA--
...AND OF COURSE, CAUCASUS SECURITY...

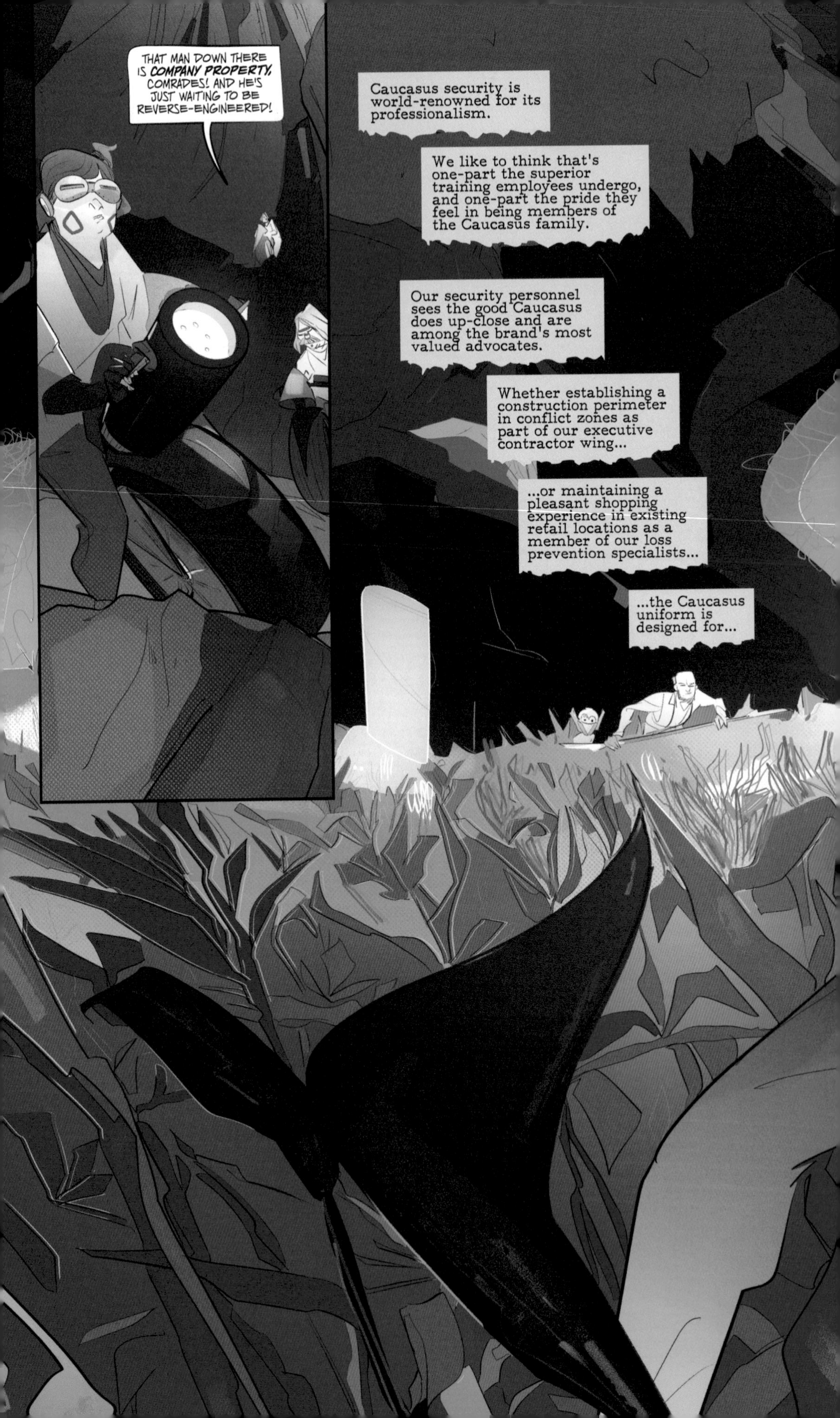

THAT MAN DOWN THERE IS COMPANY PROPERTY, COMRADES! AND HE'S JUST WAITING TO BE REVERSE-ENGINEERED!
Caucasus security is world-renowned for its professionalism.
We like to think that's one-part the superior training employees undergo, and one-part the pride they feel in being members of the Caucasus family.
Our security personnel sees the good Caucasus does up-close and are among the brand's most valued advocates.
Whether establishing a construction perimeter in conflict zones as part of our executive contractor wing...
...or maintaining a pleasant shopping experience in existing retail locations as a member of our loss prevention specialists...
...the Caucasus uniform is designed for...

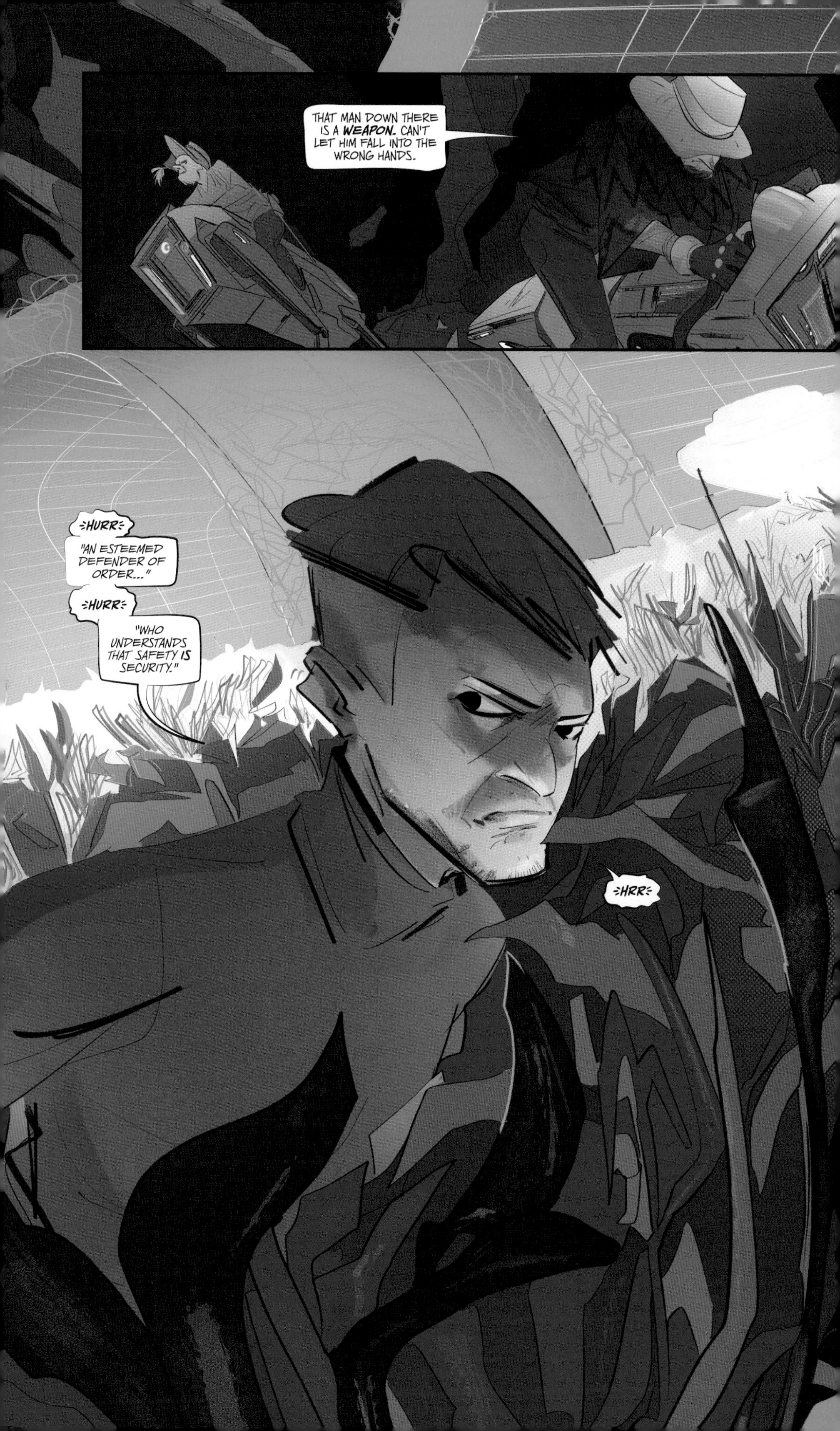
THAT MAN DOWN THERE IS A WEAPON. CAN'T LET HIM FALL INTO THE WRONG HANDS.
HURR
"AN ESTEEMED DEFENDER OF ORDER..."
HURR
"WHO UNDERSTANDS THAT SAFETY IS SECURITY."
HRR

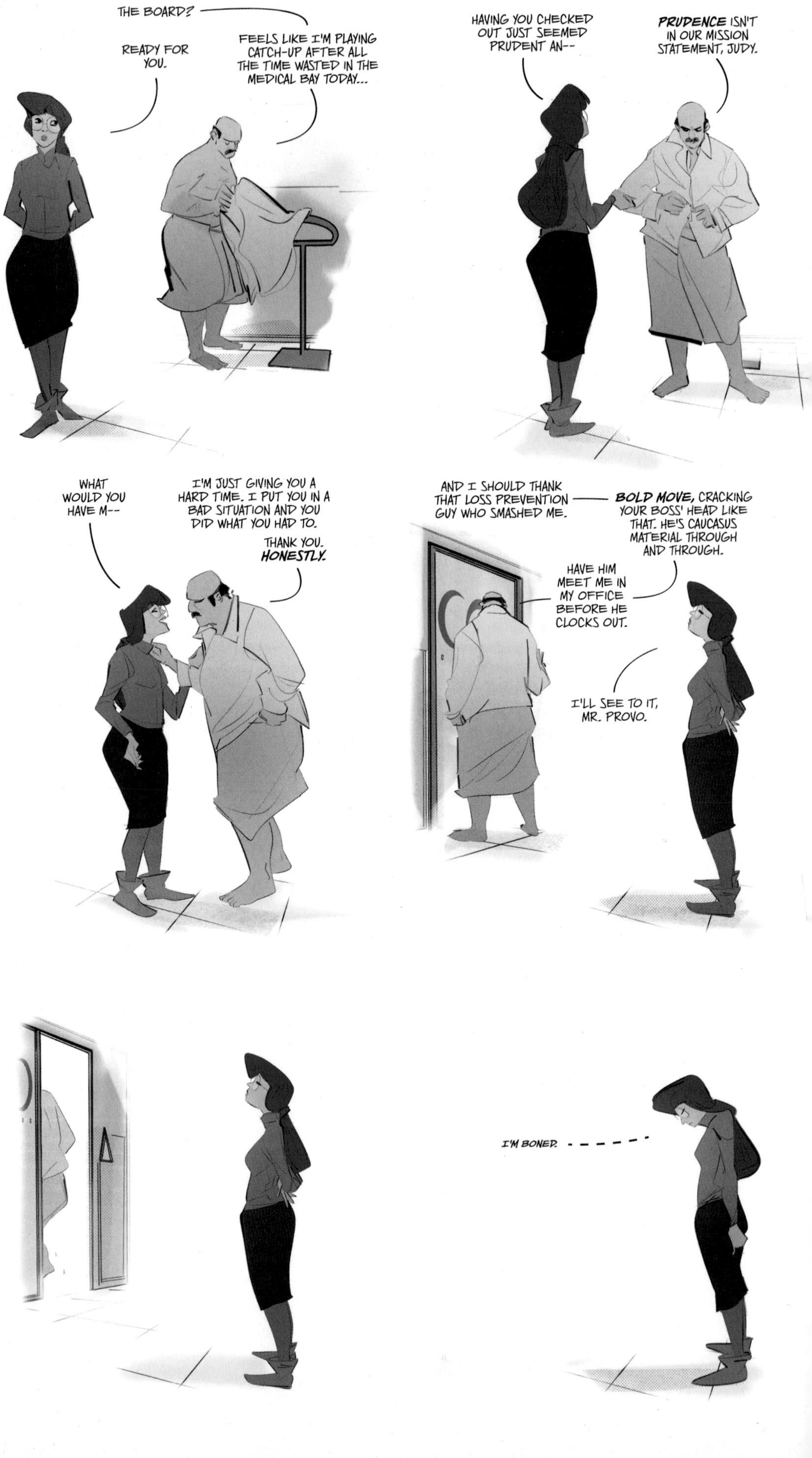
READY FOR YOU.
THE BOARD?
FEELS LIKE I'M PLAYING CATCH-UP AFTER ALL THE TIME WASTED IN THE MEDICAL BAY TODAY...
HAVING YOU CHECKED OUT JUST SEEMED PRUDENT AN--
PRUDENCE ISN'T IN OUR MISSION STATEMENT, JUDY.
WHAT WOULD YOU HAVE M--
I'M JUST GIVING YOU A HARD TIME. I PUT YOU IN A BAD SITUATION AND YOU DID WHAT YOU HAD TO.
THANK YOU. HONESTLY.
AND I SHOULD THANK THAT LOSS PREVENTION GUY WHO SMASHED ME.
BOLD MOVE, CRACKING YOUR BOSS' HEAD LIKE THAT. HE'S CAUCASUS MATERIAL THROUGH AND THROUGH.
HAVE HIM MEET ME IN MY OFFICE BEFORE HE CLOCKS OUT.
I'LL SEE TO IT, MR. PROVO.
I'M BONED.

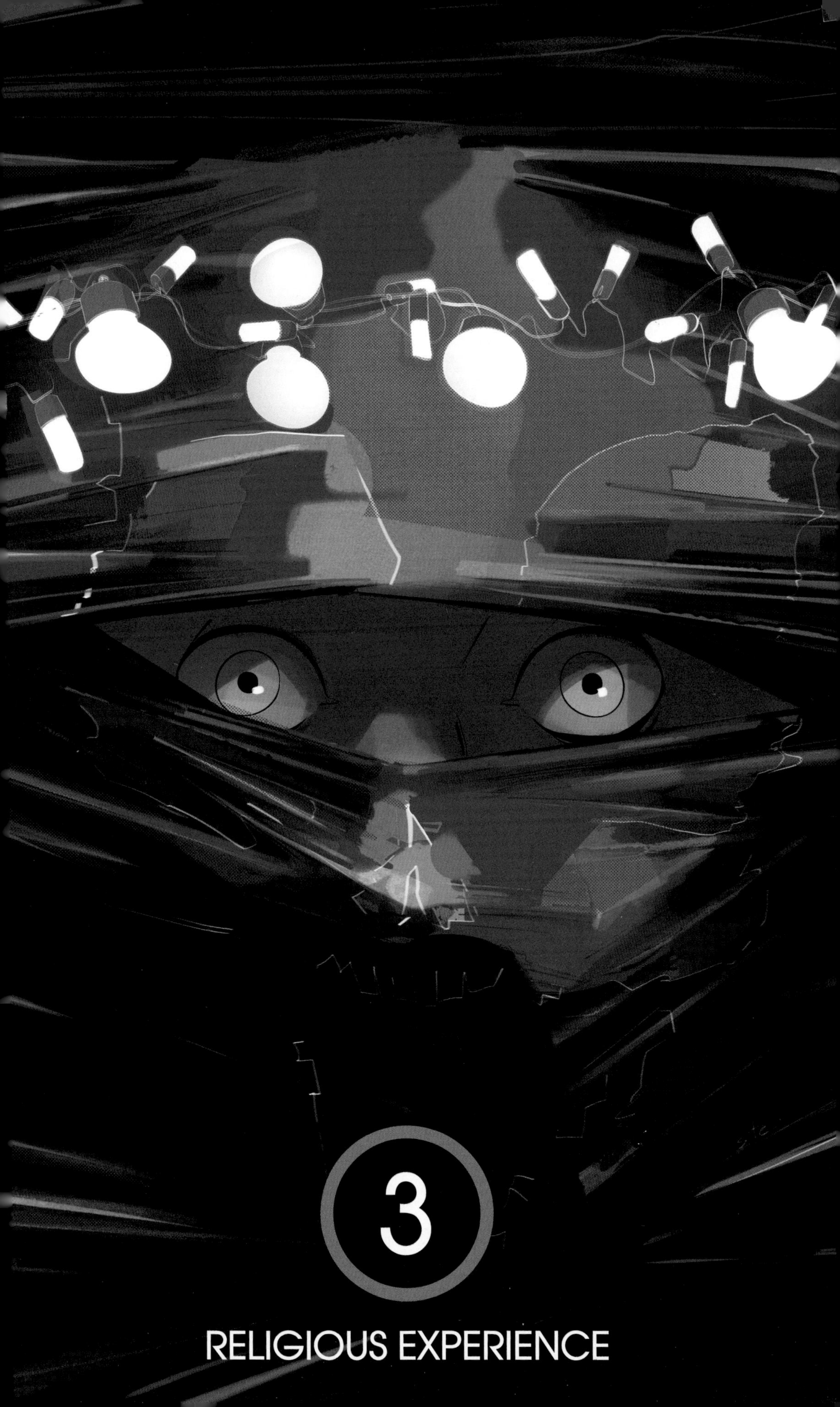

3

RELIGIOUS EXPERIENCE

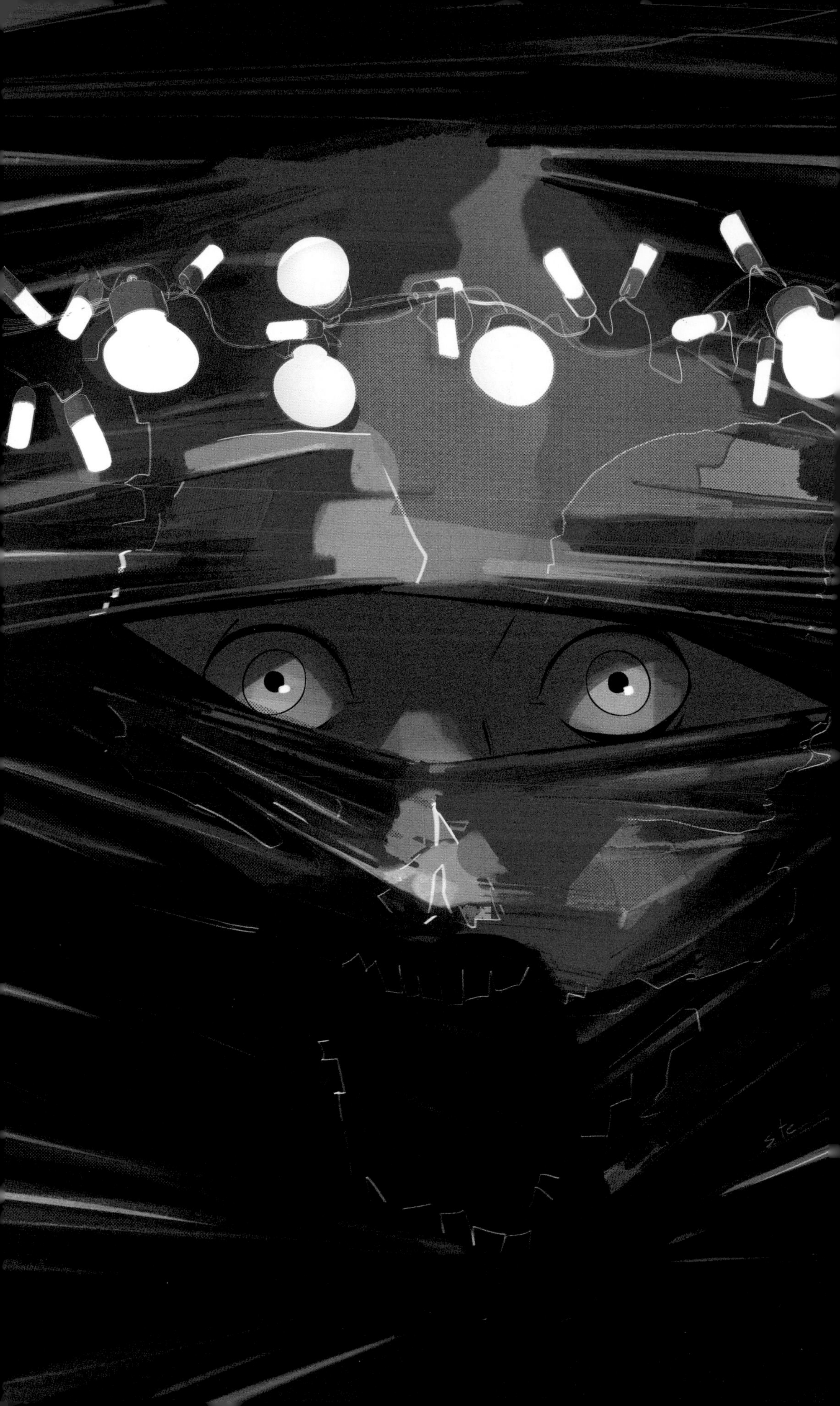

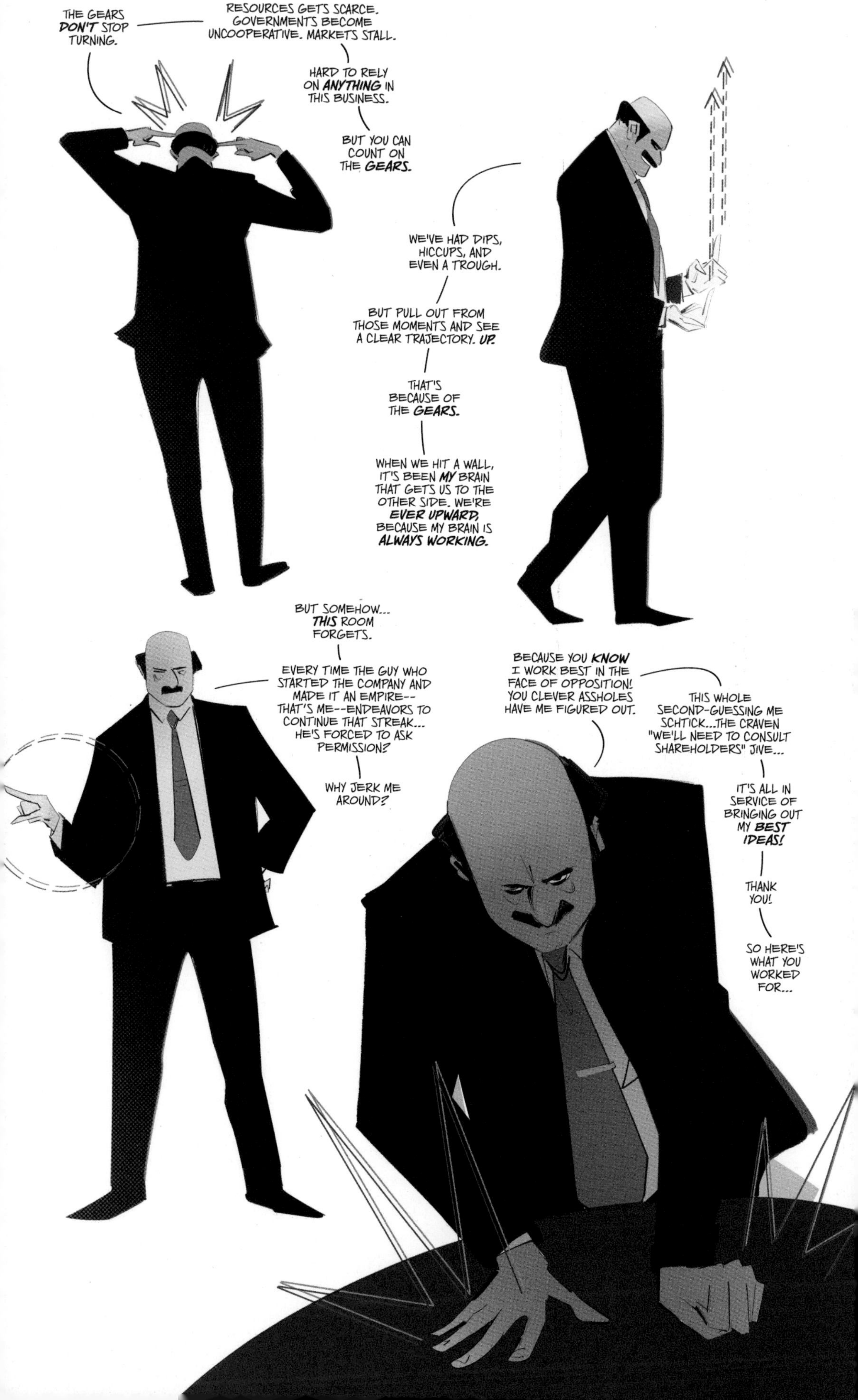
THE GEARS DON'T STOP TURNING.
RESOURCES GETS SCARCE. GOVERNMENTS BECOME UNCOOPERATIVE. MARKETS STALL.
HARD TO RELY ON ANYTHING IN THIS BUSINESS.
BUT YOU CAN COUNT ON THE GEARS.
WE'VE HAD DIPS, HICCUPS, AND EVEN A TROUGH.
BUT PULL OUT FROM THOSE MOMENTS AND SEE A CLEAR TRAJECTORY. UP.
THAT'S BECAUSE OF THE GEARS.
WHEN WE HIT A WALL, IT'S BEEN MY BRAIN THAT GETS US TO THE OTHER SIDE. WE'RE EVER UPWARD, BECAUSE MY BRAIN IS ALWAYS WORKING.
BUT SOMEHOW... THIS ROOM FORGETS.
EVERY TIME THE GUY WHO STARTED THE COMPANY AND MADE IT AN EMPIRE-- THAT'S ME--ENDEAVORS TO CONTINUE THAT STREAK... HE'S FORCED TO ASK PERMISSION?
WHY JERK ME AROUND?
BECAUSE YOU KNOW I WORK BEST IN THE FACE OF OPPOSITION! YOU CLEVER ASSHOLES HAVE ME FIGURED OUT.
THIS WHOLE SECOND-GUESSING ME SCHTICK...THE CRAVEN "WE'LL NEED TO CONSULT SHAREHOLDERS" JIVE...
IT'S ALL IN SERVICE OF BRINGING OUT MY BEST IDEAS!
THANK YOU!
SO HERE'S WHAT YOU WORKED FOR...

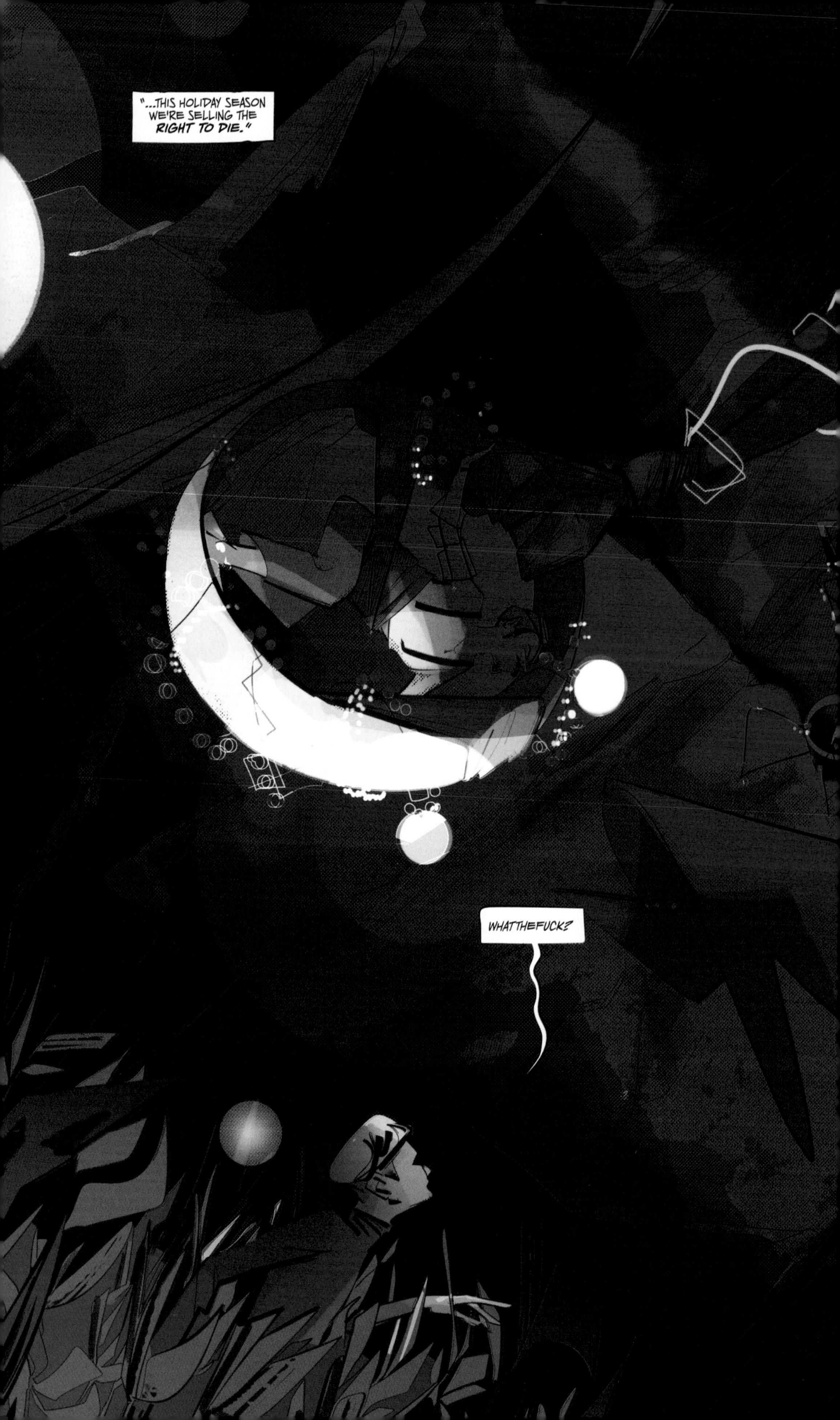
"...THIS HOLIDAY SEASON WE'RE SELLING THE RIGHT TO DIE."
WHATTHEFUCK?

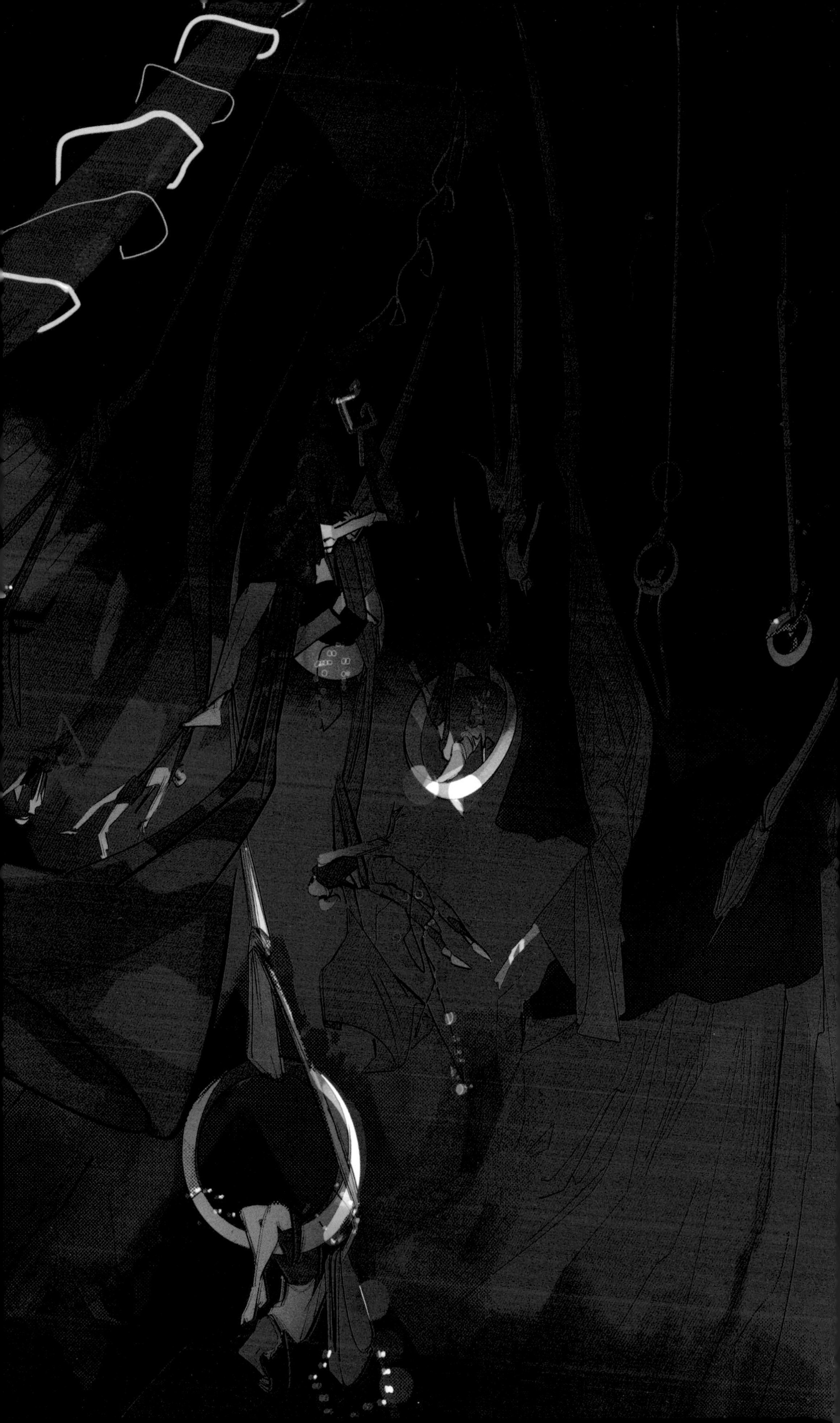

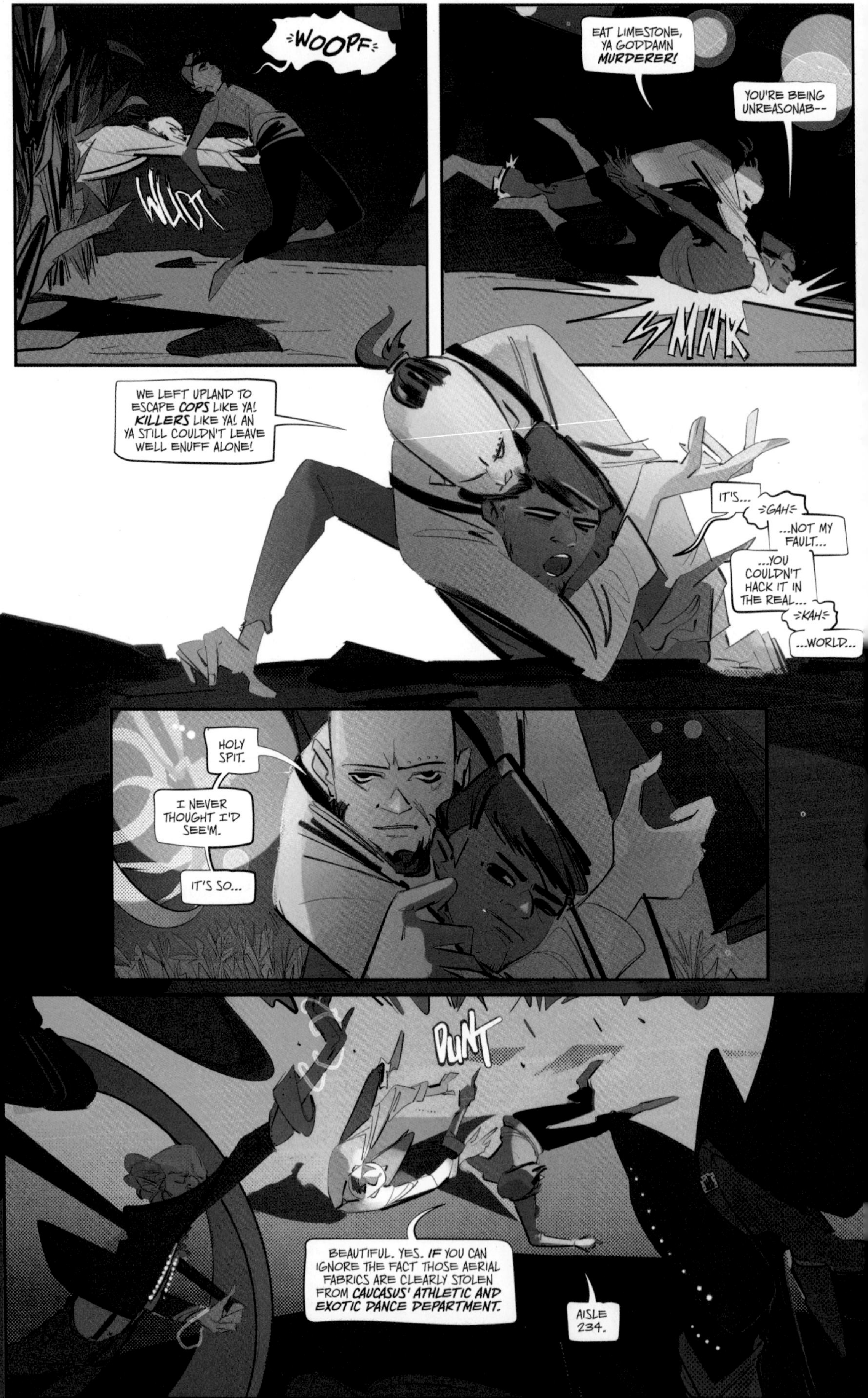

WOOPF
WUDT
EAT LIMESTONE, YA GODDAMN MURDERER!
YOU'RE BEING UNREASONAB--
SMAK
WE LEFT UPLAND TO ESCAPE COPS LIKE YA! KILLERS LIKE YA! AN YA STILL COULDN'T LEAVE WELL ENUFF ALONE!
IT'S...
GAH
...NOT MY FAULT...
...YOU COULDN'T HACK IT IN THE REAL...
KAH
...WORLD...
HOLY SPIT.
I NEVER THOUGHT I'D SEE'M.
IT'S SO...
DUNT
BEAUTIFUL. YES. IF YOU CAN IGNORE THE FACT THOSE AERIAL FABRICS ARE CLEARLY STOLEN FROM CAUCASUS' ATHLETIC AND EXOTIC DANCE DEPARTMENT.
AISLE 234.

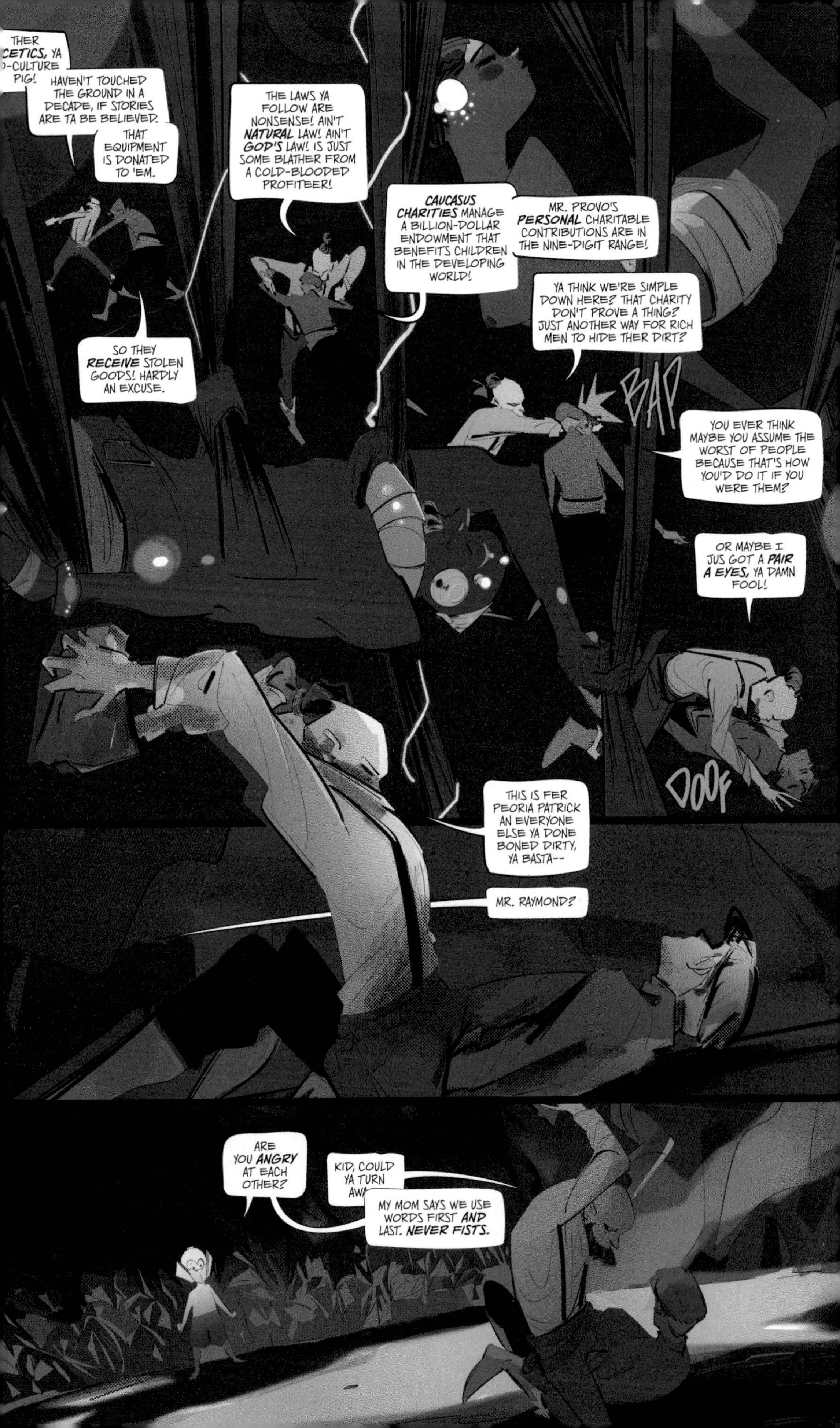
THER
CETICS, YA
-CULTURE
PIG!
HAVEN'T TOUCHED THE GROUND IN A DECADE, IF STORIES ARE TA BE BELIEVED.
THAT EQUIPMENT IS DONATED TO 'EM.
SO THEY RECEIVE STOLEN GOODS! HARDLY AN EXCUSE.
THE LAWS YA FOLLOW ARE NONSENSE! AIN'T NATURAL LAW! AIN'T GOD'S LAW! IS JUST SOME BLATHER FROM A COLD-BLOODED PROFITEER!
CAUCASUS CHARITIES MANAGE A BILLION-DOLLAR ENDOWMENT THAT BENEFITS CHILDREN IN THE DEVELOPING WORLD!
MR. PROVO'S PERSONAL CHARITABLE CONTRIBUTIONS ARE IN THE NINE-DIGIT RANGE!
YA THINK WE'RE SIMPLE DOWN HERE? THAT CHARITY DON'T PROVE A THING? JUST ANOTHER WAY FOR RICH MEN TO HIDE THER DIRT?
BAP
YOU EVER THINK MAYBE YOU ASSUME THE WORST OF PEOPLE BECAUSE THAT'S HOW YOU'D DO IT IF YOU WERE THEM?
OR MAYBE I JUS GOT A PAIR A EYES, YA DAMN FOOL!
DOOF
THIS IS FER PEORIA PATRICK AN EVERYONE ELSE YA DONE BONED DIRTY, YA BASTA--
MR. RAYMOND?
ARE YOU ANGRY AT EACH OTHER?
KID, COULD YA TURN AWA
MY MOM SAYS WE USE WORDS FIRST AND LAST. NEVER FISTS.

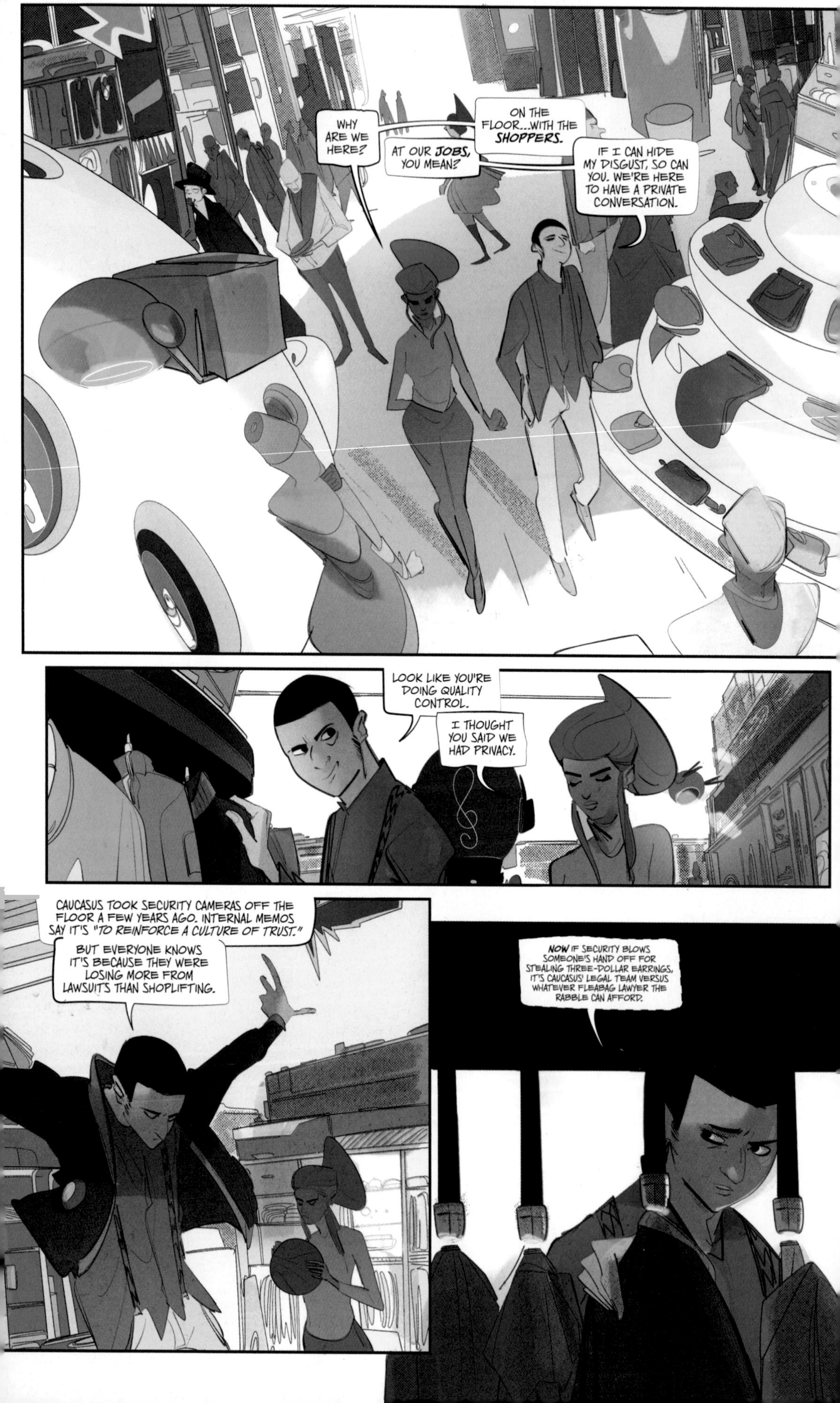
WHY ARE WE HERE?
ON THE FLOOR...WITH THE SHOPPERS.
AT OUR JOBS, YOU MEAN?
IF I CAN HIDE MY DISGUST, SO CAN YOU. WE'RE HERE TO HAVE A PRIVATE CONVERSATION.
LOOK LIKE YOU'RE DOING QUALITY CONTROL.
I THOUGHT YOU SAID WE HAD PRIVACY.
CAUCASUS TOOK SECURITY CAMERAS OFF THE FLOOR A FEW YEARS AGO. INTERNAL MEMOS SAY IT'S "TO REINFORCE A CULTURE OF TRUST."
BUT EVERYONE KNOWS IT'S BECAUSE THEY WERE LOSING MORE FROM LAWSUITS THAN SHOPLIFTING.
NOW IF SECURITY BLOWS SOMEONE'S HAND OFF FOR STEALING THREE-DOLLAR EARRINGS, IT'S CAUCASUS' LEGAL TEAM VERSUS WHATEVER FLEABAG LAWYER THE RABBLE CAN AFFORD.

BUT JUST BECAUSE THERE'S NO CAMERAS...DOESN'T MEAN WE'RE NOT BEING WATCHED.

I WAS THE ONE WHO SELECTED HER FROM THE TRAINEE POOL.

AND HERE I AM, SCARED TO DEATH OF HER.

I MEAN, YOU *ARE* A SERVILE WORM.

I'M TRYING TO MAKE US *BILLIONAIRES*, AND SOMEHOW YOU CAN'T MANAGE A KIND WORD.

LET'S GET TO BUSINESS...

NUSSBAUM IS MISSING.

IS THAT ONE OF THOSE HYPER-SPECIFIC GERMAN WORDS? FOR SOMETHING ESOTERIC LIKE "PASSIONATE LOSS" OR "AGGRIEVED FRIENDSHIP?"

NO. *NUSSBAUM* IS THE LOSS PREVENTION THUG WHO SAVED PROVO.

GETTING HIM OUT OF OUR WAY IS ESSENTIAL TO THE PLAN.

AND HE'S *MISSING.*

CALL ME DENSE BUT IF WE'RE LOOKING TO GET RID OF HIM...

...ISN'T THE FACT HE'S MISSING A *GOOD* THING?

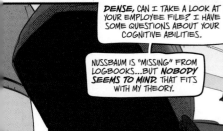

DENSE, CAN I TAKE A LOOK AT YOUR EMPLOYEE FILE? I HAVE SOME QUESTIONS ABOUT YOUR COGNITIVE ABILITIES.

NUSSBAUM IS "MISSING" FROM LOGBOOKS...BUT *NOBODY SEEMS TO MIND.* THAT FITS WITH MY THEORY.

WHICH IS?

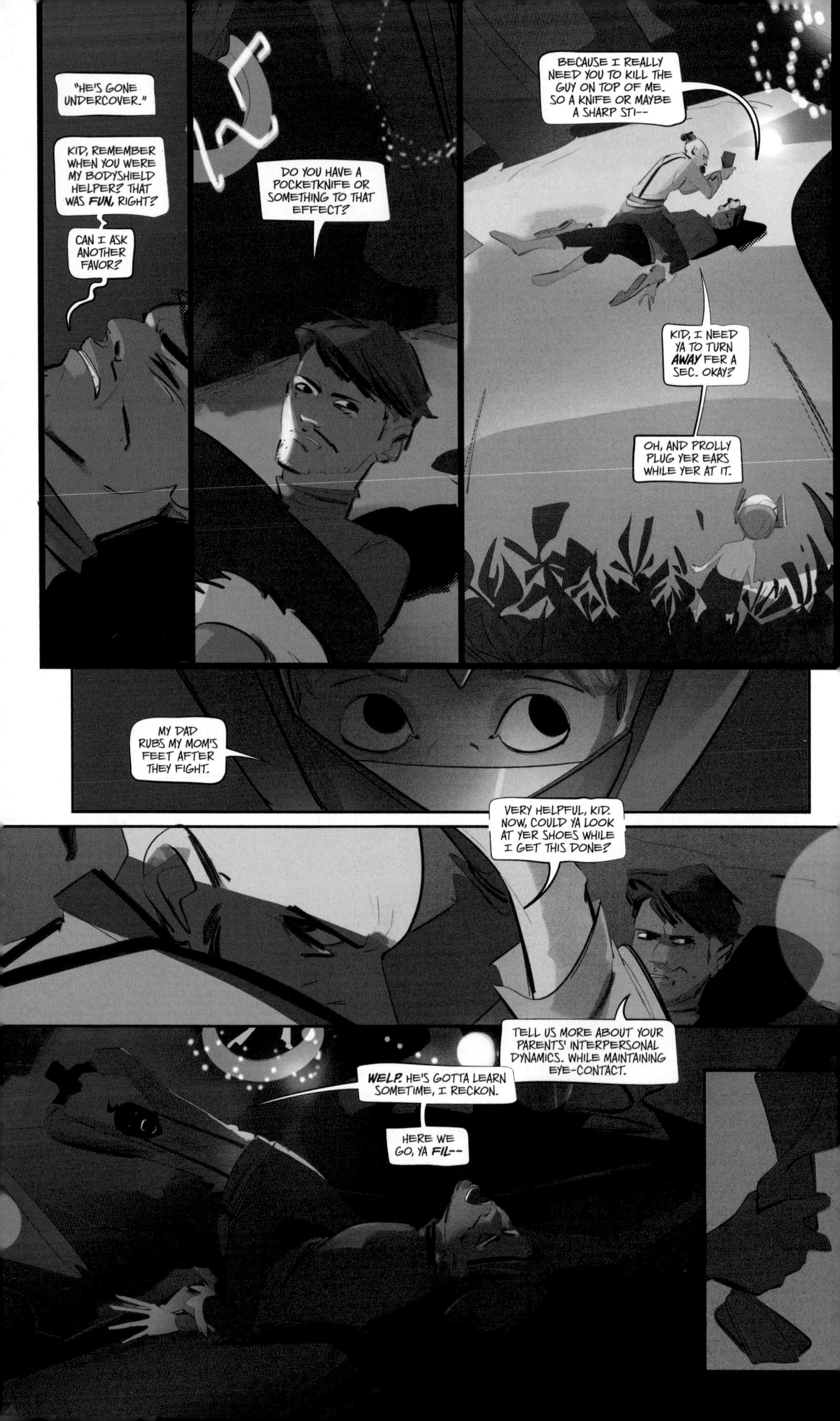
"HE'S GONE UNDERCOVER."
KID, REMEMBER WHEN YOU WERE MY BODYSHIELD HELPER? THAT WAS **FUN,** RIGHT?
CAN I ASK ANOTHER FAVOR?
DO YOU HAVE A POCKETKNIFE OR SOMETHING TO THAT EFFECT?
BECAUSE I REALLY NEED YOU TO KILL THE GUY ON TOP OF ME. SO A KNIFE OR MAYBE A SHARP STI--
KID, I NEED YA TO TURN **AWAY** FER A SEC. OKAY?
OH, AND PROLLY PLUG YER EARS WHILE YER AT IT.
MY DAD RUBS MY MOM'S FEET AFTER THEY FIGHT.
VERY HELPFUL, KID. NOW, COULD YA LOOK AT YER SHOES WHILE I GET THIS DONE?
TELL US MORE ABOUT YOUR PARENTS' INTERPERSONAL DYNAMICS. WHILE MAINTAINING EYE-CONTACT.
WELP. HE'S GOTTA LEARN SOMETIME, I RECKON.
HERE WE GO, YA **FIL--**

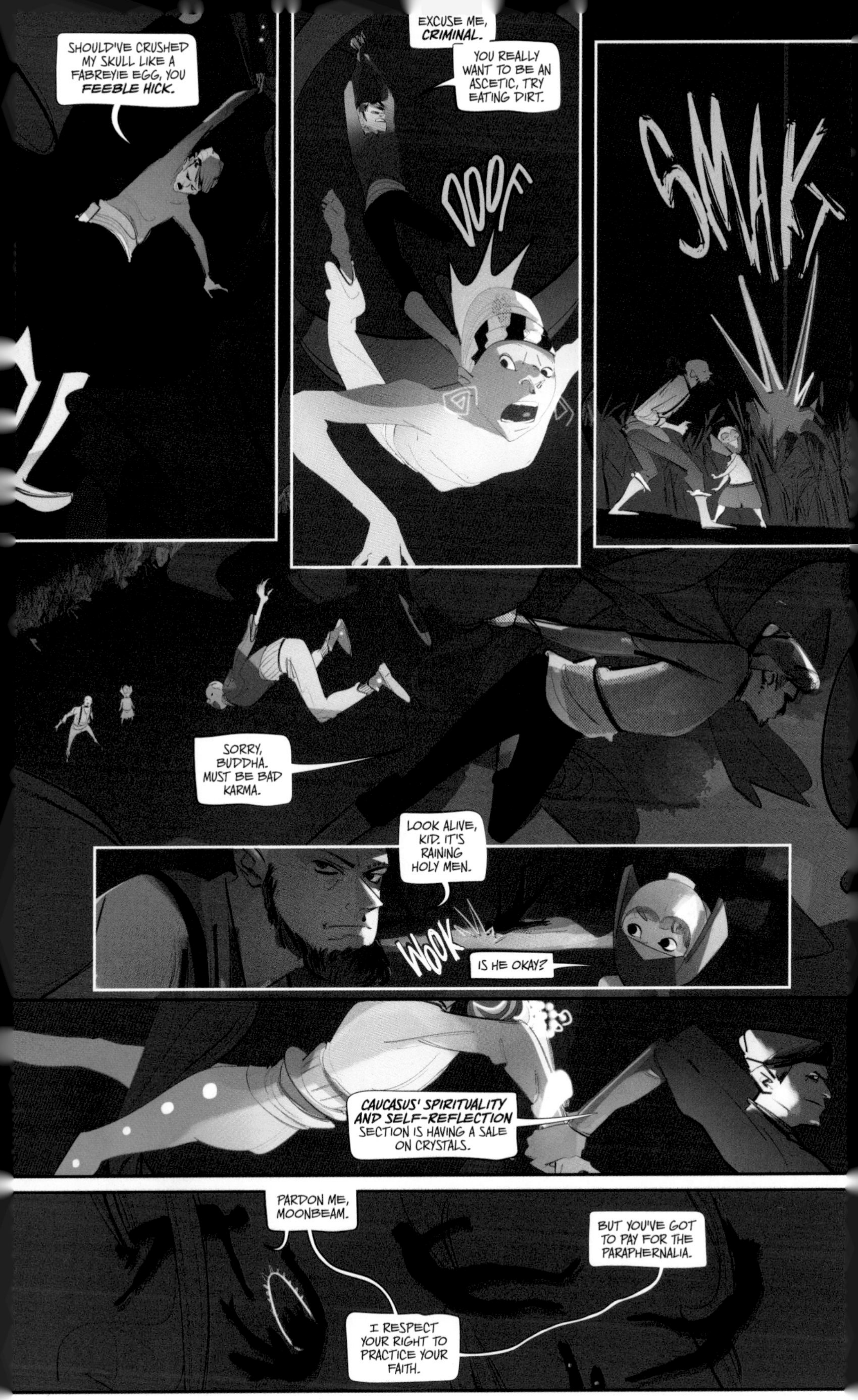
SHOULD'VE CRUSHED MY SKULL LIKE A FABREYIE EGG, YOU **FEEBLE HICK.**
EXCUSE ME, **CRIMINAL.**
YOU REALLY WANT TO BE AN ASCETIC, TRY EATING DIRT.
DOOF
SMAK
SORRY, BUDDHA. MUST BE BAD KARMA.
LOOK ALIVE, KID. IT'S RAINING HOLY MEN.
WOOK
IS HE OKAY?
CAUCASUS' SPIRITUALITY AND SELF-REFLECTION SECTION IS HAVING A SALE ON CRYSTALS.
PARDON ME, MOONBEAM.
I RESPECT YOUR RIGHT TO PRACTICE YOUR FAITH.
BUT YOU'VE GOT TO PAY FOR THE PARAPHERNALIA.

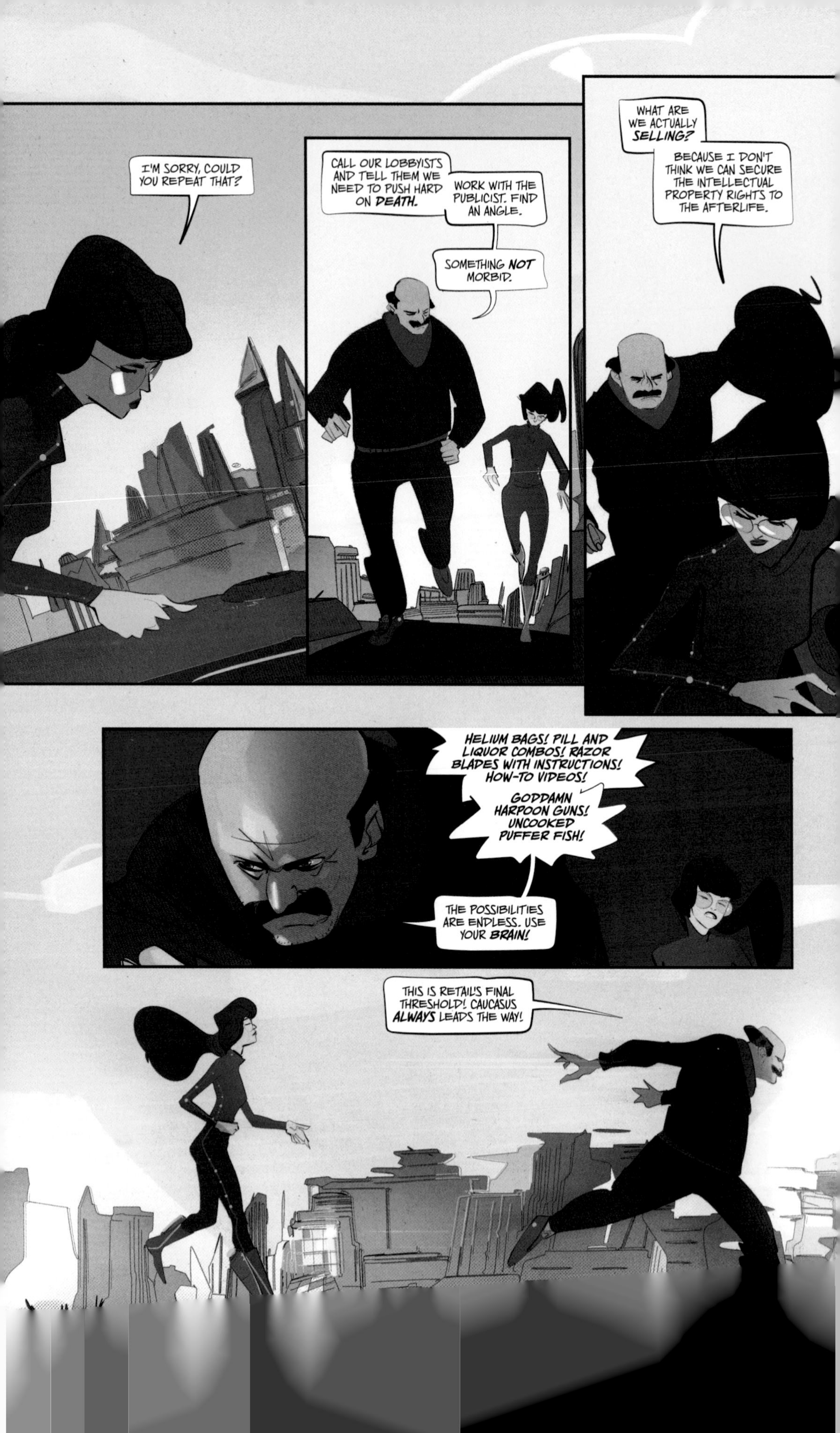
I'M SORRY, COULD YOU REPEAT THAT?
CALL OUR LOBBYISTS AND TELL THEM WE NEED TO PUSH HARD ON DEATH.
WORK WITH THE PUBLICIST. FIND AN ANGLE.
SOMETHING NOT MORBID.
WHAT ARE WE ACTUALLY SELLING?
BECAUSE I DON'T THINK WE CAN SECURE THE INTELLECTUAL PROPERTY RIGHTS TO THE AFTERLIFE.
HELIUM BAGS! PILL AND LIQUOR COMBOS! RAZOR BLADES WITH INSTRUCTIONS! HOW-TO VIDEOS!
GODDAMN HARPOON GUNS! UNCOOKED PUFFER FISH!
THE POSSIBILITIES ARE ENDLESS. USE YOUR BRAIN!
THIS IS RETAIL'S FINAL THRESHOLD! CAUCASUS ALWAYS LEADS THE WAY!

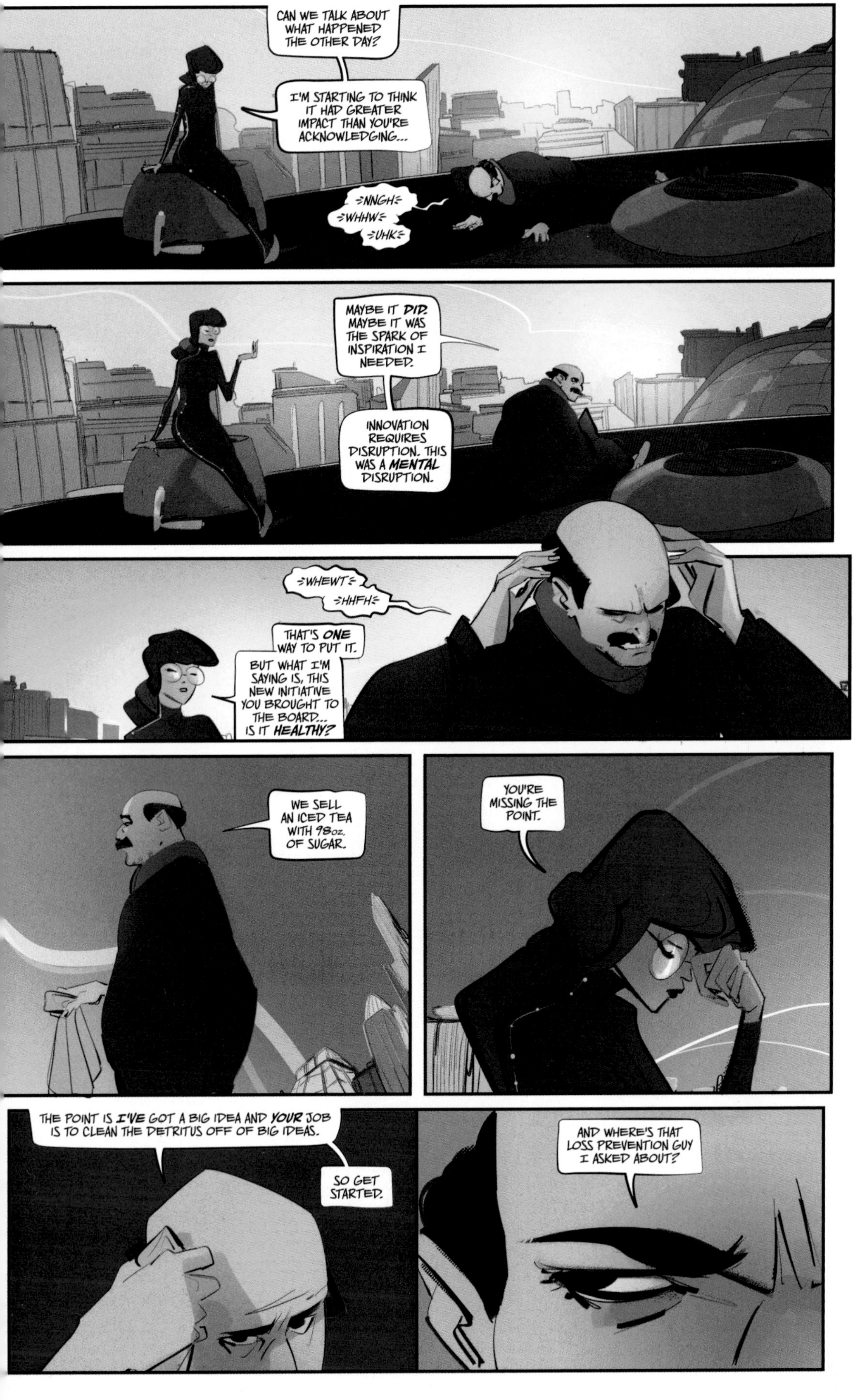
CAN WE TALK ABOUT WHAT HAPPENED THE OTHER DAY?
I'M STARTING TO THINK IT HAD GREATER IMPACT THAN YOU'RE ACKNOWLEDGING...
NNGH
WHHW
UHK
MAYBE IT DID. MAYBE IT WAS THE SPARK OF INSPIRATION I NEEDED.
INNOVATION REQUIRES DISRUPTION. THIS WAS A MENTAL DISRUPTION.
WHEWT
HHFH
THAT'S ONE WAY TO PUT IT.
BUT WHAT I'M SAYING IS, THIS NEW INITIATIVE YOU BROUGHT TO THE BOARD... IS IT HEALTHY?
WE SELL AN ICED TEA WITH 98oz. OF SUGAR.
YOU'RE MISSING THE POINT.
THE POINT IS I'VE GOT A BIG IDEA AND YOUR JOB IS TO CLEAN THE DETRITUS OFF OF BIG IDEAS.
SO GET STARTED.
AND WHERE'S THAT LOSS PREVENTION GUY I ASKED ABOUT?

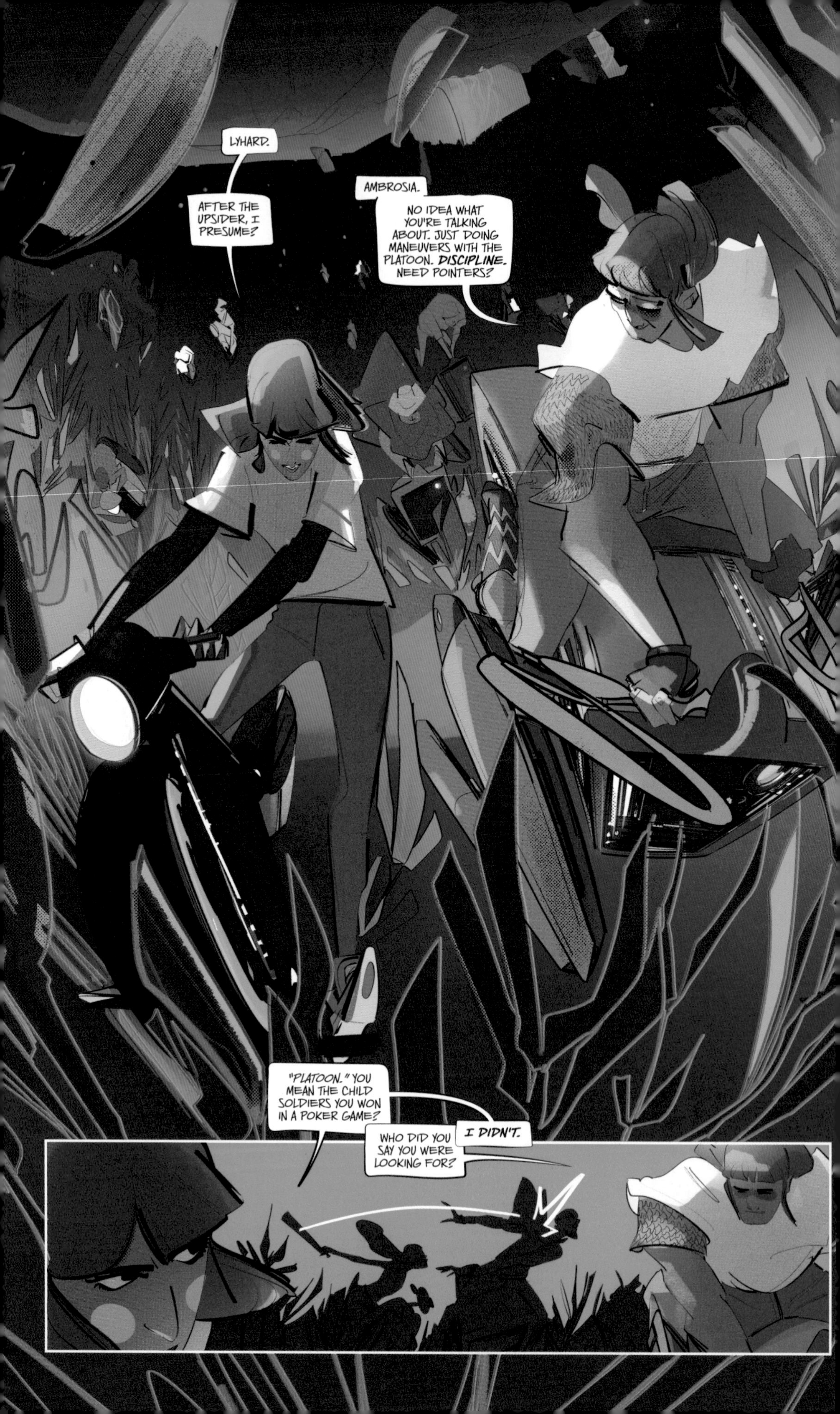
LYHARD.
AFTER THE UPSIDER, I PRESUME?
AMBROSIA.
NO IDEA WHAT YOU'RE TALKING ABOUT. JUST DOING MANEUVERS WITH THE PLATOON. DISCIPLINE. NEED POINTERS?
"PLATOON." YOU MEAN THE CHILD SOLDIERS YOU WON IN A POKER GAME?
I DIDN'T.
WHO DID YOU SAY YOU WERE LOOKING FOR?

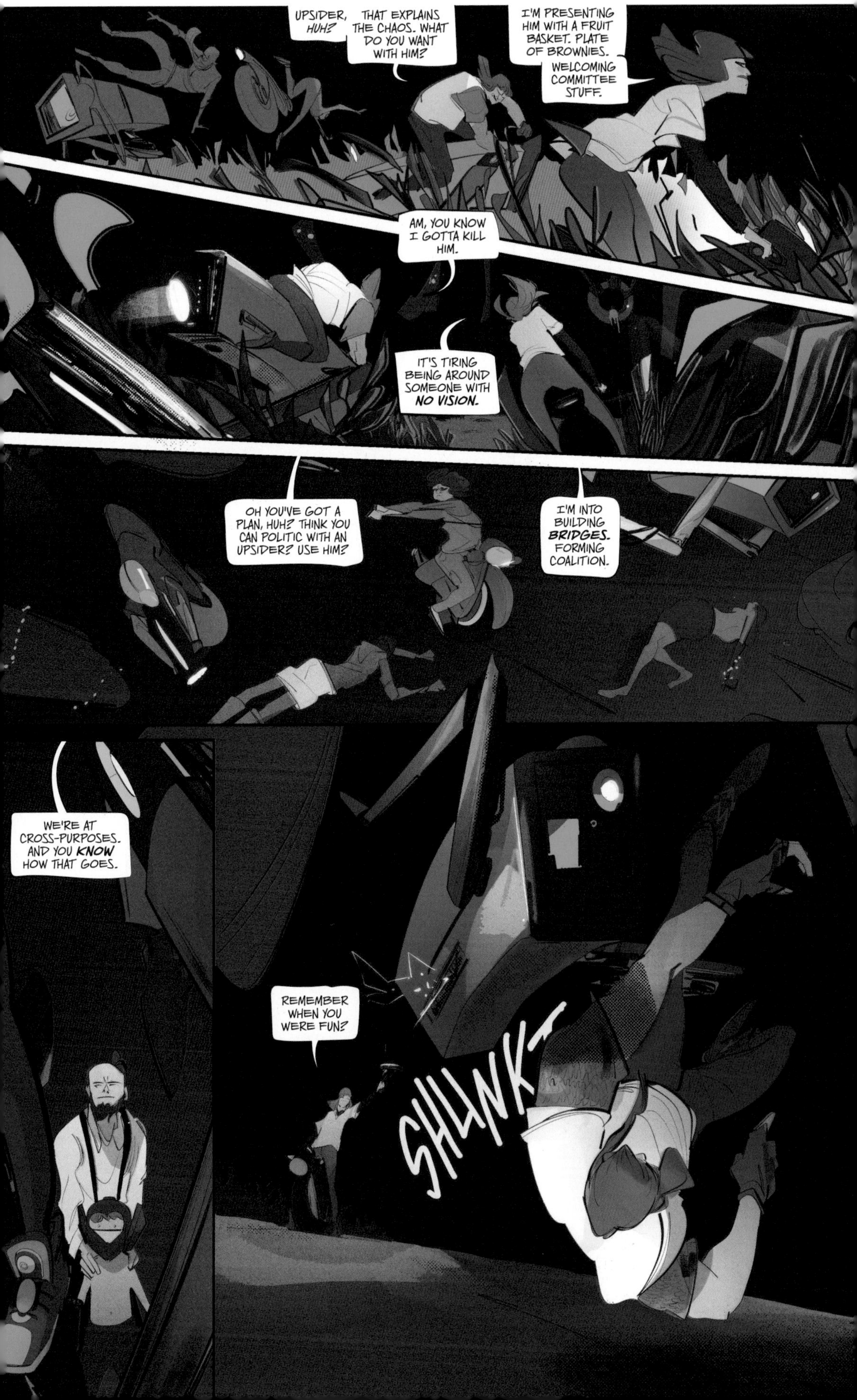

UPSIDER, HUH?
THAT EXPLAINS THE CHAOS. WHAT DO YOU WANT WITH HIM?
I'M PRESENTING HIM WITH A FRUIT BASKET. PLATE OF BROWNIES.
WELCOMING COMMITTEE STUFF.
AM, YOU KNOW I GOTTA KILL HIM.
IT'S TIRING BEING AROUND SOMEONE WITH **NO VISION.**
OH YOU'VE GOT A PLAN, HUH? THINK YOU CAN POLITIC WITH AN UPSIDER? USE HIM?
I'M INTO BUILDING **BRIDGES.** FORMING COALITION.
WE'RE AT CROSS-PURPOSES. AND YOU **KNOW** HOW THAT GOES.
REMEMBER WHEN YOU WERE FUN?
SHUNK

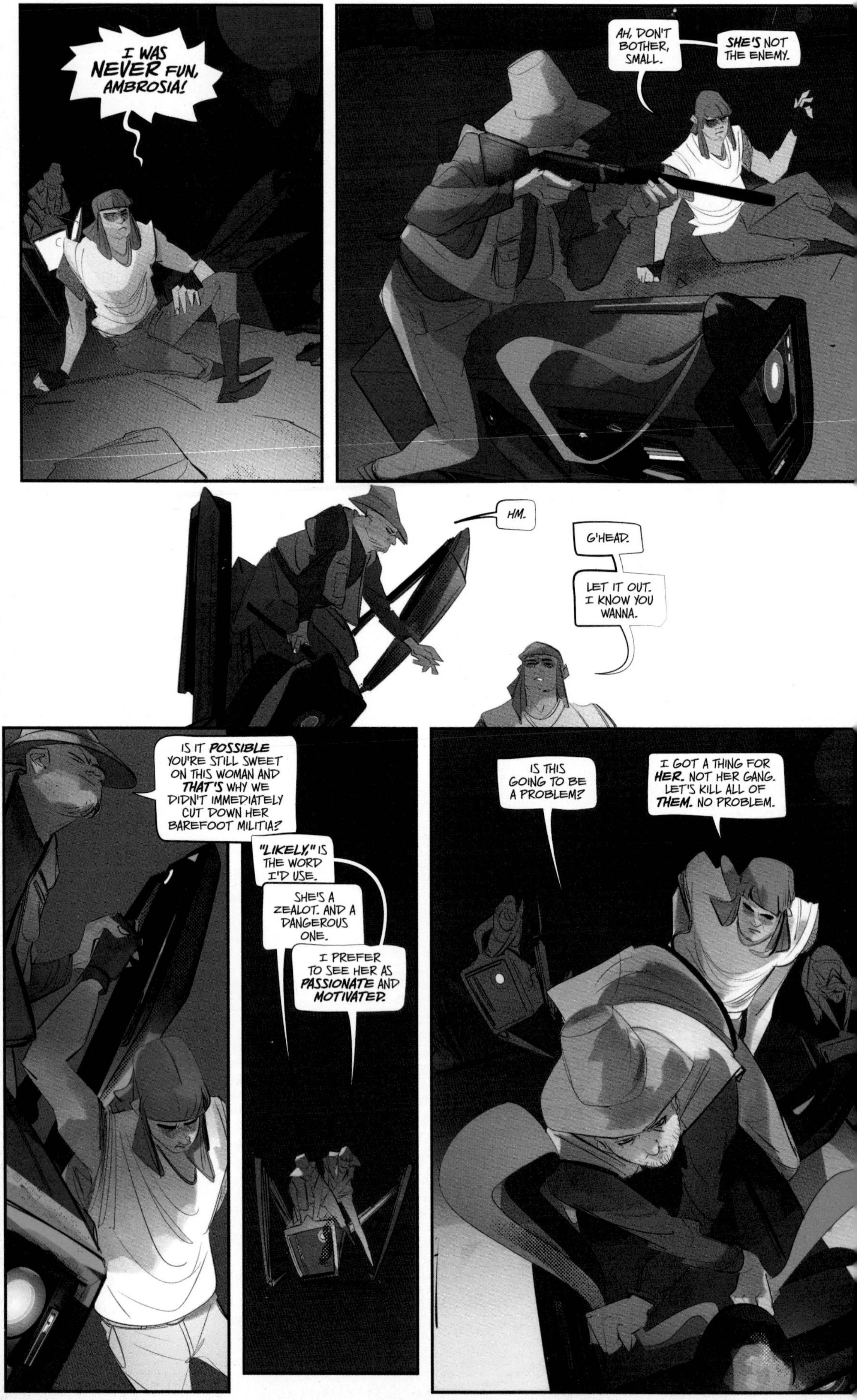
I WAS NEVER FUN, AMBROSIA!
AH, DON'T BOTHER, SMALL.
SHE'S NOT THE ENEMY.
HM.
G'HEAD.
LET IT OUT. I KNOW YOU WANNA.
IS IT POSSIBLE YOU'RE STILL SWEET ON THIS WOMAN AND THAT'S WHY WE DIDN'T IMMEDIATELY CUT DOWN HER BAREFOOT MILITIA?
"LIKELY," IS THE WORD I'D USE.
SHE'S A ZEALOT. AND A DANGEROUS ONE.
I PREFER TO SEE HER AS PASSIONATE AND MOTIVATED.
IS THIS GOING TO BE A PROBLEM?
I GOT A THING FOR HER. NOT HER GANG. LET'S KILL ALL OF THEM. NO PROBLEM.

IS THIS KARMA?
THERE'S TWO WAYS TO THE GROUND, UPSIDER! ON YOUR OWN OR WITH A BULLET'S HELP!
EVEN CAUCASUS ANTIQUES AND ONLINE BIDDING HOUSE DOESN'T SELL GUNS THAT OLD. GOOD LUCK HITTING ANYTHING.
WHOA!
WHOA!
WELL. THIS IS A PICKLE, ISN'T IT.

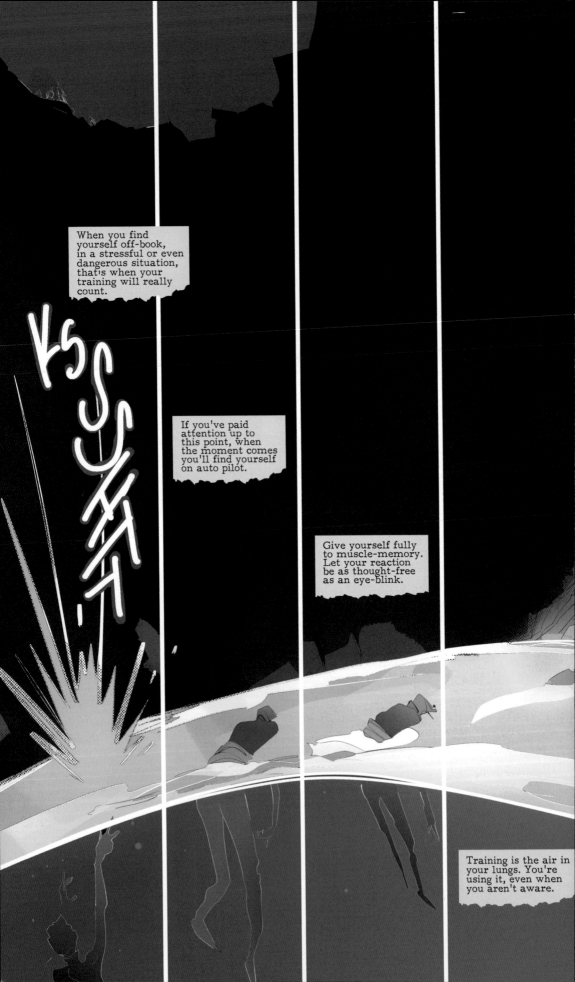

When you find yourself off-book, in a stressful or even dangerous situation, that's when your training will really count.

If you've paid attention up to this point, when the moment comes you'll find yourself on auto pilot.

Give yourself fully to muscle-memory. Let your reaction be as thought-free as an eye-blink.

Training is the air in your lungs. You're using it, even when you aren't aware.

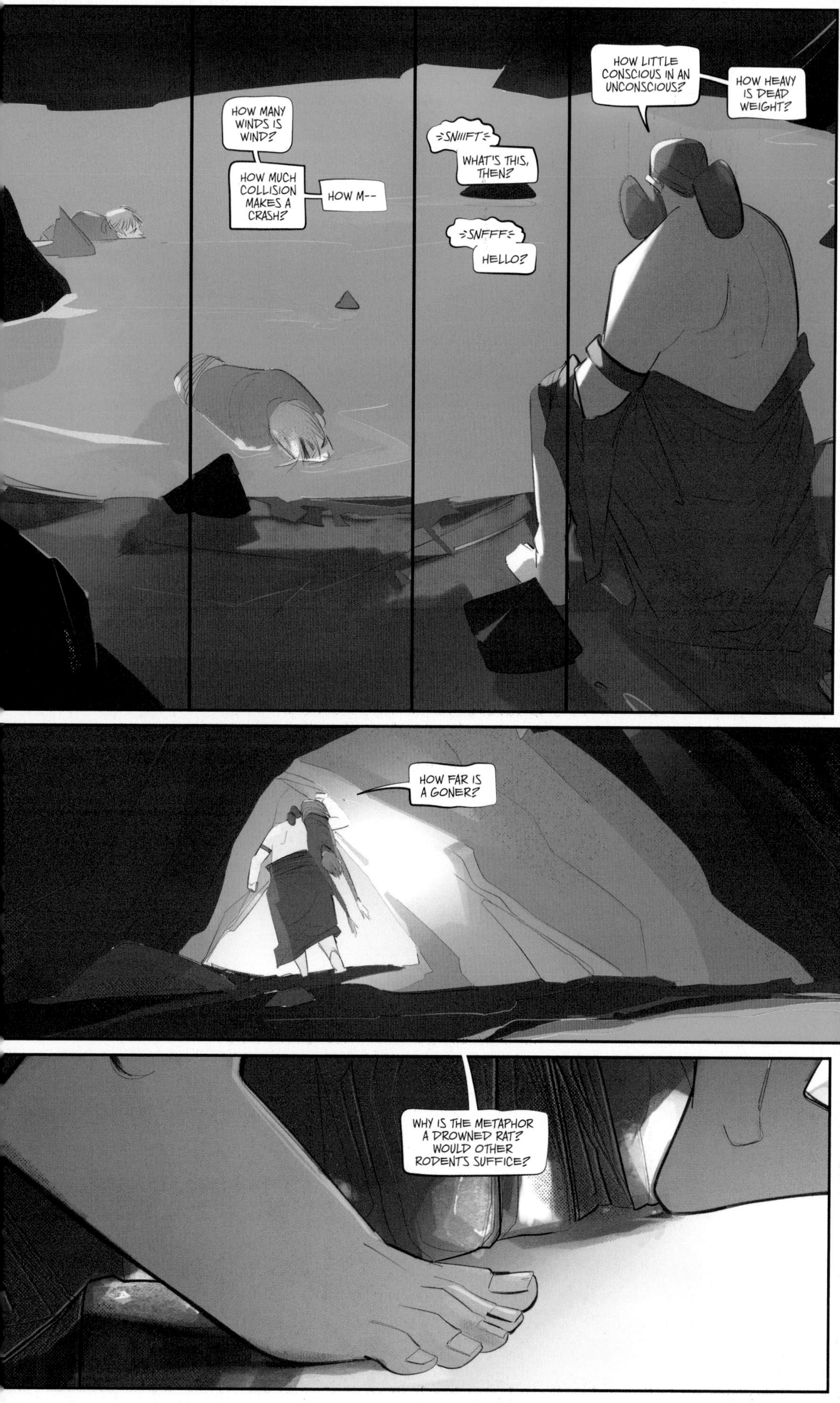
HOW MANY WINDS IS WIND?
HOW MUCH COLLISION MAKES A CRASH?
HOW M--
=SNIIIFT=
WHAT'S THIS, THEN?
=SNFFF=
HELLO?
HOW LITTLE CONSCIOUS IN AN UNCONSCIOUS?
HOW HEAVY IS DEAD WEIGHT?
HOW FAR IS A GONER?
WHY IS THE METAPHOR A DROWNED RAT? WOULD OTHER RODENTS SUFFICE?

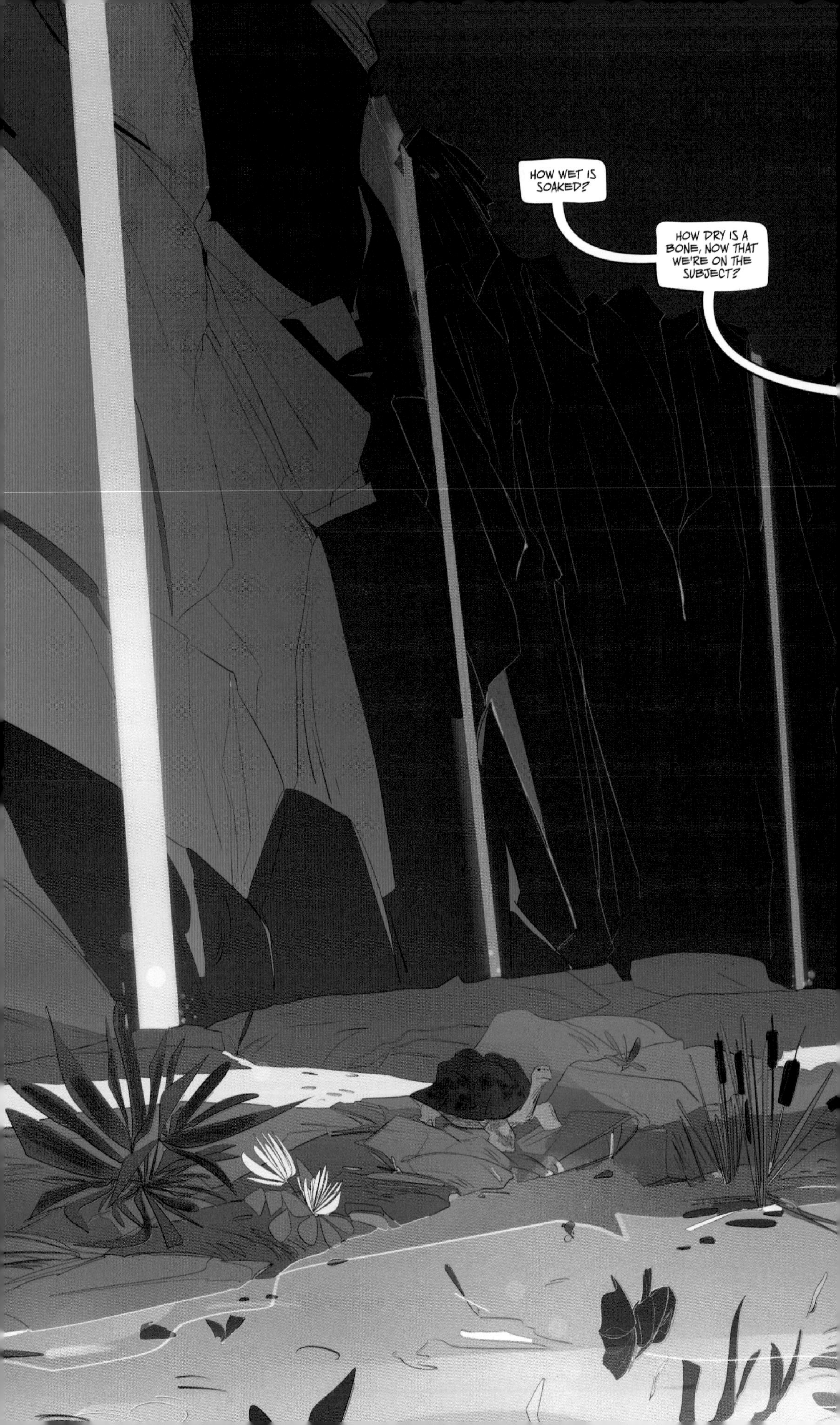
HOW WET IS SOAKED?
HOW DRY IS A BONE, NOW THAT WE'RE ON THE SUBJECT?

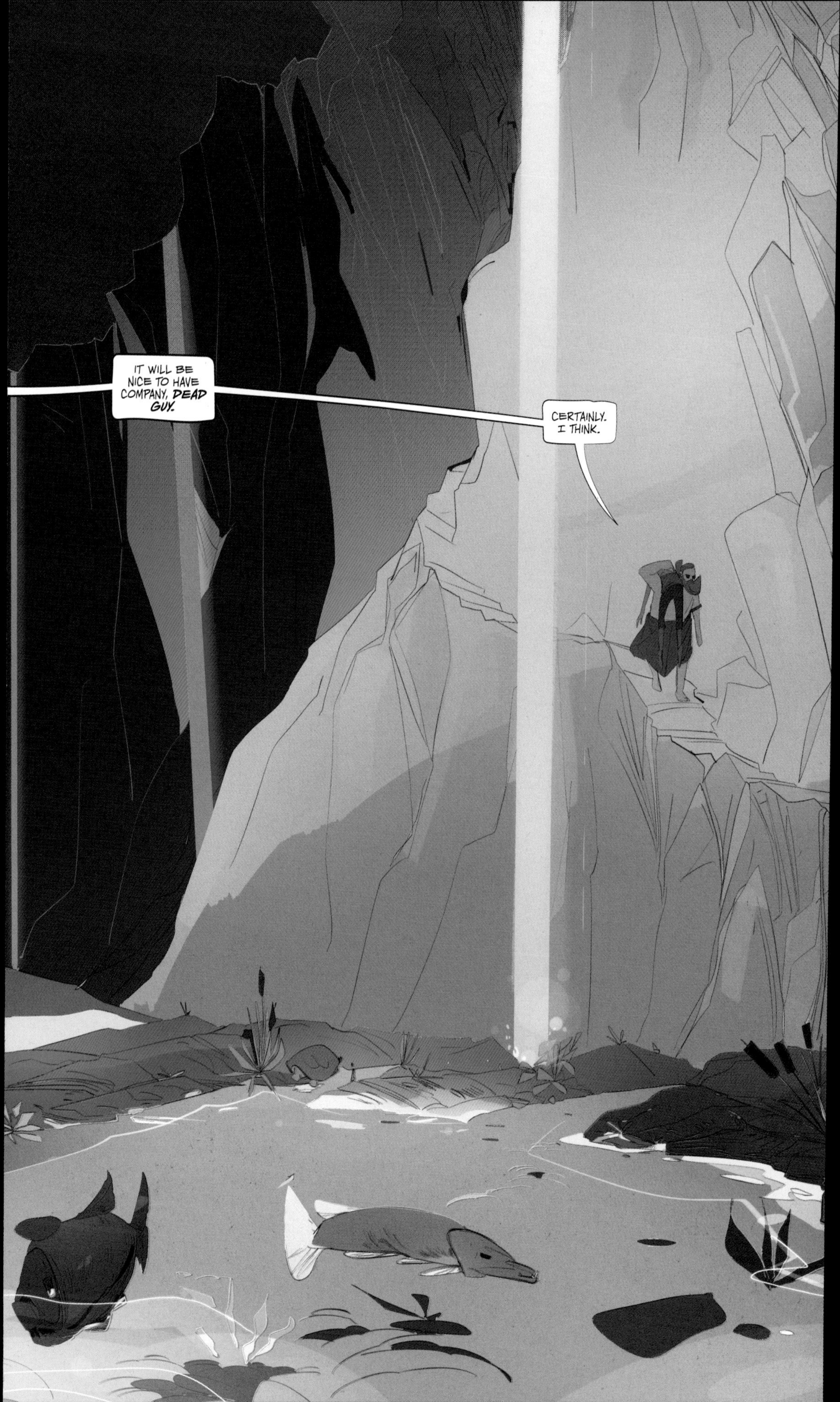
IT WILL BE NICE TO HAVE COMPANY, **DEAD GUY.**
CERTAINLY. I THINK.

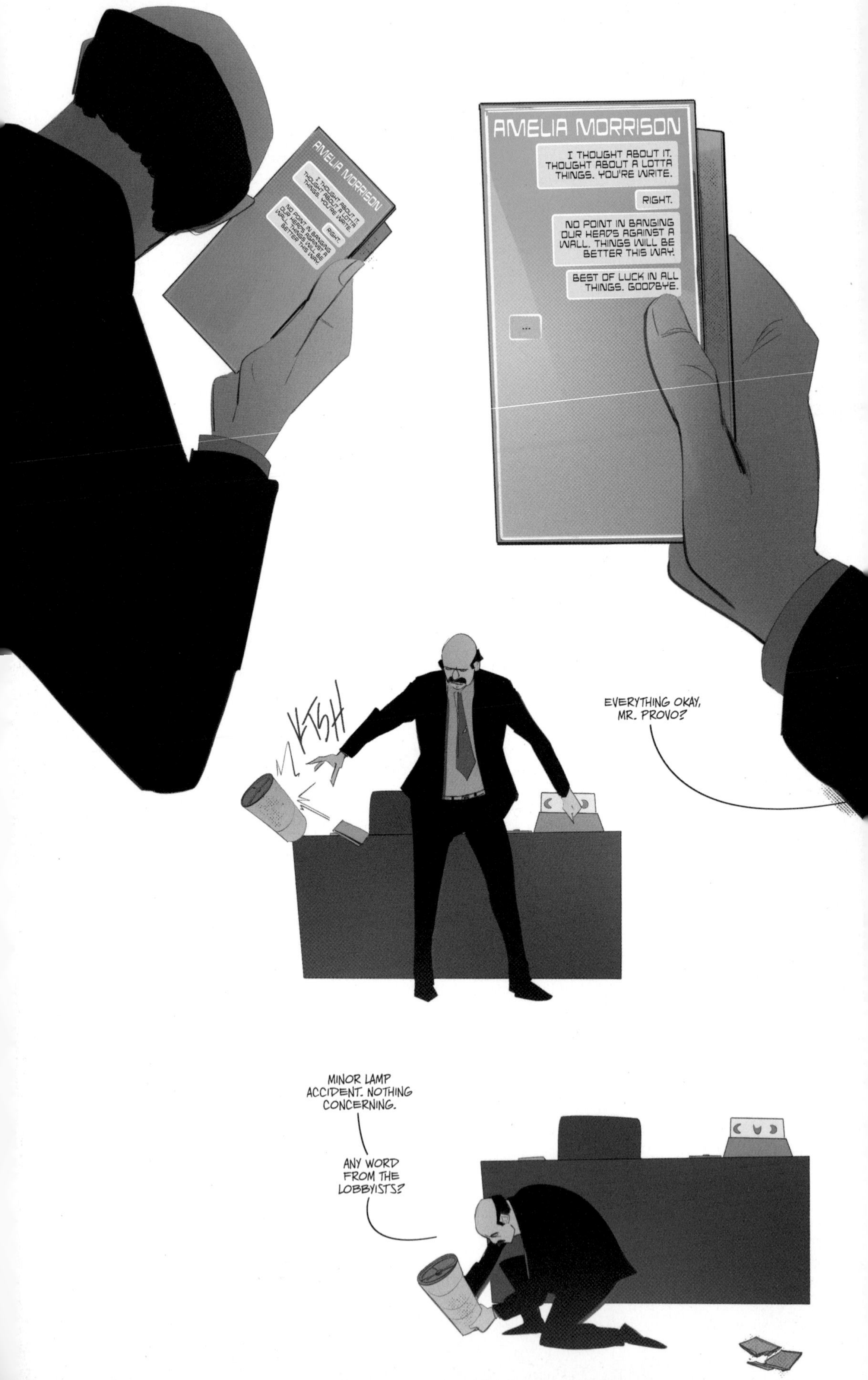
AMELIA MORRISON
I THOUGHT ABOUT IT. THOUGHT ABOUT A LOTTA THINGS. YOU'RE WRITE.
RIGHT.
NO POINT IN BANGING OUR HEADS AGAINST A WALL. THINGS WILL BE BETTER THIS WAY.
BEST OF LUCK IN ALL THINGS. GOODBYE.
...
KTSH
EVERYTHING OKAY, MR. PROVO?
MINOR LAMP ACCIDENT. NOTHING CONCERNING.
ANY WORD FROM THE LOBBYISTS?

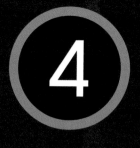

4

ROOMY INTERIOR

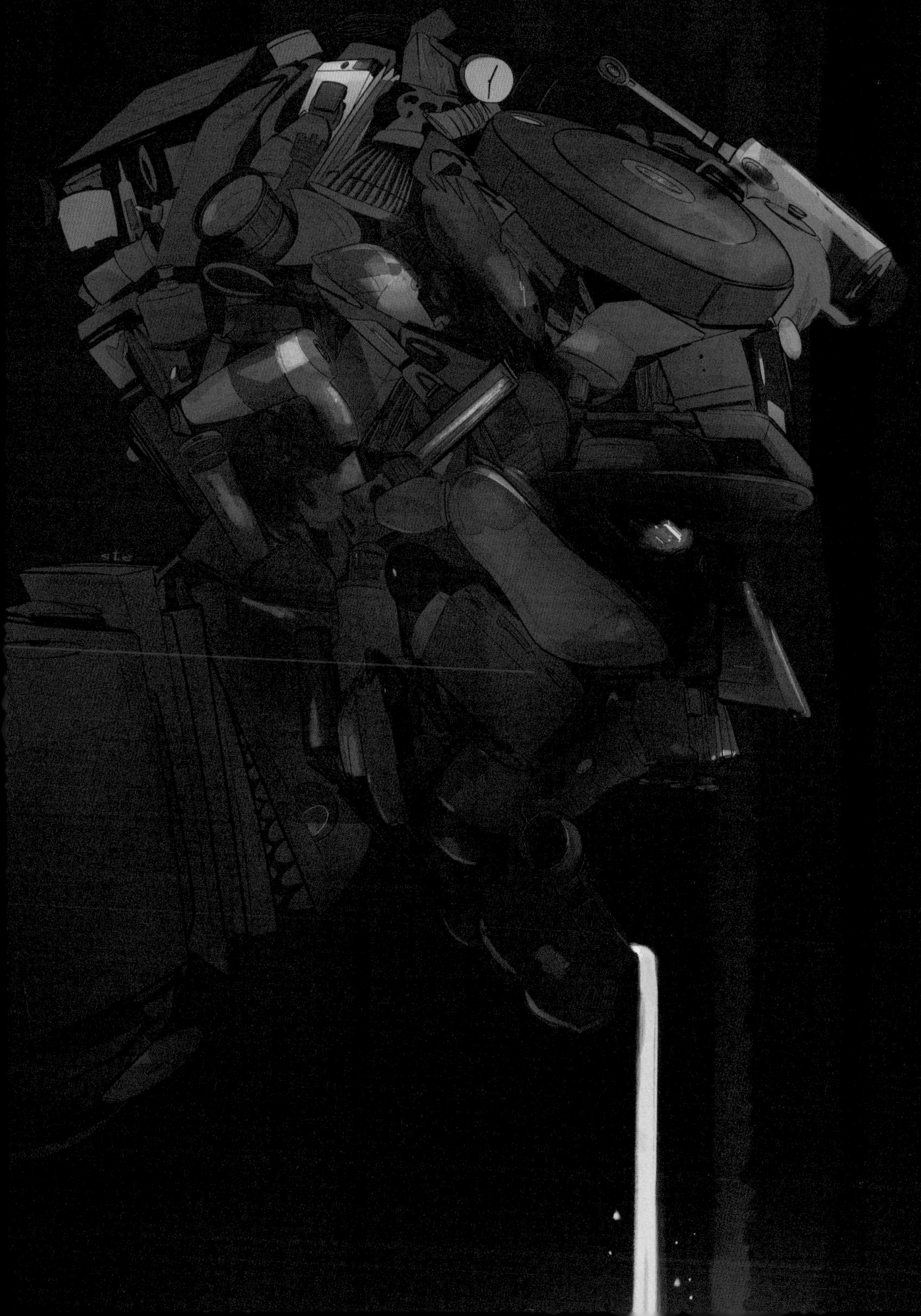

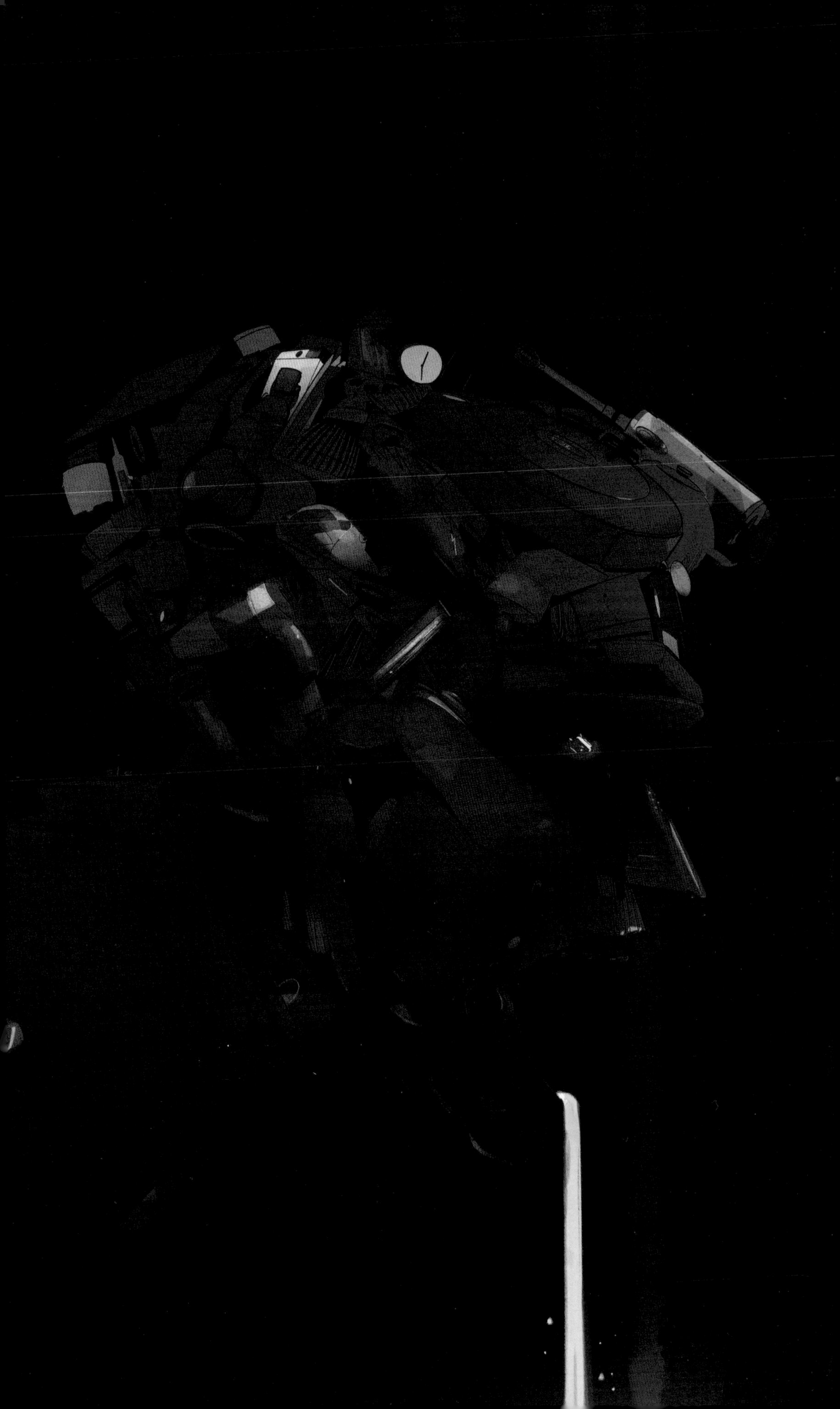

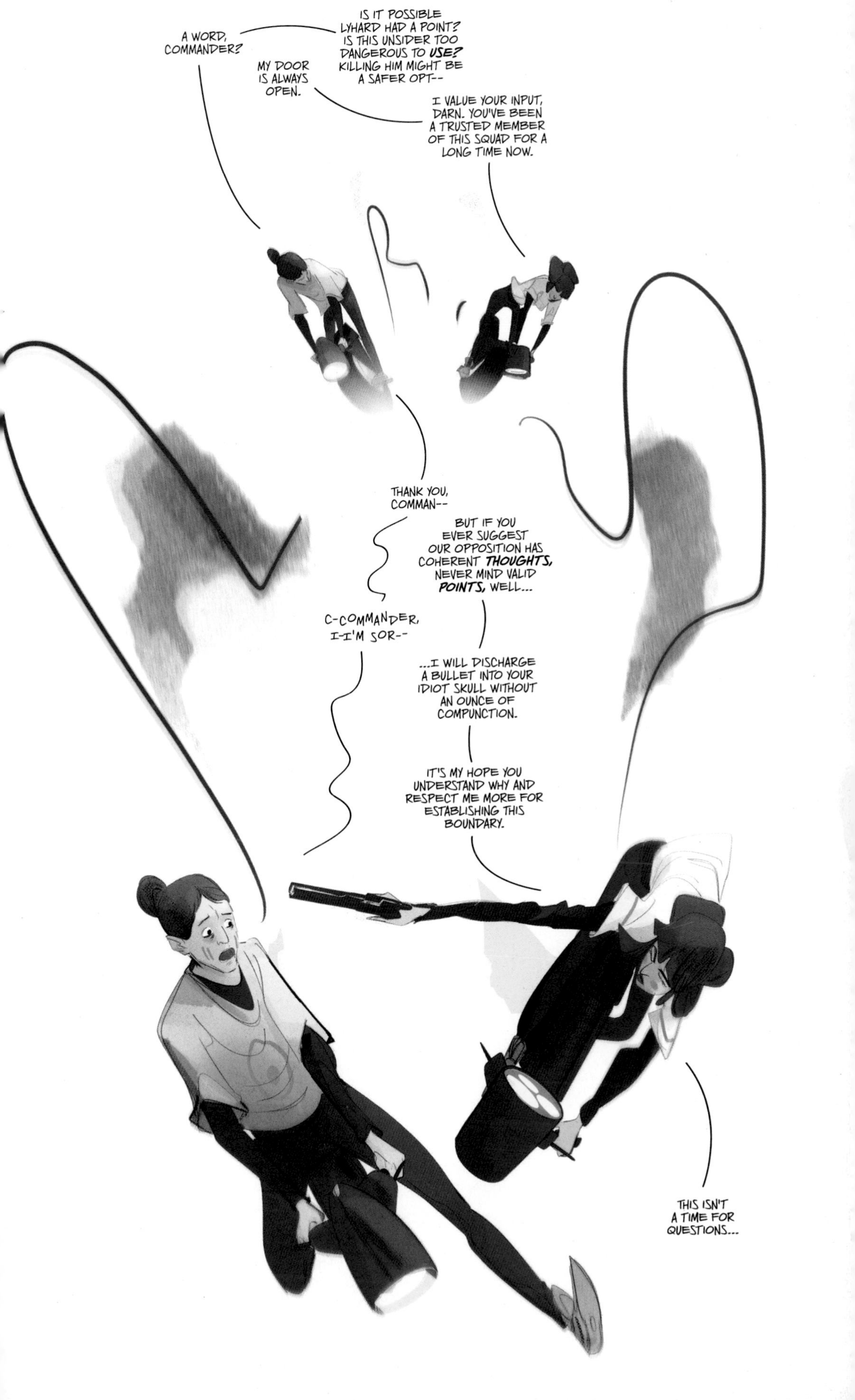
A WORD, COMMANDER?
IS IT POSSIBLE LYHARD HAD A POINT? IS THIS UNSIDER TOO DANGEROUS TO USE? KILLING HIM MIGHT BE A SAFER OPT--
MY DOOR IS ALWAYS OPEN.
I VALUE YOUR INPUT, DARN. YOU'VE BEEN A TRUSTED MEMBER OF THIS SQUAD FOR A LONG TIME NOW.
THANK YOU, COMMAN--
BUT IF YOU EVER SUGGEST OUR OPPOSITION HAS COHERENT THOUGHTS, NEVER MIND VALID POINTS, WELL...
C-COMMANDER, I-I'M SOR--
...I WILL DISCHARGE A BULLET INTO YOUR IDIOT SKULL WITHOUT AN OUNCE OF COMPUNCTION.
IT'S MY HOPE YOU UNDERSTAND WHY AND RESPECT ME MORE FOR ESTABLISHING THIS BOUNDARY.
THIS ISN'T A TIME FOR QUESTIONS...

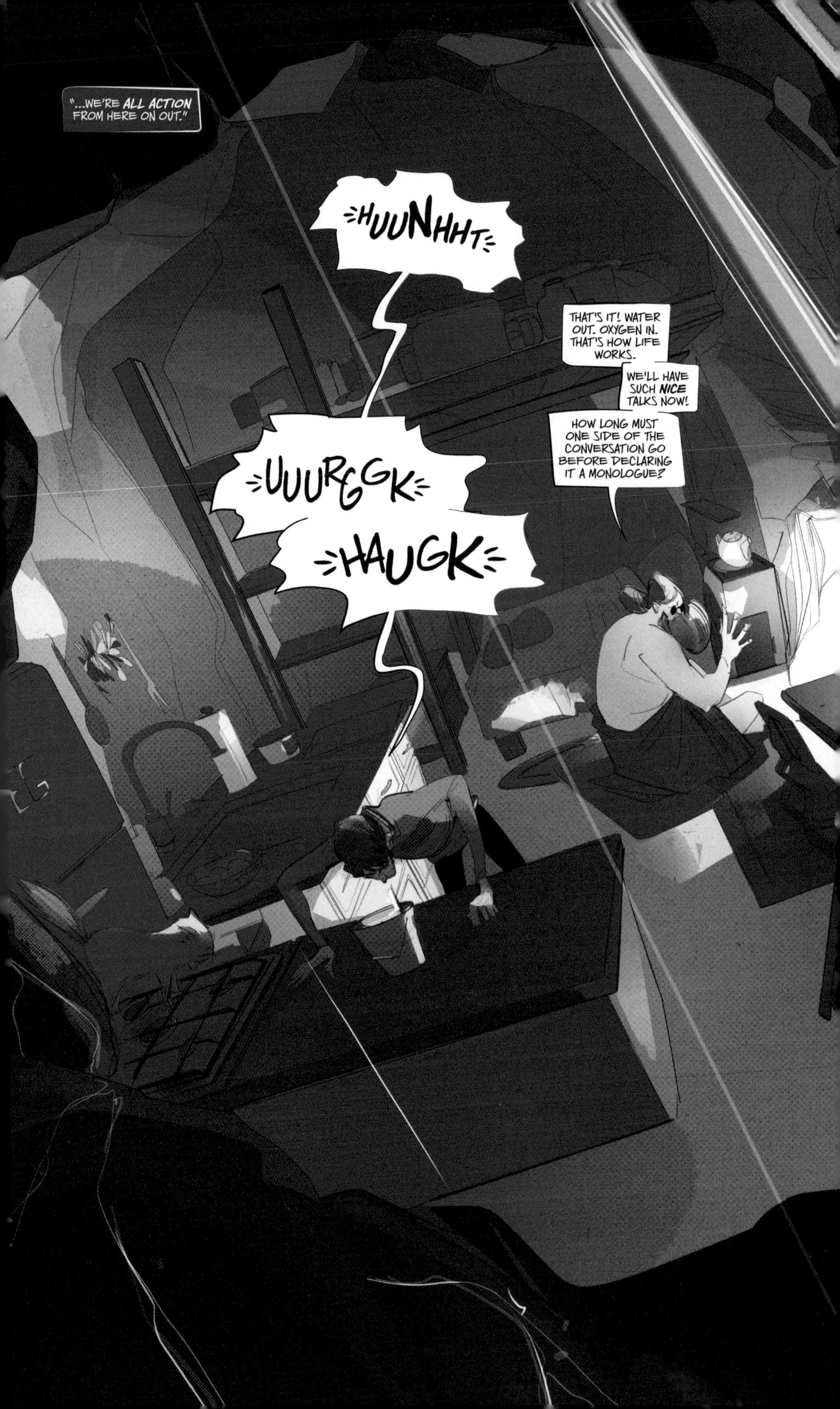
"...WE'RE ALL ACTION FROM HERE ON OUT."
HUUNHHT
UUURGGK
HAUGK
THAT'S IT! WATER OUT. OXYGEN IN. THAT'S HOW LIFE WORKS.
WE'LL HAVE SUCH NICE TALKS NOW!
HOW LONG MUST ONE SIDE OF THE CONVERSATION GO BEFORE DECLARING IT A MONOLOGUE?

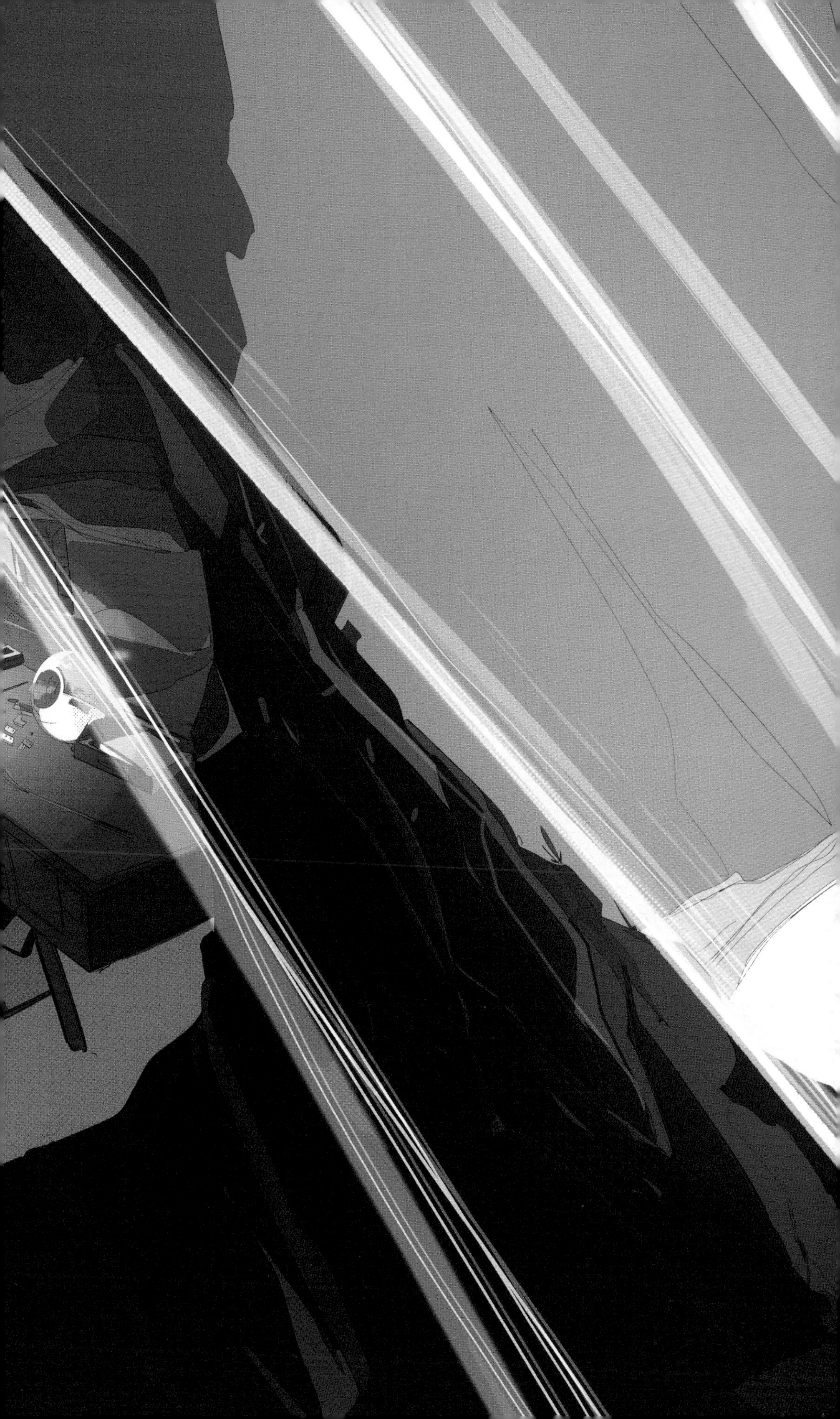

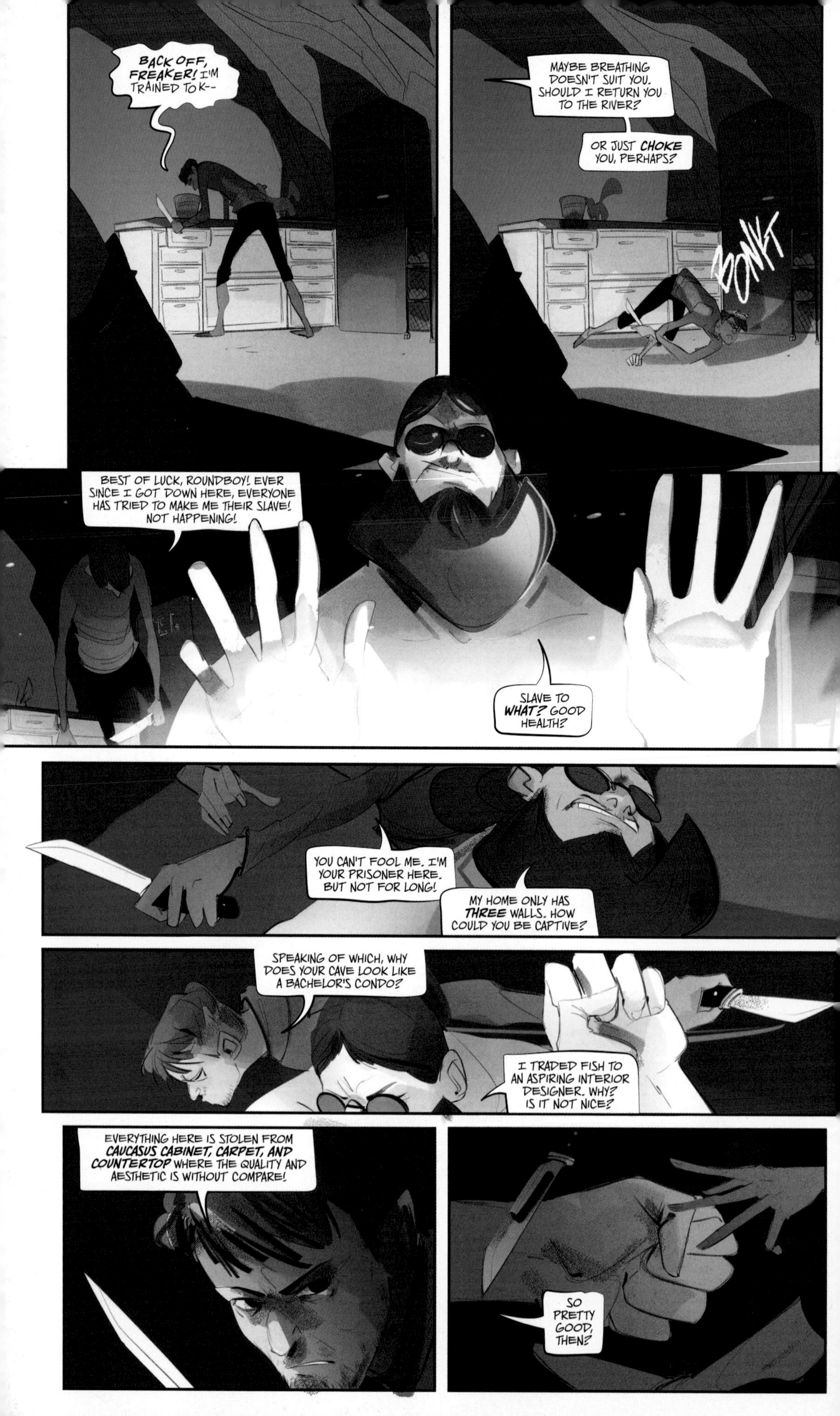
BACK OFF, FREAKER! I'M TRAINED TO K--
MAYBE BREATHING DOESN'T SUIT YOU. SHOULD I RETURN YOU TO THE RIVER?
OR JUST CHOKE YOU, PERHAPS?
BONK
BEST OF LUCK, ROUNDBOY! EVER SINCE I GOT DOWN HERE, EVERYONE HAS TRIED TO MAKE ME THEIR SLAVE! NOT HAPPENING!
SLAVE TO WHAT? GOOD HEALTH?
YOU CAN'T FOOL ME. I'M YOUR PRISONER HERE. BUT NOT FOR LONG!
MY HOME ONLY HAS THREE WALLS. HOW COULD YOU BE CAPTIVE?
SPEAKING OF WHICH, WHY DOES YOUR CAVE LOOK LIKE A BACHELOR'S CONDO?
I TRADED FISH TO AN ASPIRING INTERIOR DESIGNER. WHY? IS IT NOT NICE?
EVERYTHING HERE IS STOLEN FROM CAUCASUS CABINET, CARPET, AND COUNTERTOP WHERE THE QUALITY AND AESTHETIC IS WITHOUT COMPARE!
SO PRETTY GOOD, THEN?

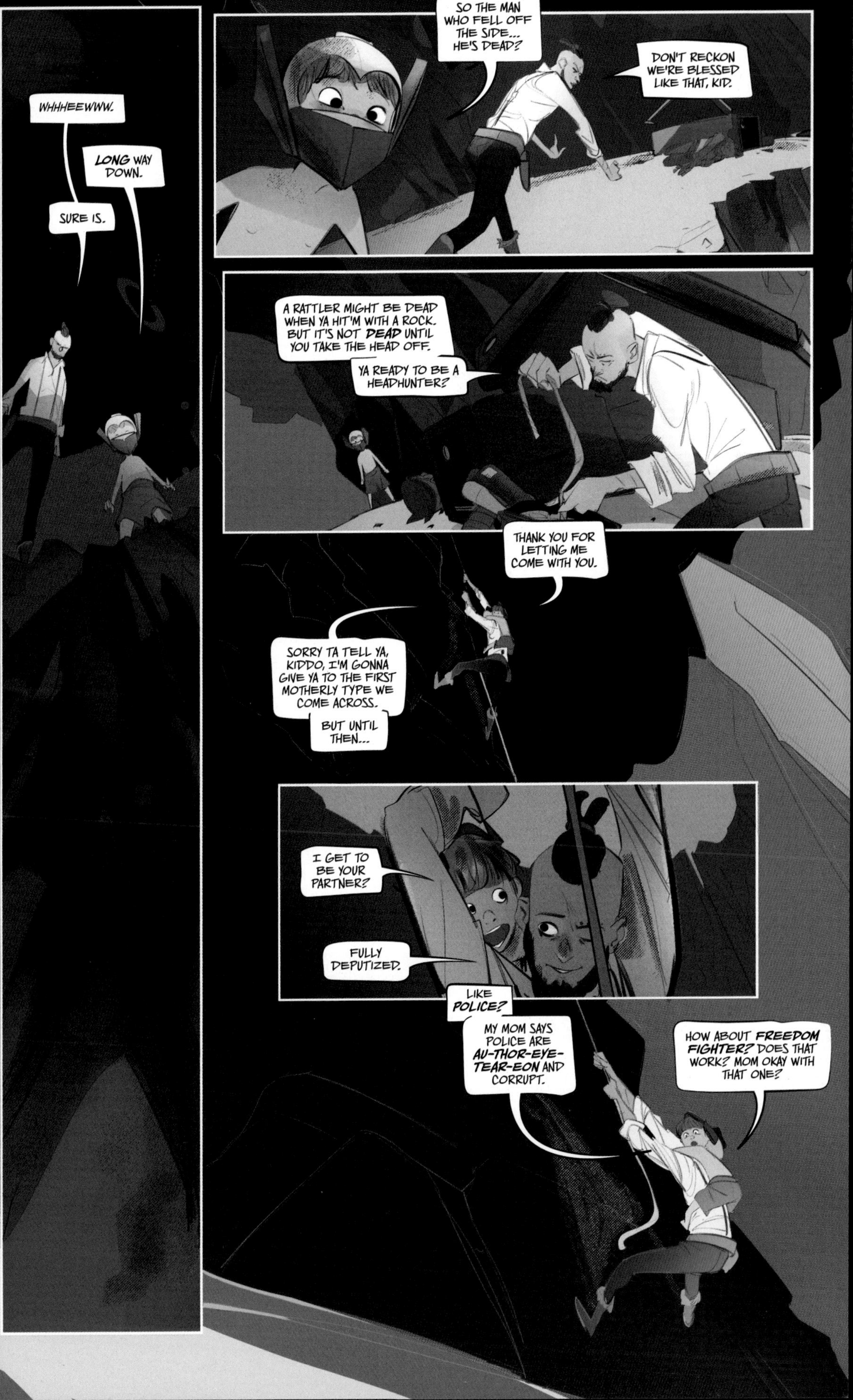
WHHHEEWWW.
LONG WAY DOWN.
SURE IS.
SO THE MAN WHO FELL OFF THE SIDE... HE'S DEAD?
DON'T RECKON WE'RE BLESSED LIKE THAT, KID.
A RATTLER MIGHT BE DEAD WHEN YA HIT'M WITH A ROCK. BUT IT'S NOT DEAD UNTIL YOU TAKE THE HEAD OFF.
YA READY TO BE A HEADHUNTER?
THANK YOU FOR LETTING ME COME WITH YOU.
SORRY TA TELL YA, KIDDO, I'M GONNA GIVE YA TO THE FIRST MOTHERLY TYPE WE COME ACROSS.
BUT UNTIL THEN...
I GET TO BE YOUR PARTNER?
FULLY DEPUTIZED.
LIKE POLICE?
MY MOM SAYS POLICE ARE AU-THOR-EYE-TEAR-EON AND CORRUPT.
HOW ABOUT FREEDOM FIGHTER? DOES THAT WORK? MOM OKAY WITH THAT ONE?

I DON'T THINK WE HAVE ENOUGH ROPE.

THAT A FACT?

WHAT WILL WE DO?

SPLSH

CLUB

≈GASHP≈

SCHWUP

HOLD ON TIGHT, KID! SOMETIMES REVENGE DON'T COME EASY!

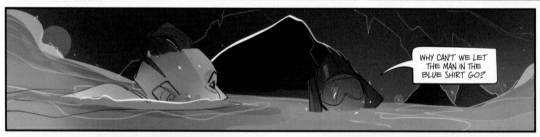

WHY CAN'T WE LET THE MAN IN THE BLUE SHIRT GO?

LEMME GIVE YA A QUICK LESSON ON LIFE AND HOW YA CAN BEST STAY LIVING IT...

IF YA LET IT GO TOO LONG...IF YA DON'T KILL THE GERM WITH SOME MEDICINE...THEN THE INFECTION SPREADS.

SOON YA CAN'T THINK STRAIGHT OR SLEEP. YA GET WEAK.

AND I DON'T WANT THAT FER US, KID. WE'RE GONNA STAY HEALTHY, YA HEAR?

OW.

PUNT

WHAT SOMEONE DOES TO YA, THAT'S A GERM. AND YA GOTTA FIGHT THAT GERM OR YA GET SICK.

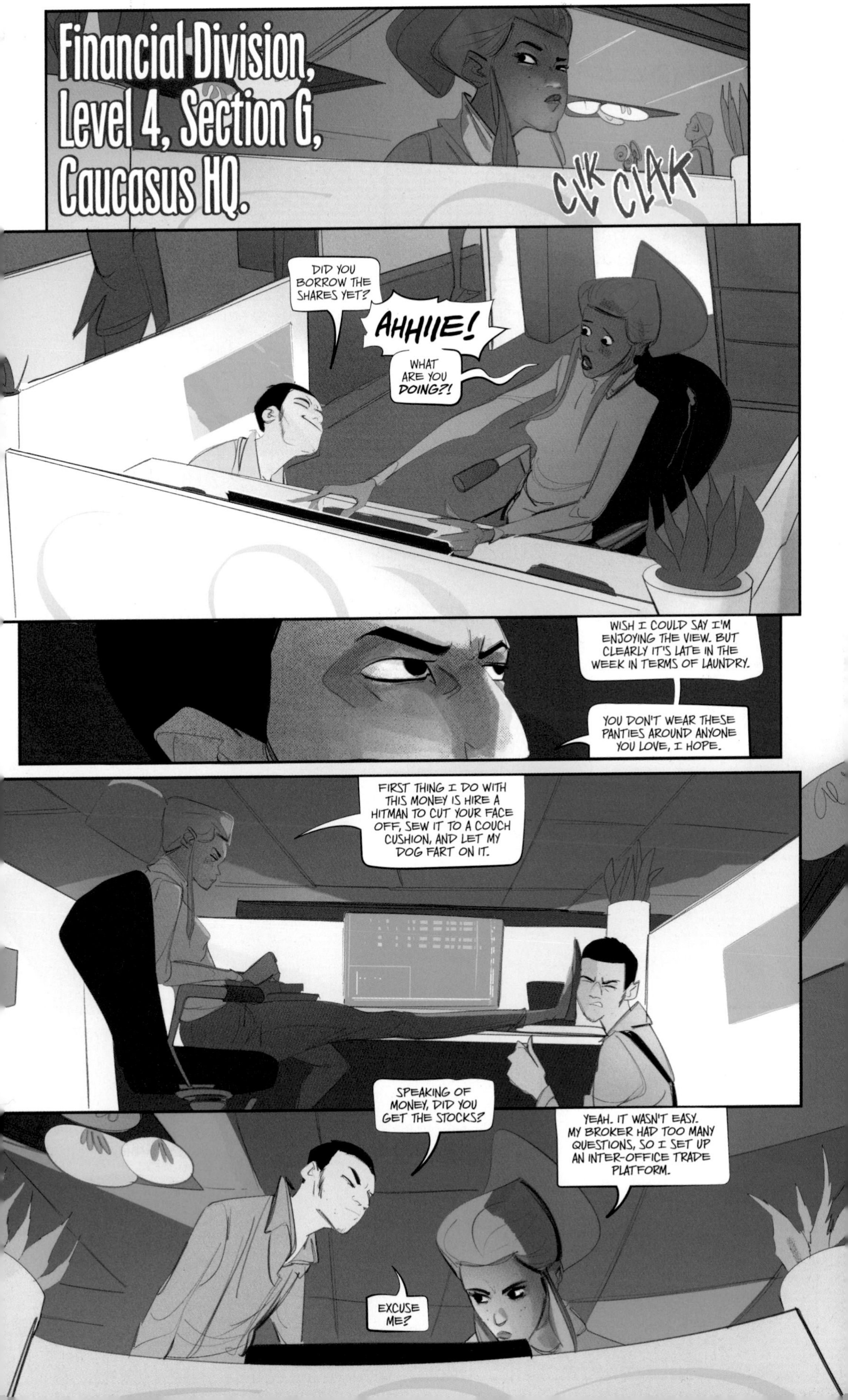
Financial Division, Level 4, Section G, Caucasus HQ.
CLIK CLAK
DID YOU BORROW THE SHARES YET?
AHHIIE!
WHAT ARE YOU DOING?!
WISH I COULD SAY I'M ENJOYING THE VIEW. BUT CLEARLY IT'S LATE IN THE WEEK IN TERMS OF LAUNDRY.
YOU DON'T WEAR THESE PANTIES AROUND ANYONE YOU LOVE, I HOPE.
FIRST THING I DO WITH THIS MONEY IS HIRE A HITMAN TO CUT YOUR FACE OFF, SEW IT TO A COUCH CUSHION, AND LET MY DOG FART ON IT.
SPEAKING OF MONEY, DID YOU GET THE STOCKS?
YEAH. IT WASN'T EASY. MY BROKER HAD TOO MANY QUESTIONS, SO I SET UP AN INTER-OFFICE TRADE PLATFORM.
EXCUSE ME?

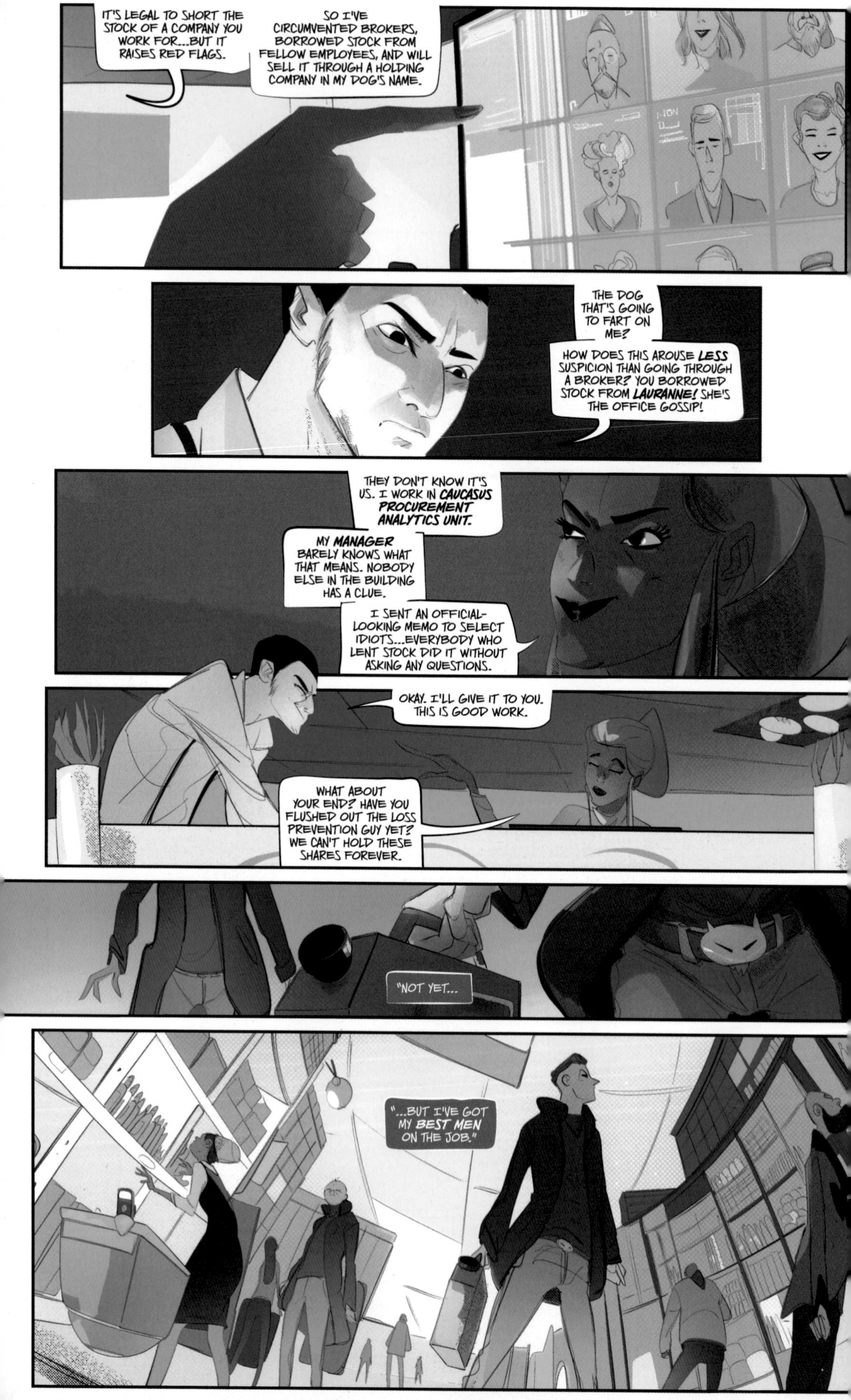
IT'S LEGAL TO SHORT THE STOCK OF A COMPANY YOU WORK FOR...BUT IT RAISES RED FLAGS.
SO I'VE CIRCUMVENTED BROKERS, BORROWED STOCK FROM FELLOW EMPLOYEES, AND WILL SELL IT THROUGH A HOLDING COMPANY IN MY DOG'S NAME.
THE DOG THAT'S GOING TO FART ON ME?
HOW DOES THIS AROUSE **LESS** SUSPICION THAN GOING THROUGH A BROKER? YOU BORROWED STOCK FROM **LAURANNE!** SHE'S THE OFFICE GOSSIP!
THEY DON'T KNOW IT'S US. I WORK IN **CAUCASUS PROCUREMENT ANALYTICS UNIT.**
MY **MANAGER** BARELY KNOWS WHAT THAT MEANS. NOBODY ELSE IN THE BUILDING HAS A CLUE.
I SENT AN OFFICIAL-LOOKING MEMO TO SELECT IDIOTS...EVERYBODY WHO LENT STOCK DID IT WITHOUT ASKING ANY QUESTIONS.
OKAY. I'LL GIVE IT TO YOU. THIS IS GOOD WORK.
WHAT ABOUT YOUR END? HAVE YOU FLUSHED OUT THE LOSS PREVENTION GUY YET? WE CAN'T HOLD THESE SHARES FOREVER.
"NOT YET...
"...BUT I'VE GOT MY **BEST MEN** ON THE JOB."

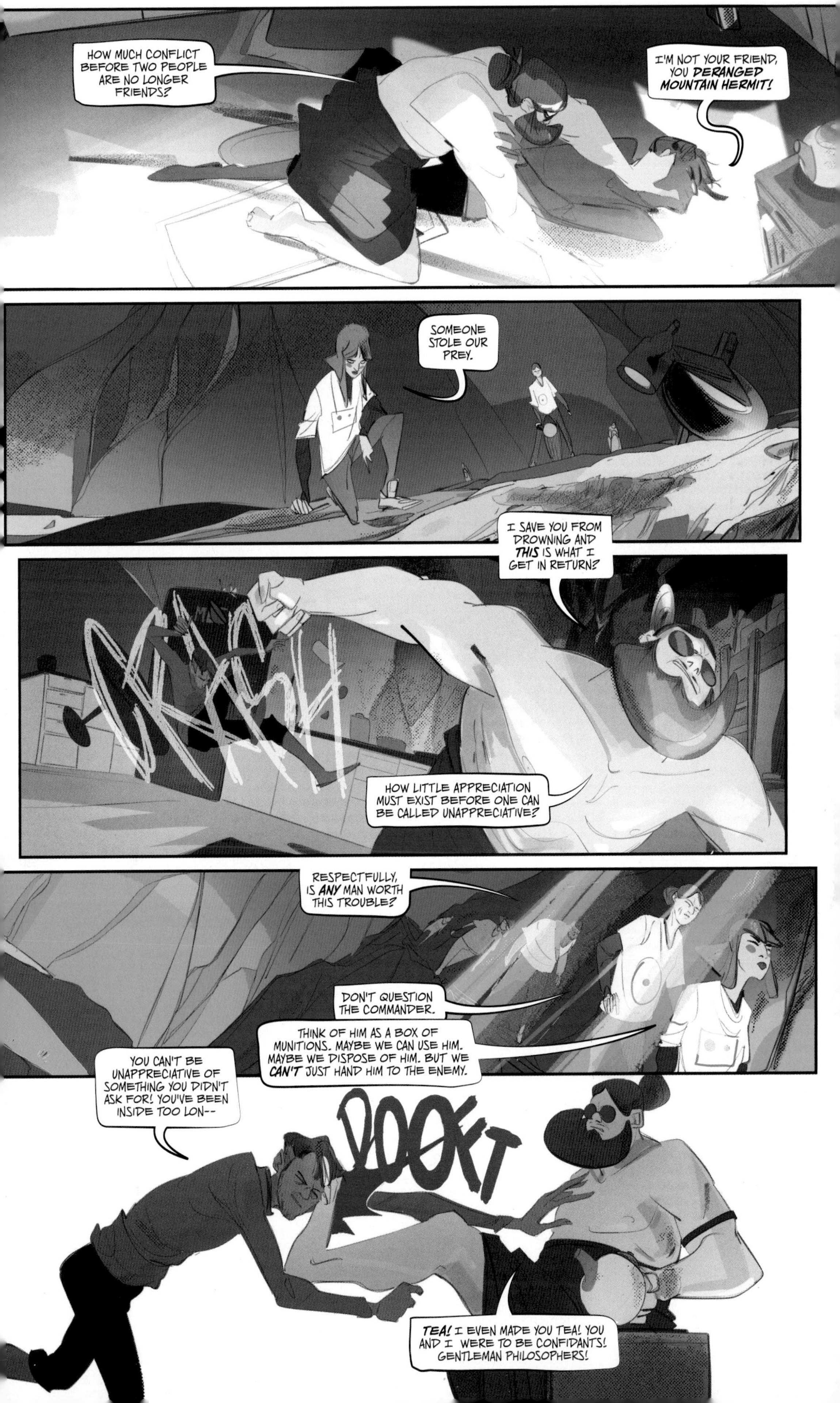
HOW MUCH CONFLICT BEFORE TWO PEOPLE ARE NO LONGER FRIENDS?
I'M NOT YOUR FRIEND, YOU DERANGED MOUNTAIN HERMIT!
SOMEONE STOLE OUR PREY.
I SAVE YOU FROM DROWNING AND THIS IS WHAT I GET IN RETURN?
CRASH
HOW LITTLE APPRECIATION MUST EXIST BEFORE ONE CAN BE CALLED UNAPPRECIATIVE?
RESPECTFULLY, IS ANY MAN WORTH THIS TROUBLE?
DON'T QUESTION THE COMMANDER.
THINK OF HIM AS A BOX OF MUNITIONS. MAYBE WE CAN USE HIM. MAYBE WE DISPOSE OF HIM. BUT WE CAN'T JUST HAND HIM TO THE ENEMY.
YOU CAN'T BE UNAPPRECIATIVE OF SOMETHING YOU DIDN'T ASK FOR! YOU'VE BEEN INSIDE TOO LON--
DOOKT
TEA! I EVEN MADE YOU TEA! YOU AND I WERE TO BE CONFIDANTS! GENTLEMAN PHILOSOPHERS!

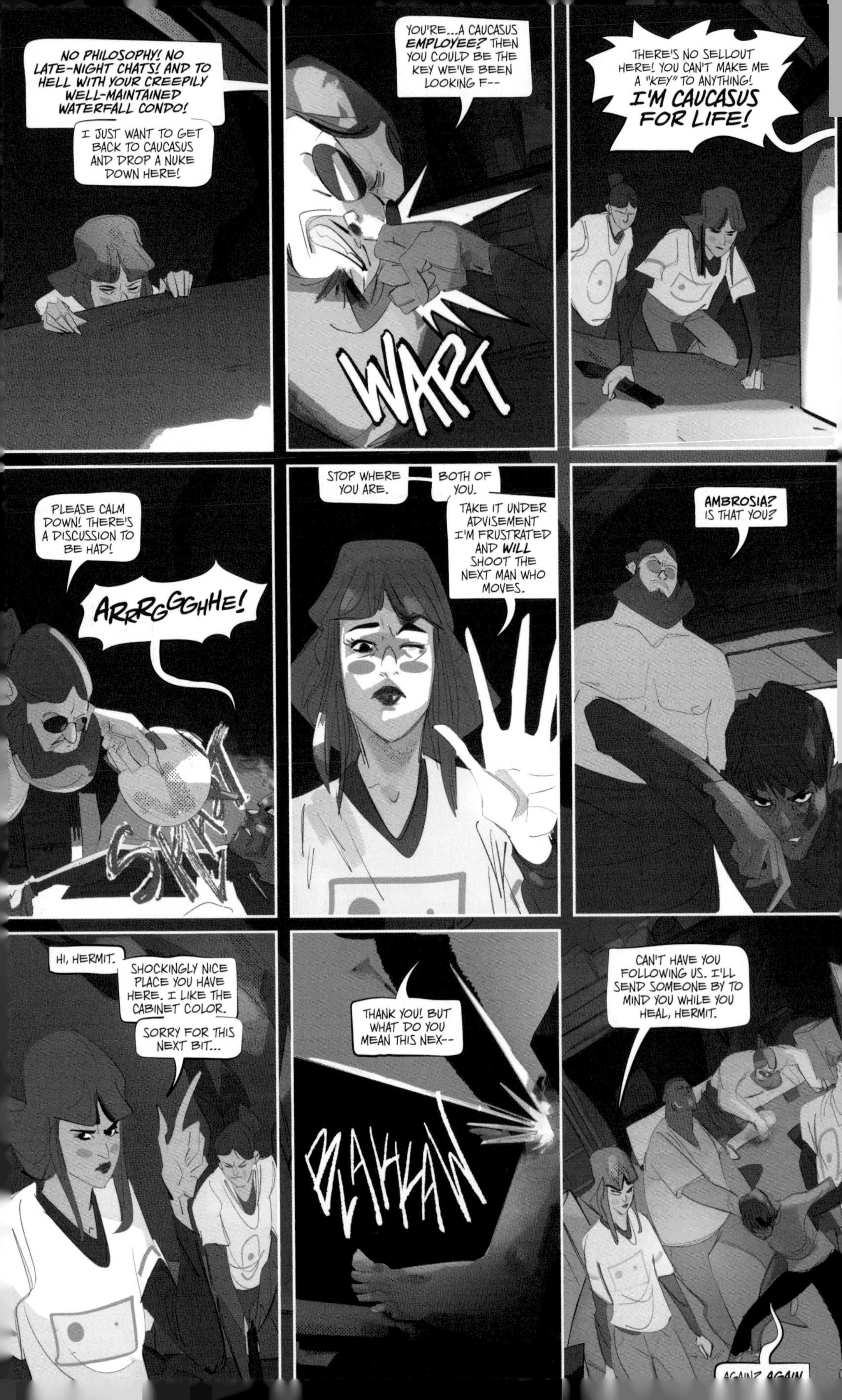

NO PHILOSOPHY! NO LATE-NIGHT CHATS! AND TO HELL WITH YOUR CREEPILY WELL-MAINTAINED WATERFALL CONDO!
I JUST WANT TO GET BACK TO CAUCASUS AND DROP A NUKE DOWN HERE!
YOU'RE...A CAUCASUS EMPLOYEE? THEN YOU COULD BE THE KEY WE'VE BEEN LOOKING F--
WAPT
THERE'S NO SELLOUT HERE! YOU CAN'T MAKE ME A "KEY" TO ANYTHING! I'M CAUCASUS FOR LIFE!
PLEASE CALM DOWN! THERE'S A DISCUSSION TO BE HAD!
ARRRGGGHHE!
STOP WHERE YOU ARE.
BOTH OF YOU.
TAKE IT UNDER ADVISEMENT I'M FRUSTRATED AND WILL SHOOT THE NEXT MAN WHO MOVES.
AMBROSIA? IS THAT YOU?
HI, HERMIT.
SHOCKINGLY NICE PLACE YOU HAVE HERE. I LIKE THE CABINET COLOR.
SORRY FOR THIS NEXT BIT...
THANK YOU! BUT WHAT DO YOU MEAN THIS NEX--
BLAKKAW
CAN'T HAVE YOU FOLLOWING US. I'LL SEND SOMEONE BY TO MIND YOU WHILE YOU HEAL, HERMIT.
AGAIN? AGAIN

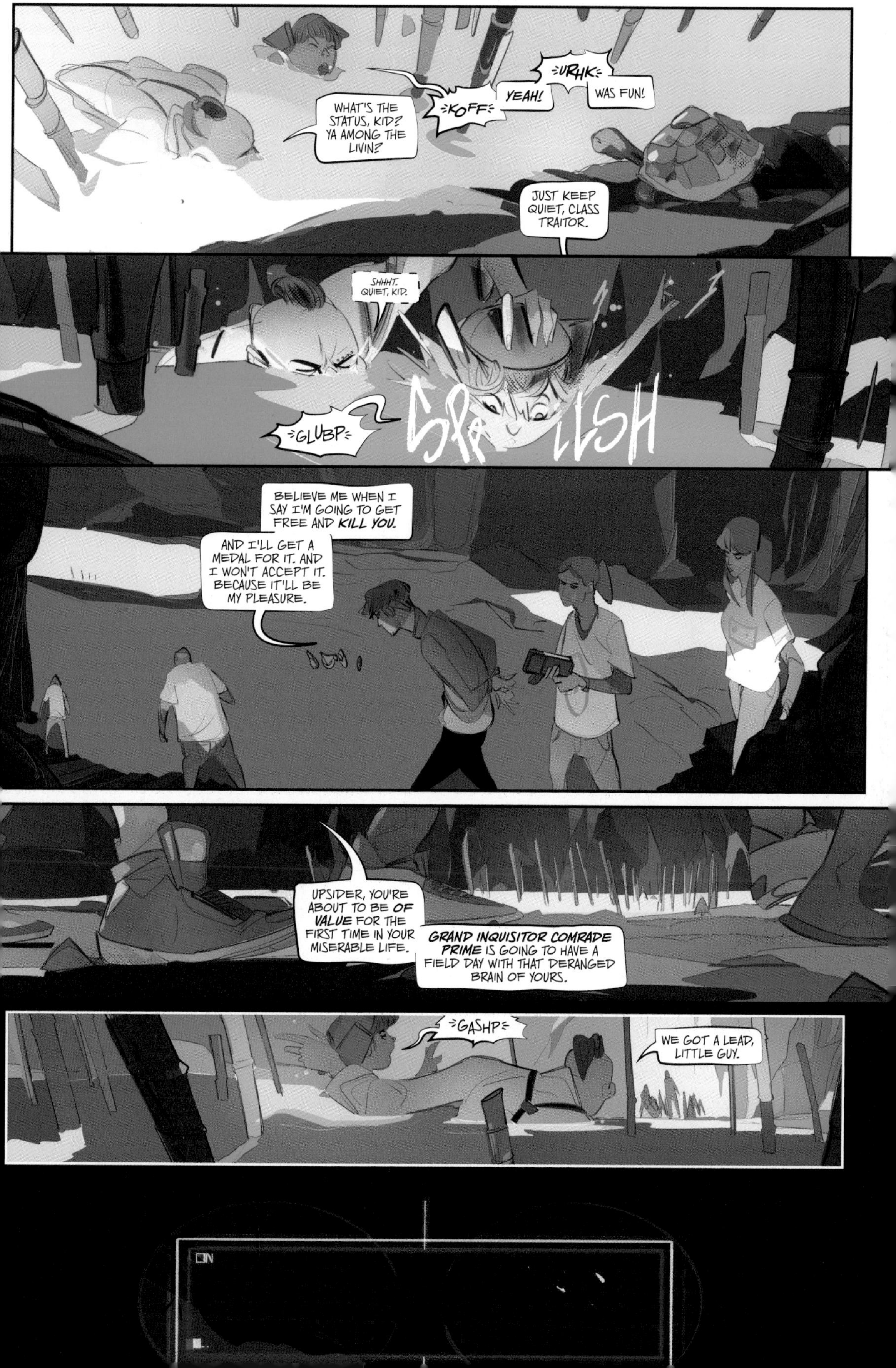
WHAT'S THE STATUS, KID? YA AMONG THE LIVIN?
KOFF
YEAH!
URHK
WAS FUN!
JUST KEEP QUIET, CLASS TRAITOR.
SHHHT. QUIET, KID.
GLUBP
BELIEVE ME WHEN I SAY I'M GOING TO GET FREE AND **KILL YOU.**
AND I'LL GET A MEDAL FOR IT. AND I WON'T ACCEPT IT. BECAUSE IT'LL BE MY PLEASURE.
UPSIDER, YOU'RE ABOUT TO BE **OF VALUE** FOR THE FIRST TIME IN YOUR MISERABLE LIFE.
GRAND INQUISITOR COMRADE PRIME IS GOING TO HAVE A FIELD DAY WITH THAT DERANGED BRAIN OF YOURS.
GASHP
WE GOT A LEAD, LITTLE GUY.

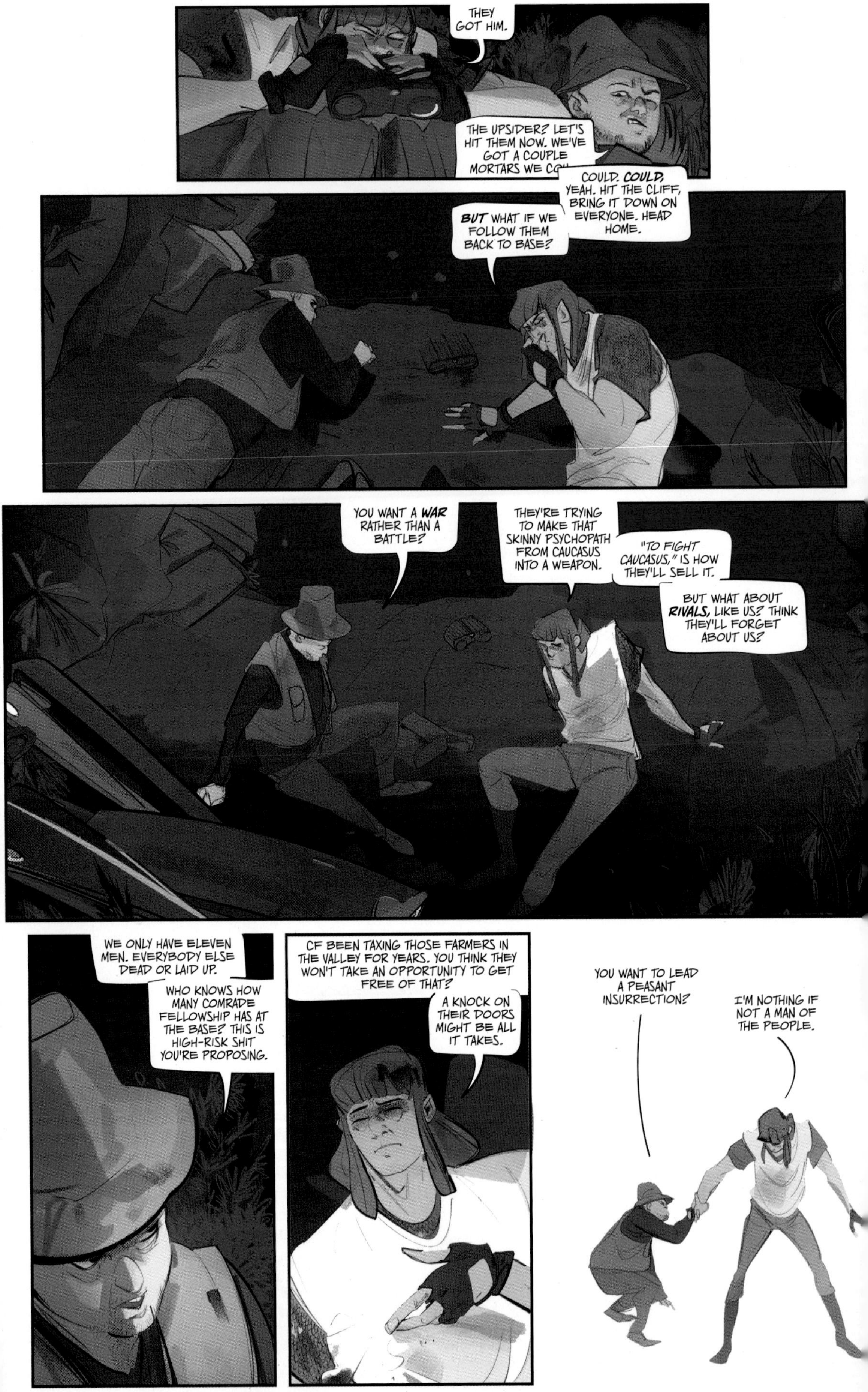
THEY GOT HIM.
THE UPSIDER? LET'S HIT THEM NOW. WE'VE GOT A COUPLE MORTARS WE CO—
COULD. *COULD*, YEAH. HIT THE CLIFF, BRING IT DOWN ON EVERYONE. HEAD HOME.
BUT WHAT IF WE FOLLOW THEM BACK TO BASE?
YOU WANT A *WAR* RATHER THAN A BATTLE?
THEY'RE TRYING TO MAKE THAT SKINNY PSYCHOPATH FROM CAUCASUS INTO A WEAPON.
"TO FIGHT CAUCASUS," IS HOW THEY'LL SELL IT.
BUT WHAT ABOUT *RIVALS*, LIKE US? THINK THEY'LL FORGET ABOUT US?
WE ONLY HAVE ELEVEN MEN. EVERYBODY ELSE DEAD OR LAID UP.
WHO KNOWS HOW MANY COMRADE FELLOWSHIP HAS AT THE BASE? THIS IS HIGH-RISK SHIT YOU'RE PROPOSING.
CF BEEN TAXING THOSE FARMERS IN THE VALLEY FOR YEARS. YOU THINK THEY WON'T TAKE AN OPPORTUNITY TO GET FREE OF THAT?
A KNOCK ON THEIR DOORS MIGHT BE ALL IT TAKES.
YOU WANT TO LEAD A PEASANT INSURRECTION?
I'M NOTHING IF NOT A MAN OF THE PEOPLE.

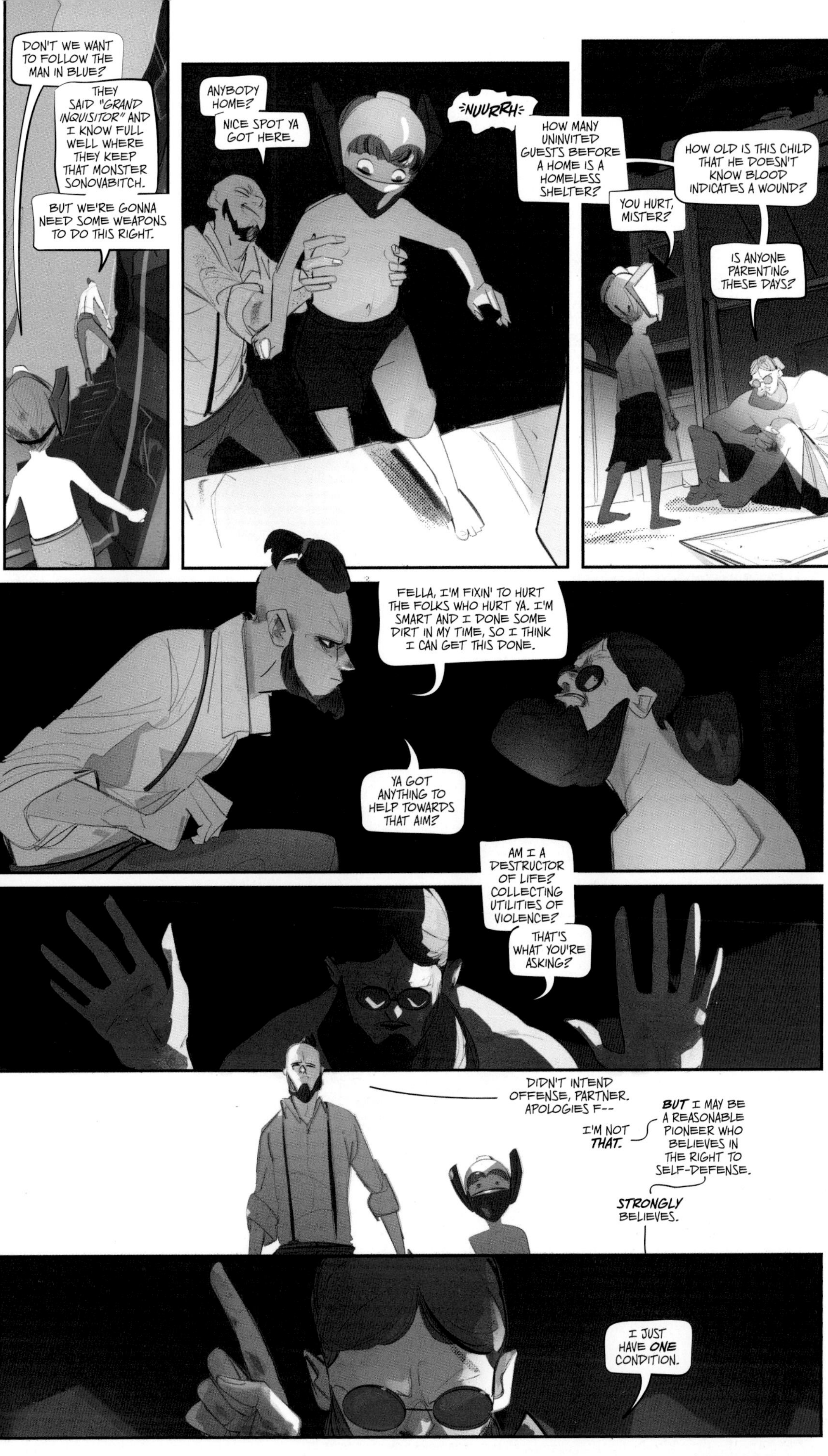
DON'T WE WANT TO FOLLOW THE MAN IN BLUE?
THEY SAID "GRAND INQUISITOR" AND I KNOW FULL WELL WHERE THEY KEEP THAT MONSTER SONOVABITCH.
BUT WE'RE GONNA NEED SOME WEAPONS TO DO THIS RIGHT.
ANYBODY HOME?
NICE SPOT YA GOT HERE.
NUURRH
HOW MANY UNINVITED GUESTS BEFORE A HOME IS A HOMELESS SHELTER?
HOW OLD IS THIS CHILD THAT HE DOESN'T KNOW BLOOD INDICATES A WOUND?
YOU HURT, MISTER?
IS ANYONE PARENTING THESE DAYS?
FELLA, I'M FIXIN' TO HURT THE FOLKS WHO HURT YA. I'M SMART AND I DONE SOME DIRT IN MY TIME, SO I THINK I CAN GET THIS DONE.
YA GOT ANYTHING TO HELP TOWARDS THAT AIM?
AM I A DESTRUCTOR OF LIFE? COLLECTING UTILITIES OF VIOLENCE?
THAT'S WHAT YOU'RE ASKING?
DIDN'T INTEND OFFENSE, PARTNER. APOLOGIES F--
I'M NOT THAT.
BUT I MAY BE A REASONABLE PIONEER WHO BELIEVES IN THE RIGHT TO SELF-DEFENSE.
STRONGLY BELIEVES.
I JUST HAVE ONE CONDITION.

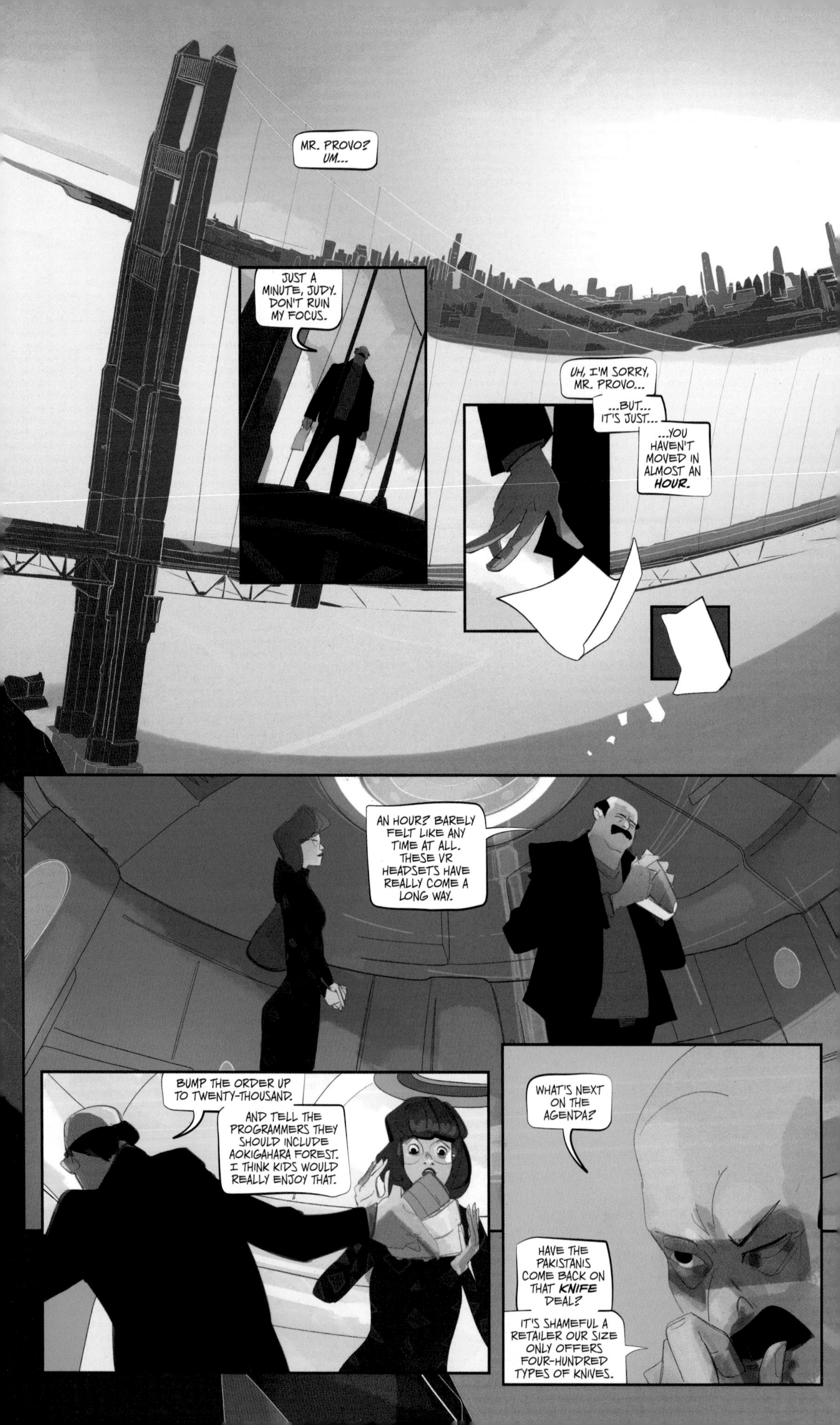
MR. PROVO? UM...
JUST A MINUTE, JUDY. DON'T RUIN MY FOCUS.
UH, I'M SORRY, MR. PROVO...
...BUT... IT'S JUST...
...YOU HAVEN'T MOVED IN ALMOST AN HOUR.
AN HOUR? BARELY FELT LIKE ANY TIME AT ALL. THESE VR HEADSETS HAVE REALLY COME A LONG WAY.
BUMP THE ORDER UP TO TWENTY-THOUSAND.
AND TELL THE PROGRAMMERS THEY SHOULD INCLUDE AOKIGAHARA FOREST. I THINK KIDS WOULD REALLY ENJOY THAT.
WHAT'S NEXT ON THE AGENDA?
HAVE THE PAKISTANIS COME BACK ON THAT KNIFE DEAL?
IT'S SHAMEFUL A RETAILER OUR SIZE ONLY OFFERS FOUR-HUNDRED TYPES OF KNIVES.

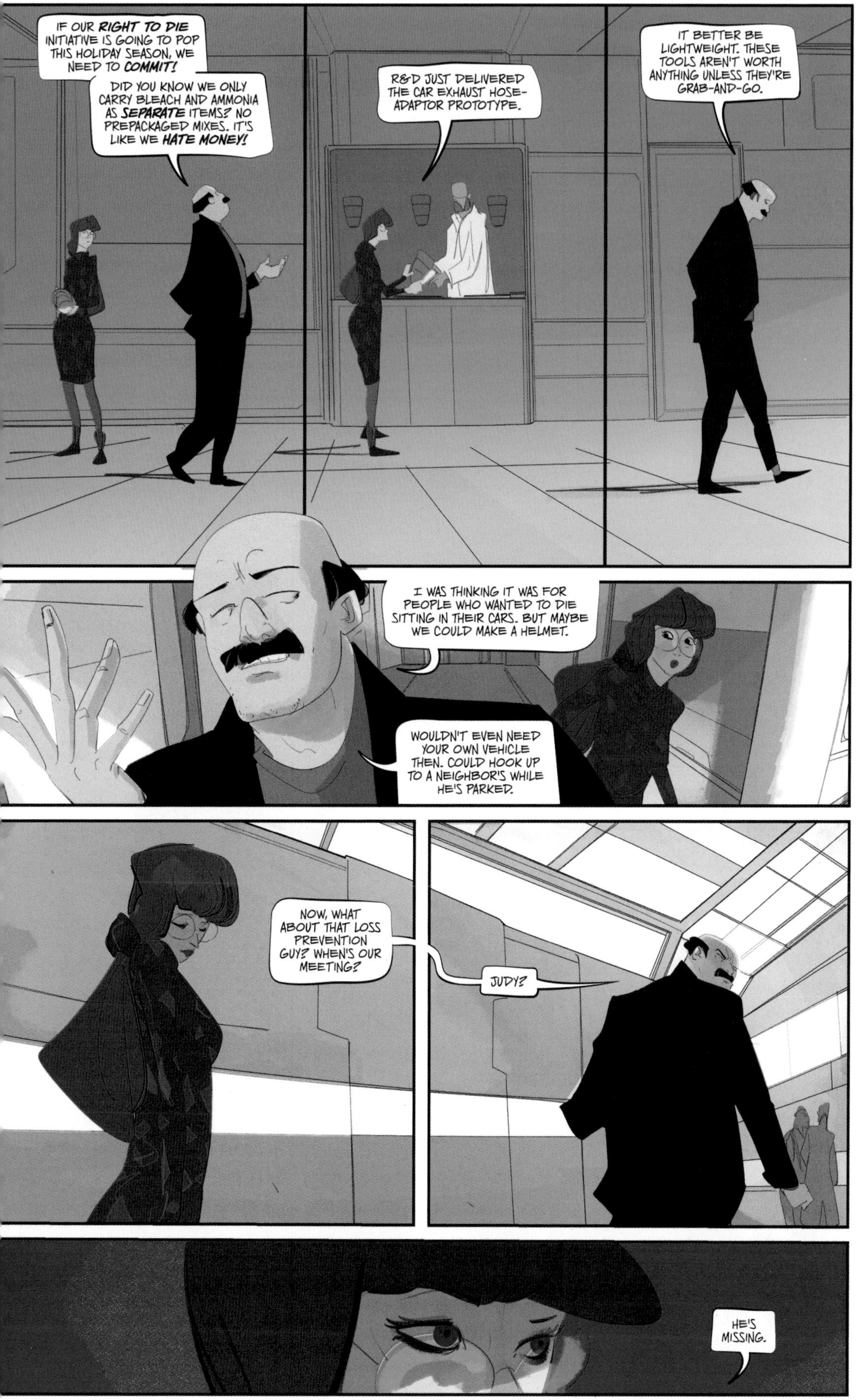
IF OUR RIGHT TO DIE INITIATIVE IS GOING TO POP THIS HOLIDAY SEASON, WE NEED TO COMMIT!
DID YOU KNOW WE ONLY CARRY BLEACH AND AMMONIA AS SEPARATE ITEMS? NO PREPACKAGED MIXES. IT'S LIKE WE HATE MONEY!
R&D JUST DELIVERED THE CAR EXHAUST HOSE-ADAPTOR PROTOTYPE.
IT BETTER BE LIGHTWEIGHT. THESE TOOLS AREN'T WORTH ANYTHING UNLESS THEY'RE GRAB-AND-GO.
I WAS THINKING IT WAS FOR PEOPLE WHO WANTED TO DIE SITTING IN THEIR CARS. BUT MAYBE WE COULD MAKE A HELMET.
WOULDN'T EVEN NEED YOUR OWN VEHICLE THEN. COULD HOOK UP TO A NEIGHBOR'S WHILE HE'S PARKED.
NOW, WHAT ABOUT THAT LOSS PREVENTION GUY? WHEN'S OUR MEETING?
JUDY?
HE'S MISSING.

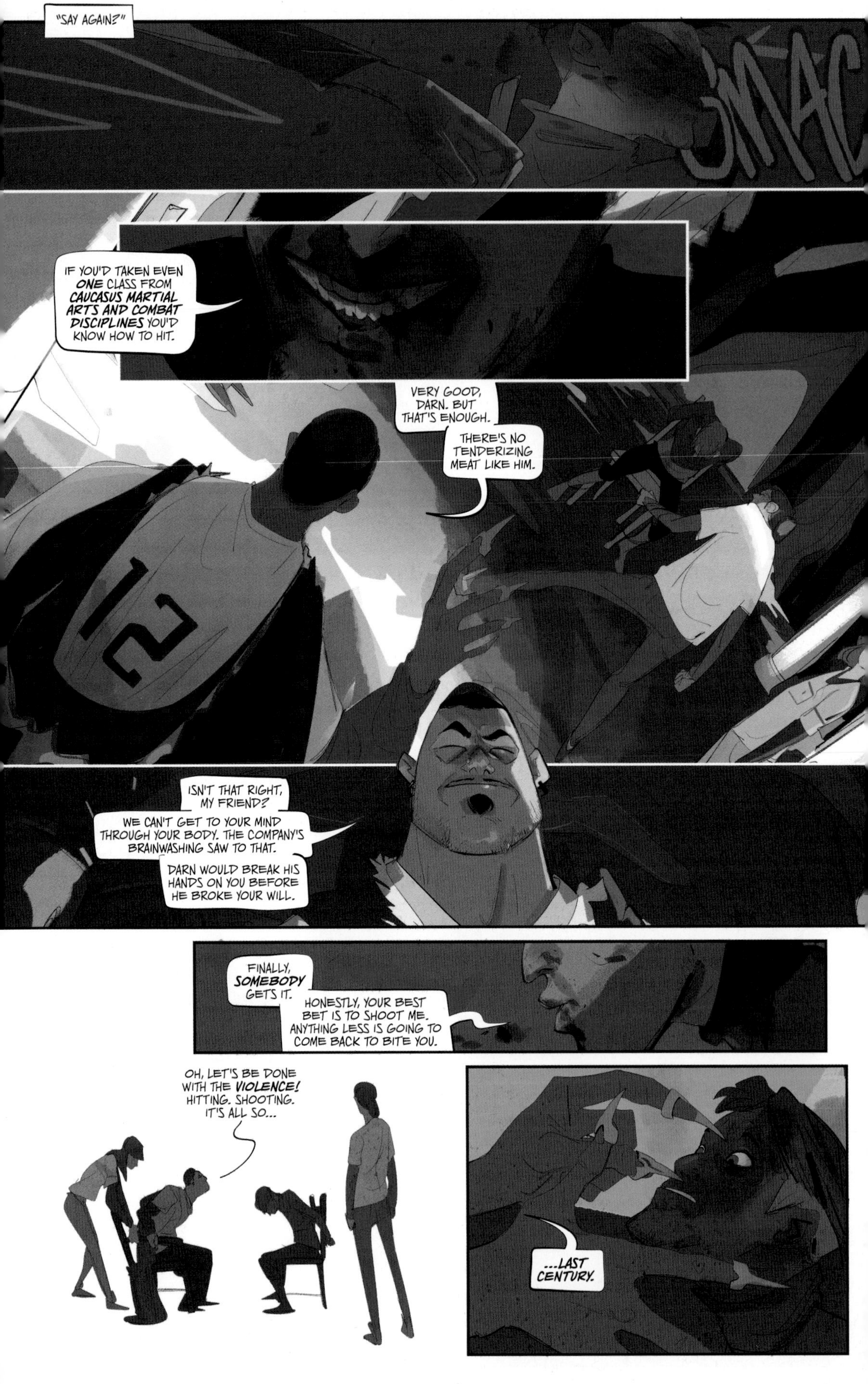
"SAY AGAIN?"
SMAC
IF YOU'D TAKEN EVEN ONE CLASS FROM CAUCASUS MARTIAL ARTS AND COMBAT DISCIPLINES YOU'D KNOW HOW TO HIT.
VERY GOOD, DARN. BUT THAT'S ENOUGH.
THERE'S NO TENDERIZING MEAT LIKE HIM.
ISN'T THAT RIGHT, MY FRIEND?
WE CAN'T GET TO YOUR MIND THROUGH YOUR BODY. THE COMPANY'S BRAINWASHING SAW TO THAT.
DARN WOULD BREAK HIS HANDS ON YOU BEFORE HE BROKE YOUR WILL.
FINALLY, SOMEBODY GETS IT.
HONESTLY, YOUR BEST BET IS TO SHOOT ME. ANYTHING LESS IS GOING TO COME BACK TO BITE YOU.
OH, LET'S BE DONE WITH THE VIOLENCE! HITTING. SHOOTING. IT'S ALL SO...
...LAST CENTURY.

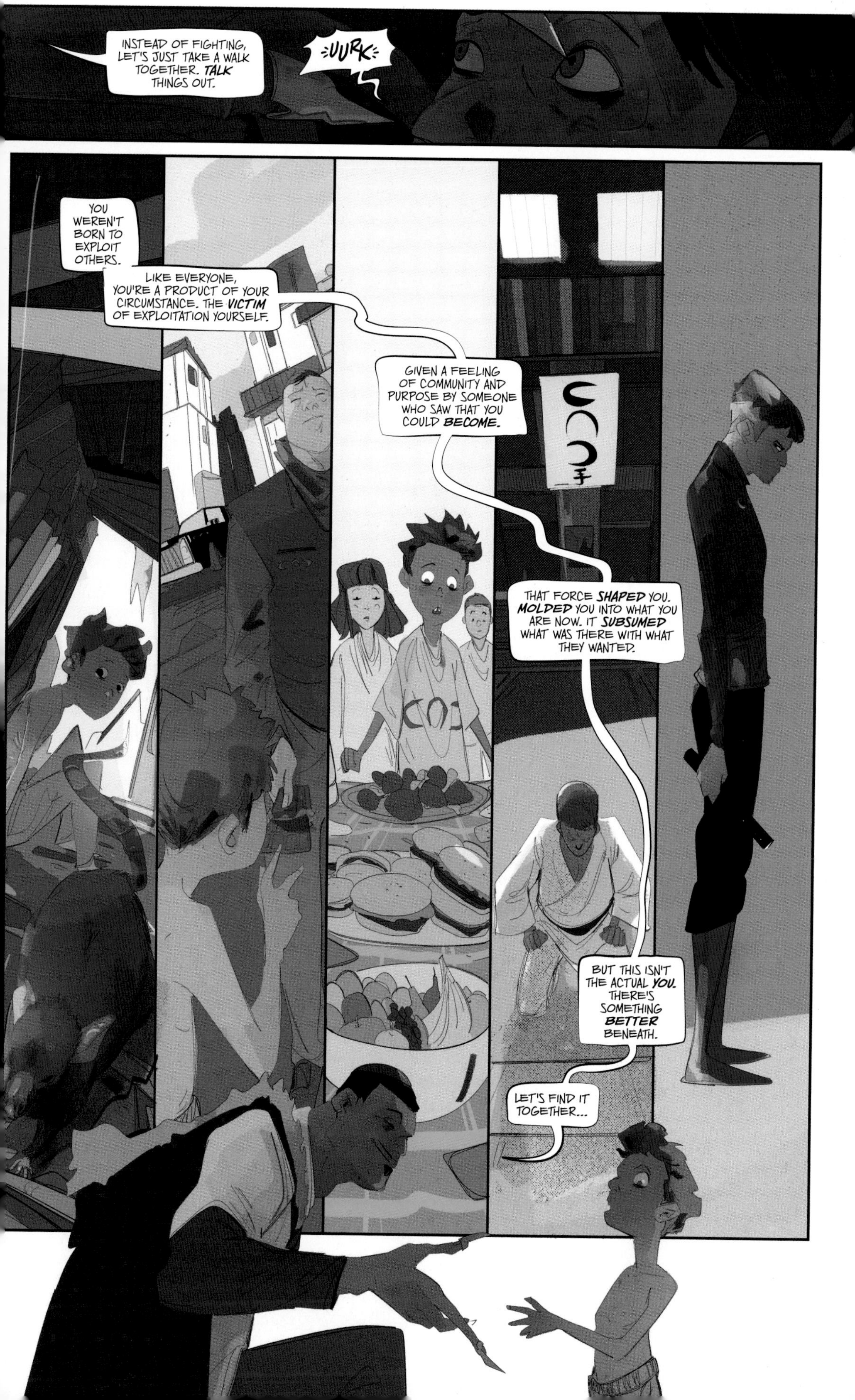

INSTEAD OF FIGHTING, LET'S JUST TAKE A WALK TOGETHER. TALK THINGS OUT.
UURK
YOU WEREN'T BORN TO EXPLOIT OTHERS.
LIKE EVERYONE, YOU'RE A PRODUCT OF YOUR CIRCUMSTANCE. THE VICTIM OF EXPLOITATION YOURSELF.
GIVEN A FEELING OF COMMUNITY AND PURPOSE BY SOMEONE WHO SAW THAT YOU COULD BECOME.
THAT FORCE SHAPED YOU. MOLDED YOU INTO WHAT YOU ARE NOW. IT SUBSUMED WHAT WAS THERE WITH WHAT THEY WANTED.
BUT THIS ISN'T THE ACTUAL YOU. THERE'S SOMETHING BETTER BENEATH.
LET'S FIND IT TOGETHER...

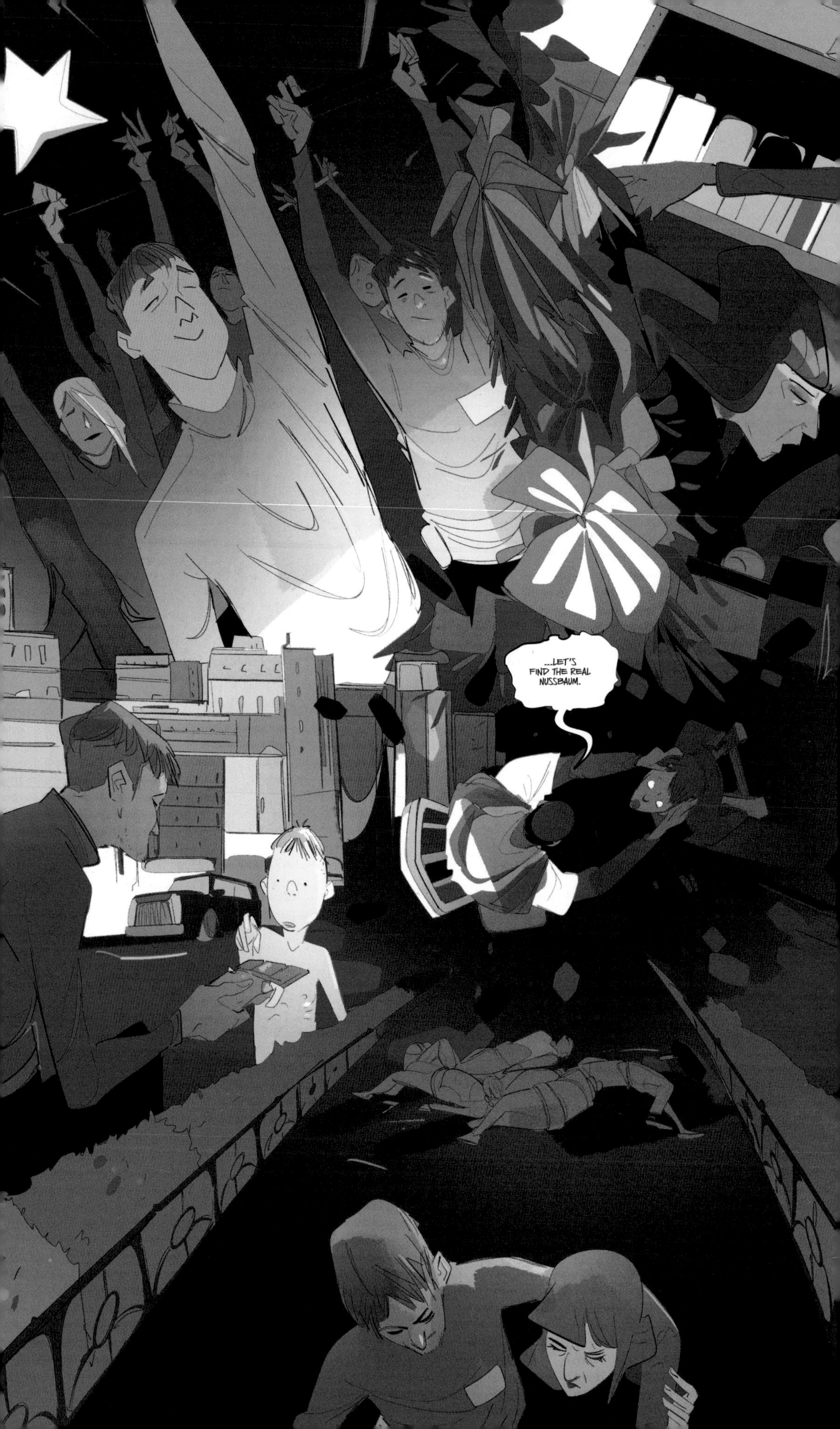
...LET'S FIND THE REAL NUSSBAUM.

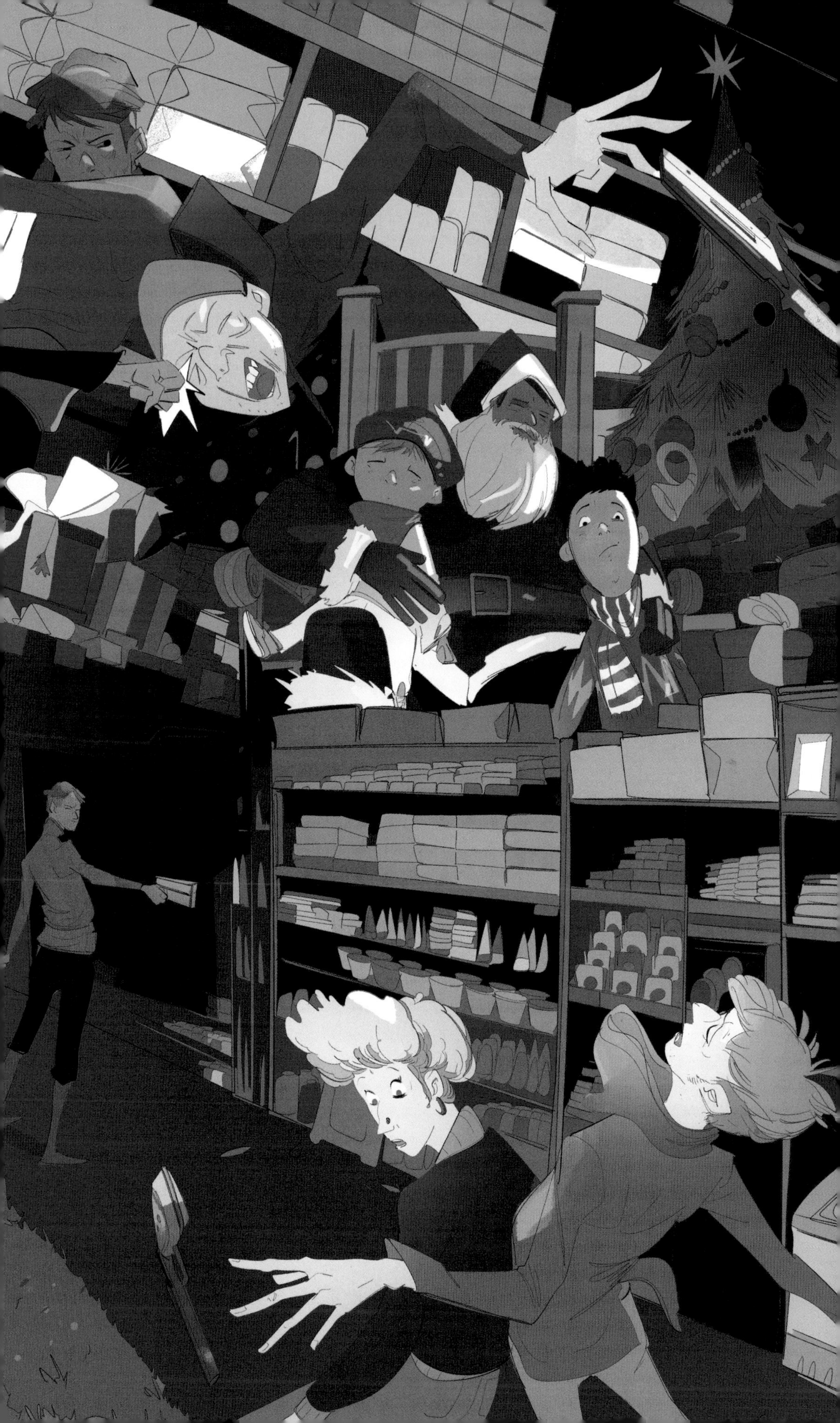

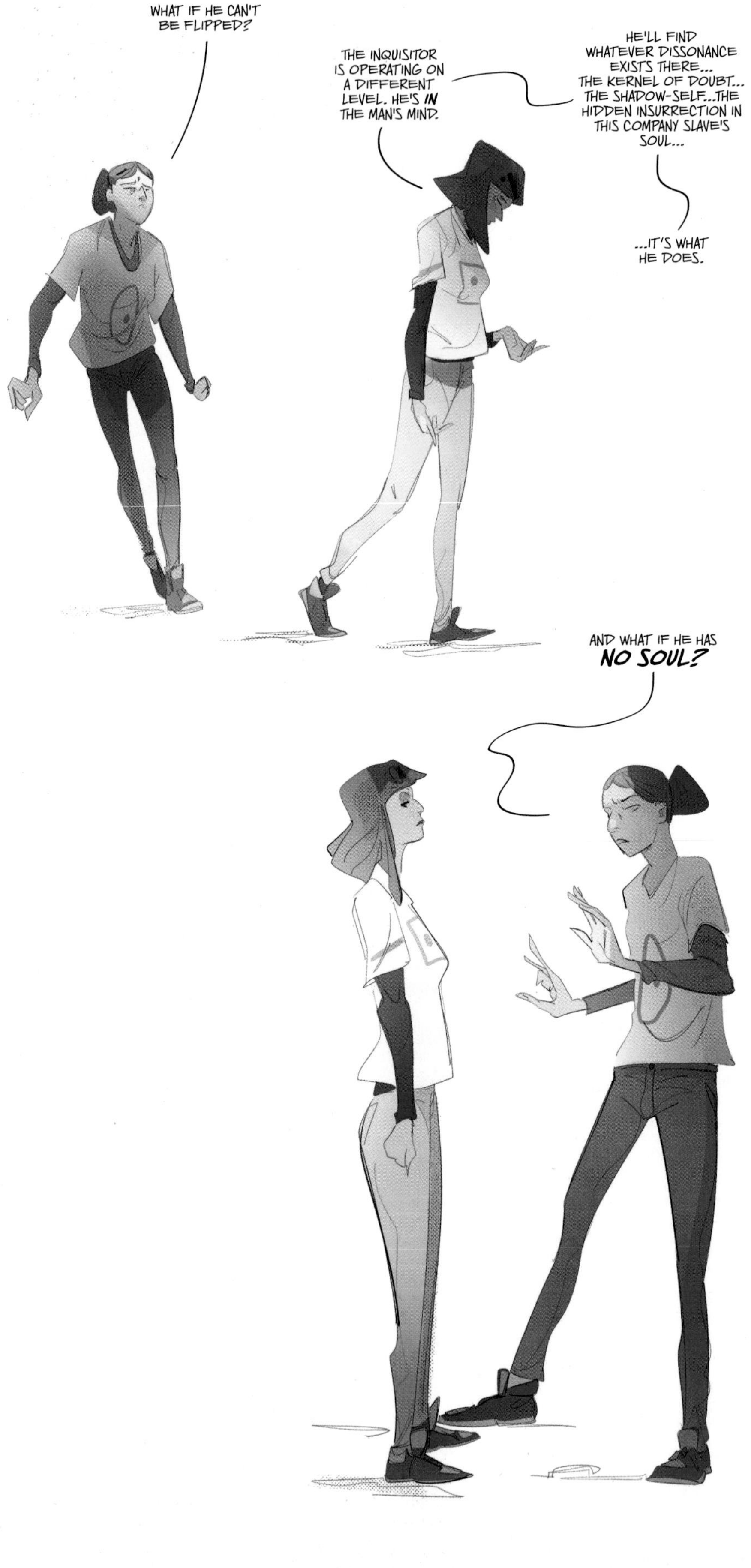
WHAT IF HE CAN'T BE FLIPPED?
THE INQUISITOR IS OPERATING ON A DIFFERENT LEVEL. HE'S *IN* THE MAN'S MIND.
HE'LL FIND WHATEVER DISSONANCE EXISTS THERE... THE KERNEL OF DOUBT... THE SHADOW-SELF...THE HIDDEN INSURRECTION IN THIS COMPANY SLAVE'S SOUL...
...IT'S WHAT HE DOES.
AND WHAT IF HE HAS **NO SOUL?**

5

FIRST TO MARKET

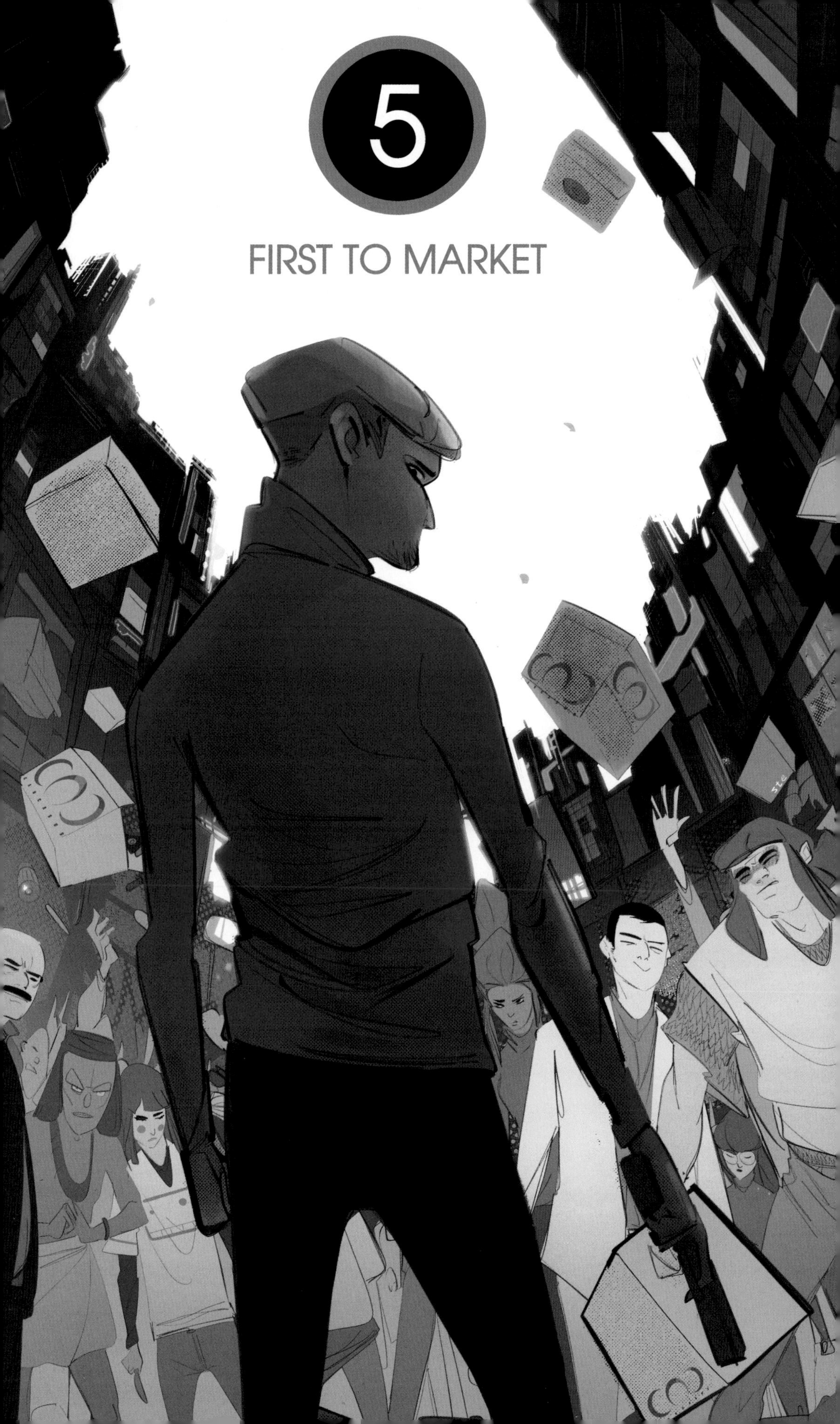

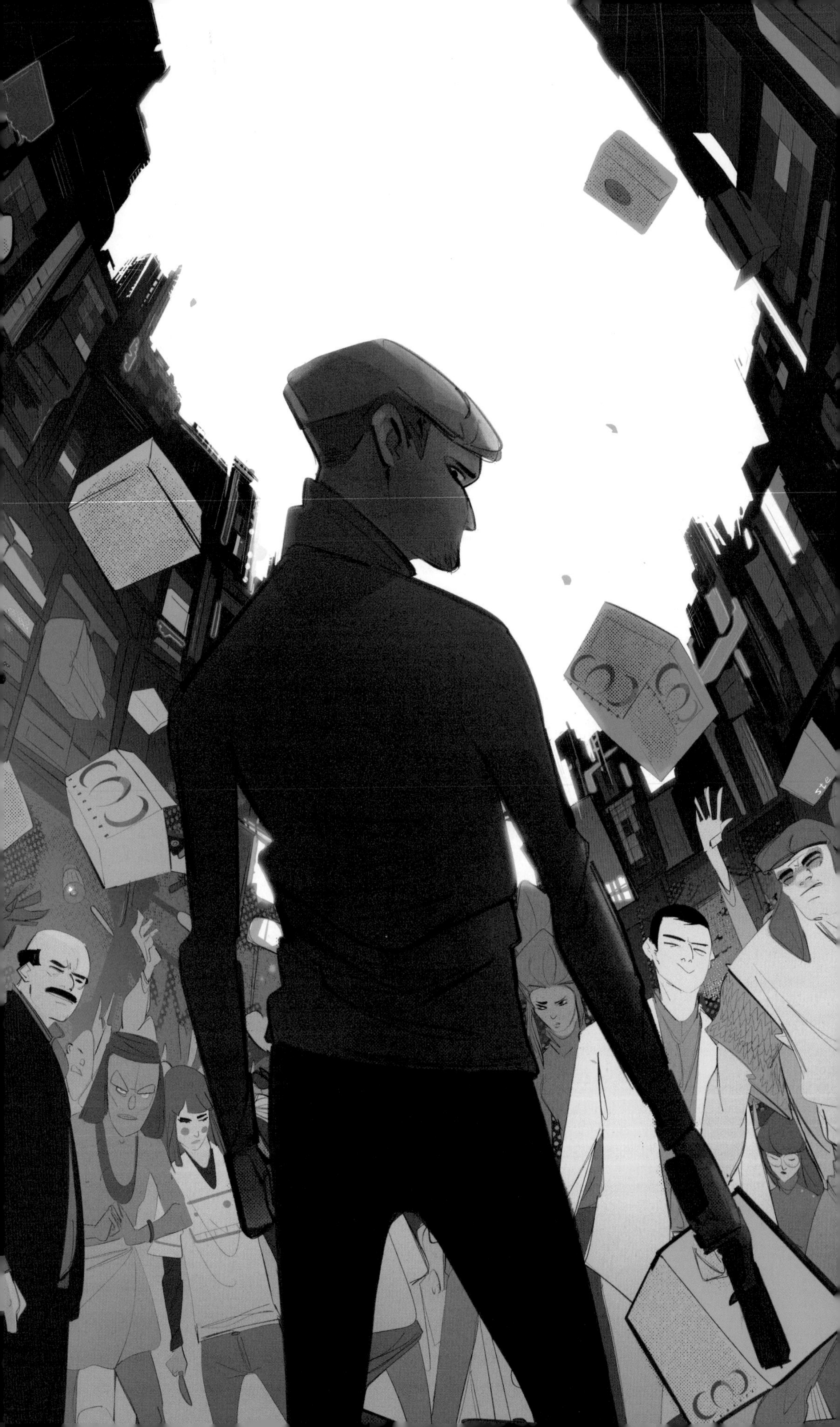

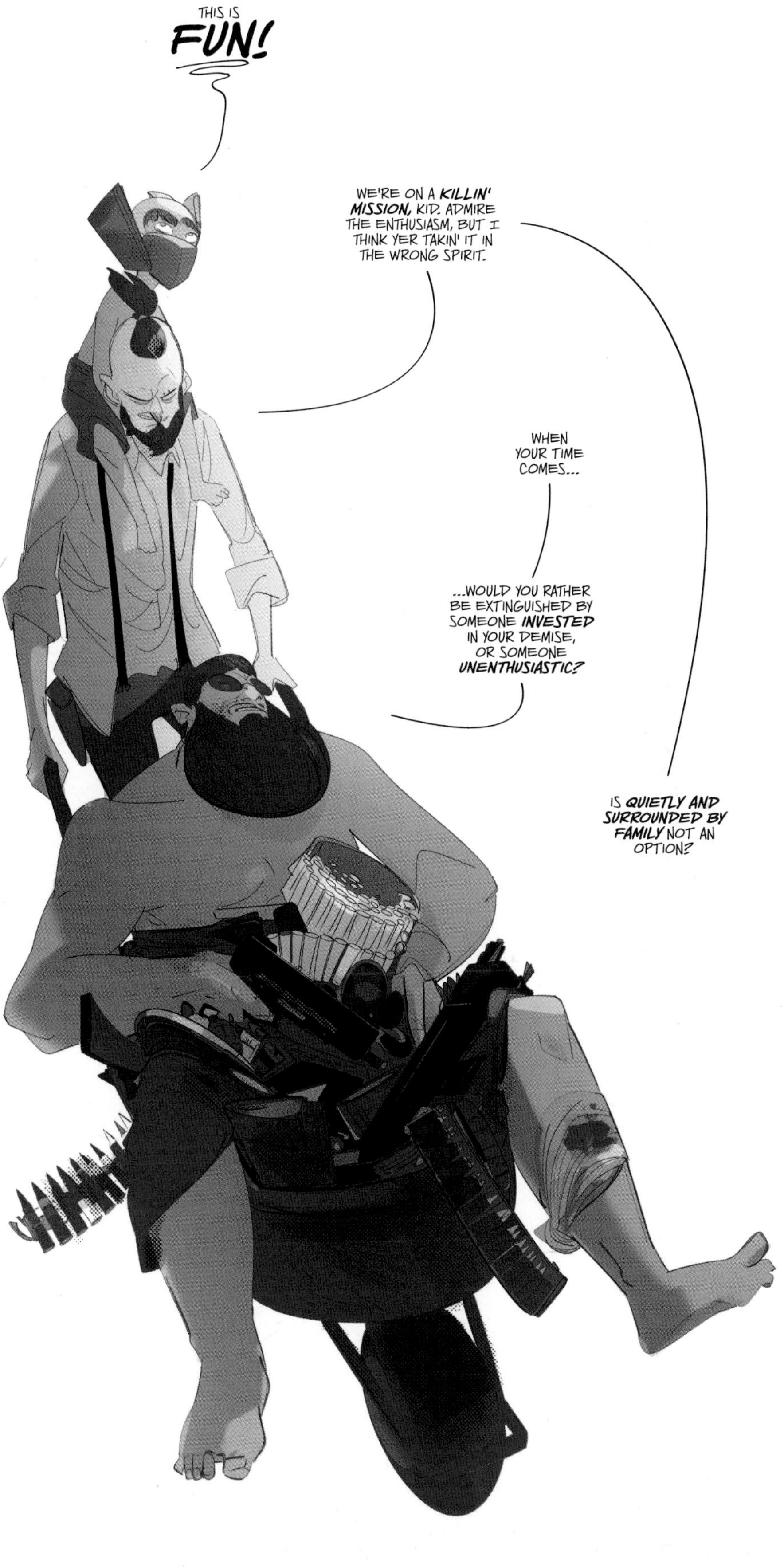
THIS IS FUN!
WE'RE ON A KILLIN' MISSION, KID. ADMIRE THE ENTHUSIASM, BUT I THINK YER TAKIN' IT IN THE WRONG SPIRIT.
WHEN YOUR TIME COMES...
...WOULD YOU RATHER BE EXTINGUISHED BY SOMEONE INVESTED IN YOUR DEMISE, OR SOMEONE UNENTHUSIASTIC?
IS QUIETLY AND SURROUNDED BY FAMILY NOT AN OPTION?

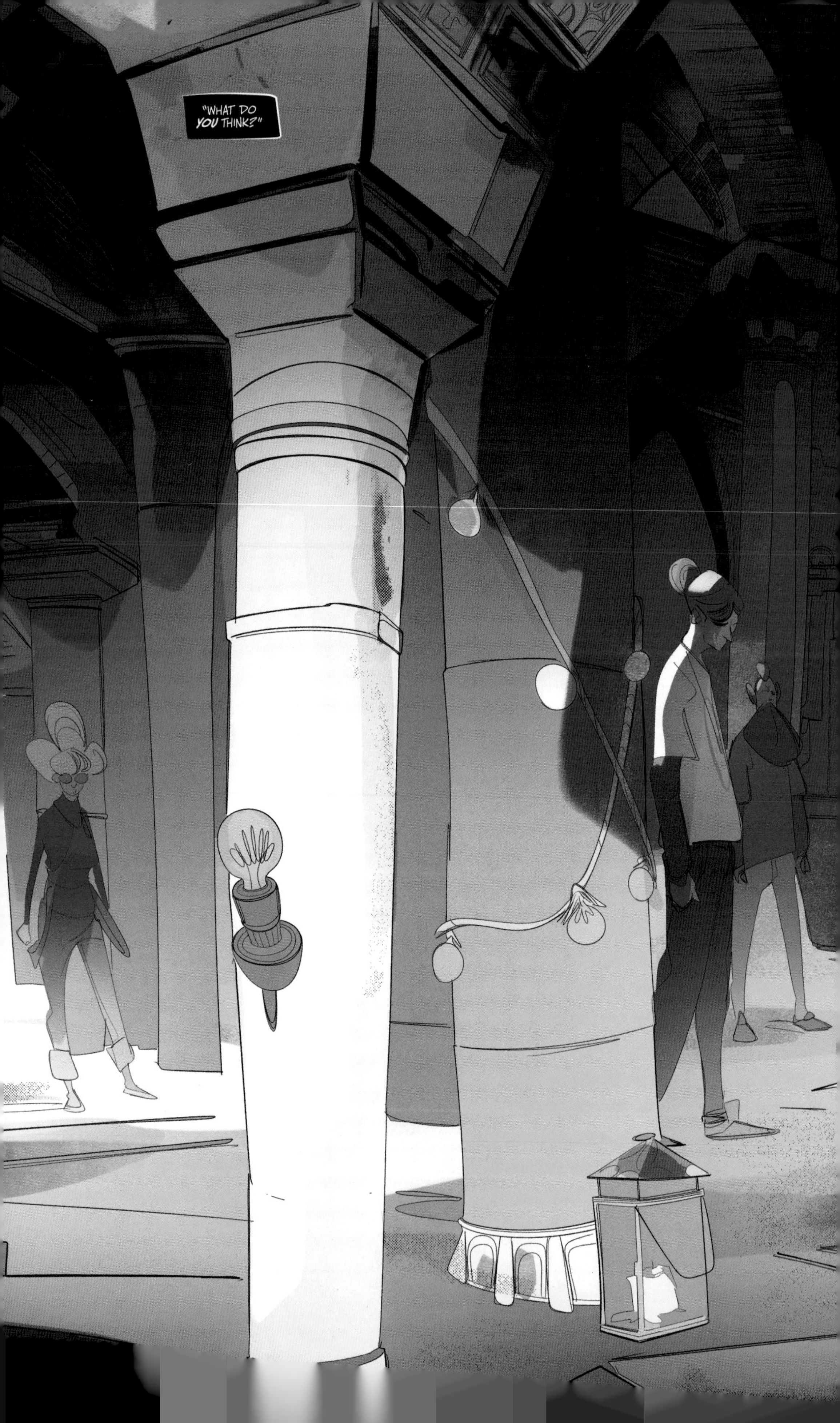
"WHAT DO YOU THINK?"

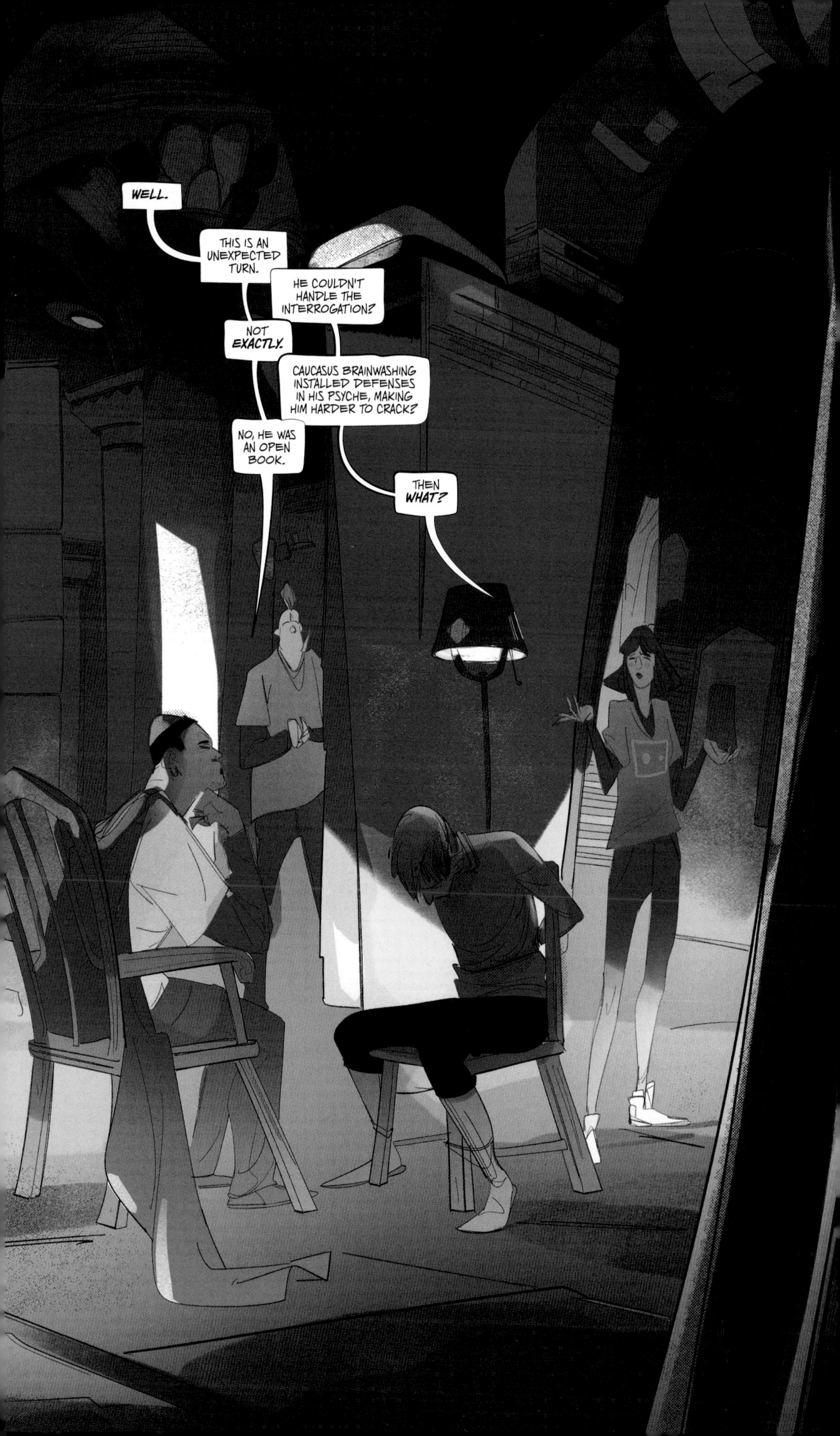
WELL.
THIS IS AN UNEXPECTED TURN.
HE COULDN'T HANDLE THE INTERROGATION?
NOT EXACTLY.
CAUCASUS BRAINWASHING INSTALLED DEFENSES IN HIS PSYCHE, MAKING HIM HARDER TO CRACK?
NO, HE WAS AN OPEN BOOK.
THEN WHAT?

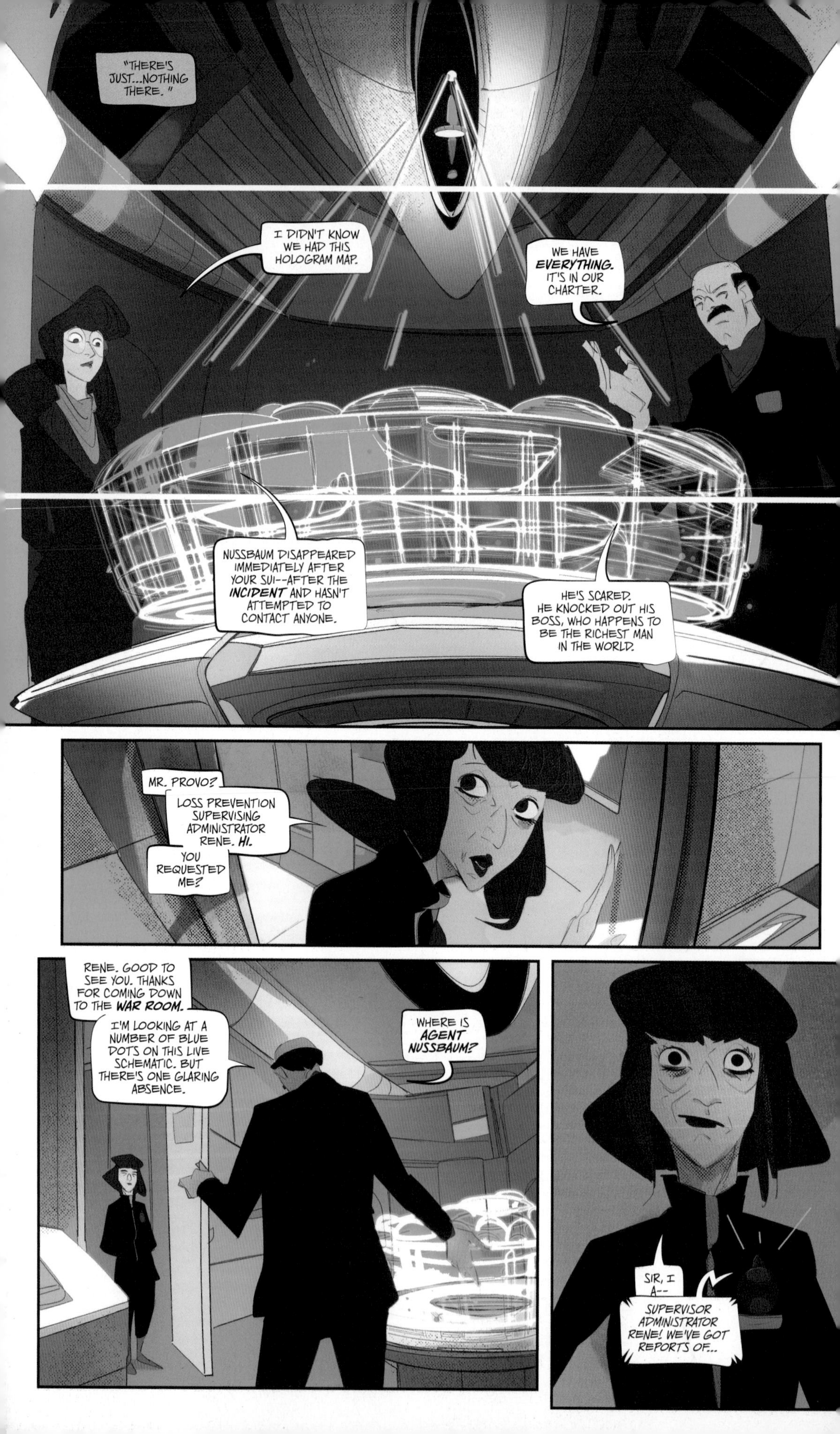
"THERE'S JUST...NOTHING THERE."
I DIDN'T KNOW WE HAD THIS HOLOGRAM MAP.
WE HAVE EVERYTHING. IT'S IN OUR CHARTER.
NUSSBAUM DISAPPEARED IMMEDIATELY AFTER YOUR SUI--AFTER THE INCIDENT AND HASN'T ATTEMPTED TO CONTACT ANYONE.
HE'S SCARED. HE KNOCKED OUT HIS BOSS, WHO HAPPENS TO BE THE RICHEST MAN IN THE WORLD.
MR. PROVO?
LOSS PREVENTION SUPERVISING ADMINISTRATOR RENE. HI.
YOU REQUESTED ME?
RENE. GOOD TO SEE YOU. THANKS FOR COMING DOWN TO THE WAR ROOM.
I'M LOOKING AT A NUMBER OF BLUE DOTS ON THIS LIVE SCHEMATIC. BUT THERE'S ONE GLARING ABSENCE.
WHERE IS AGENT NUSSBAUM?
SIR, I A--
SUPERVISOR ADMINISTRATOR RENE! WE'VE GOT REPORTS OF...

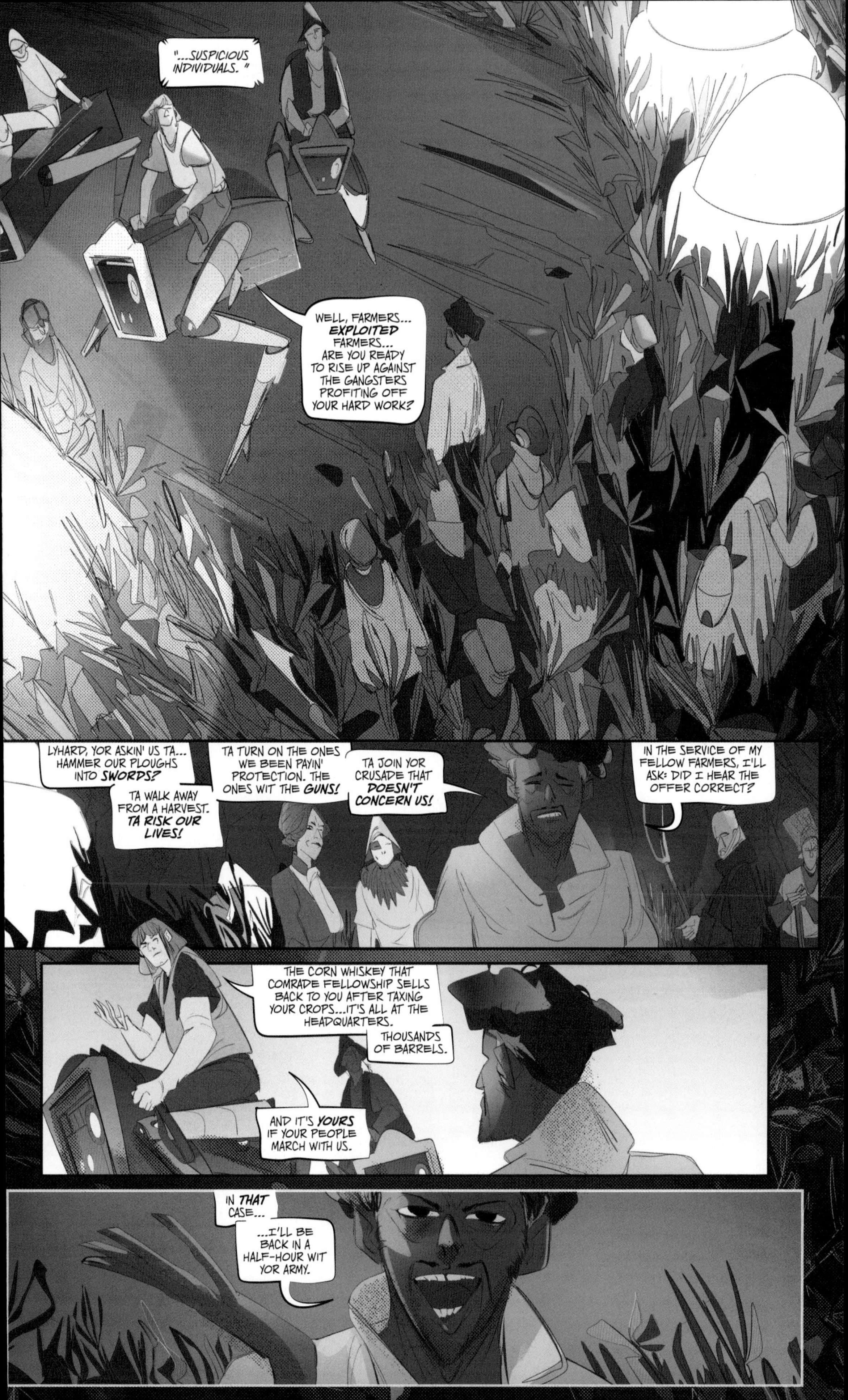
"...SUSPICIOUS INDIVIDUALS."
WELL, FARMERS... EXPLOITED FARMERS... ARE YOU READY TO RISE UP AGAINST THE GANGSTERS PROFITING OFF YOUR HARD WORK?
LYHARD, YOR ASKIN' US TA... HAMMER OUR PLOUGHS INTO SWORDS?
TA WALK AWAY FROM A HARVEST. TA RISK OUR LIVES!
TA TURN ON THE ONES WE BEEN PAYIN' PROTECTION. THE ONES WIT THE GUNS!
TA JOIN YOR CRUSADE THAT DOESN'T CONCERN US!
IN THE SERVICE OF MY FELLOW FARMERS, I'LL ASK: DID I HEAR THE OFFER CORRECT?
THE CORN WHISKEY THAT COMRADE FELLOWSHIP SELLS BACK TO YOU AFTER TAXING YOUR CROPS...IT'S ALL AT THE HEADQUARTERS.
THOUSANDS OF BARRELS.
AND IT'S YOURS IF YOUR PEOPLE MARCH WITH US.
IN THAT CASE...
...I'LL BE BACK IN A HALF-HOUR WIT YOR ARMY.

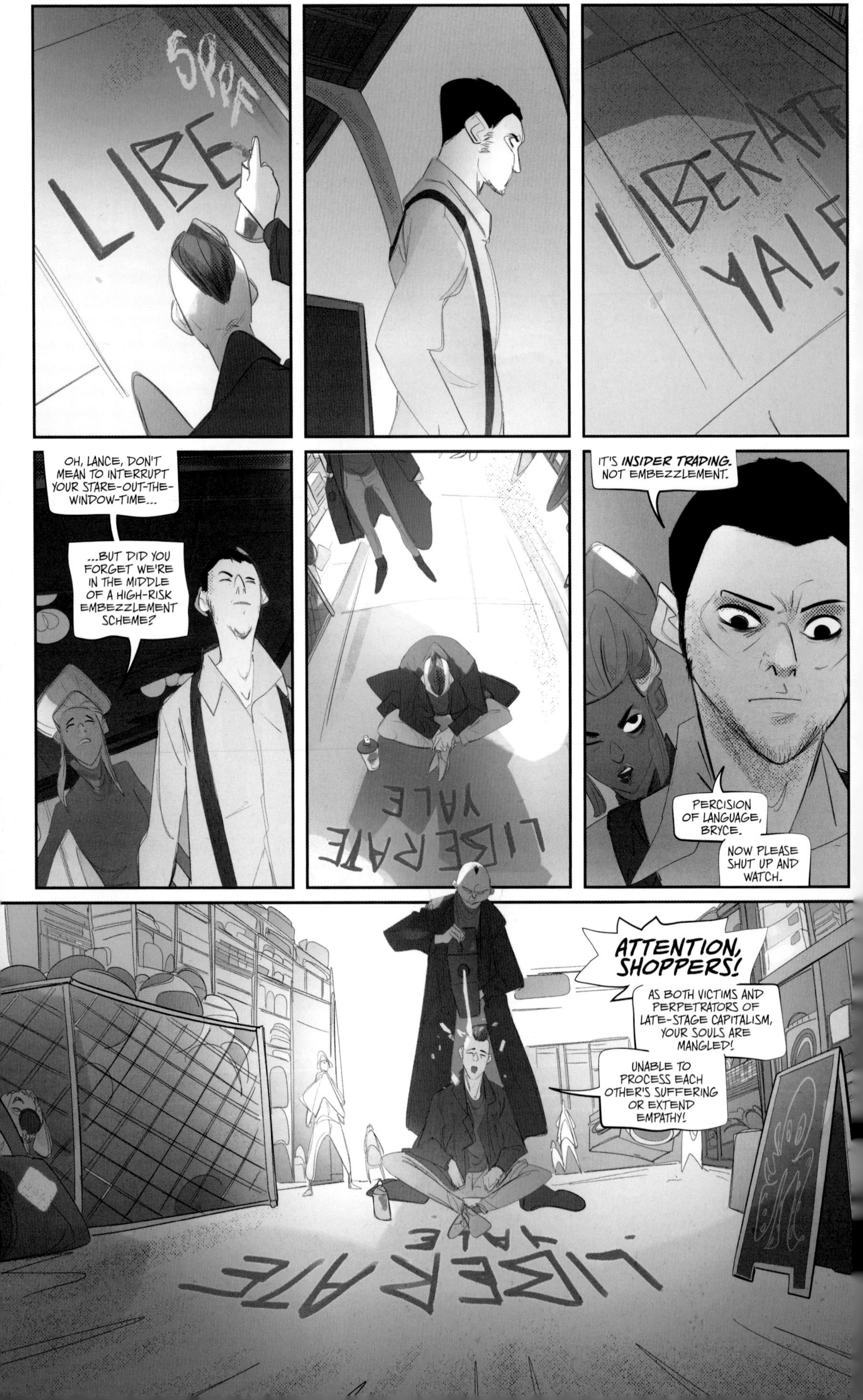
5PPF
LIBE
LIBERATE
YALE
OH, LANCE, DON'T MEAN TO INTERRUPT YOUR STARE-OUT-THE-WINDOW-TIME...
...BUT DID YOU FORGET WE'RE IN THE MIDDLE OF A HIGH-RISK EMBEZZLEMENT SCHEME?
IT'S **INSIDER TRADING.** NOT EMBEZZLEMENT.
PERCISION OF LANGUAGE, BRYCE.
NOW PLEASE SHUT UP AND WATCH.
ATTENTION, SHOPPERS!
AS BOTH VICTIMS AND PERPETRATORS OF LATE-STAGE CAPITALISM, YOUR SOULS ARE MANGLED!
UNABLE TO PROCESS EACH OTHER'S SUFFERING OR EXTEND EMPATHY!

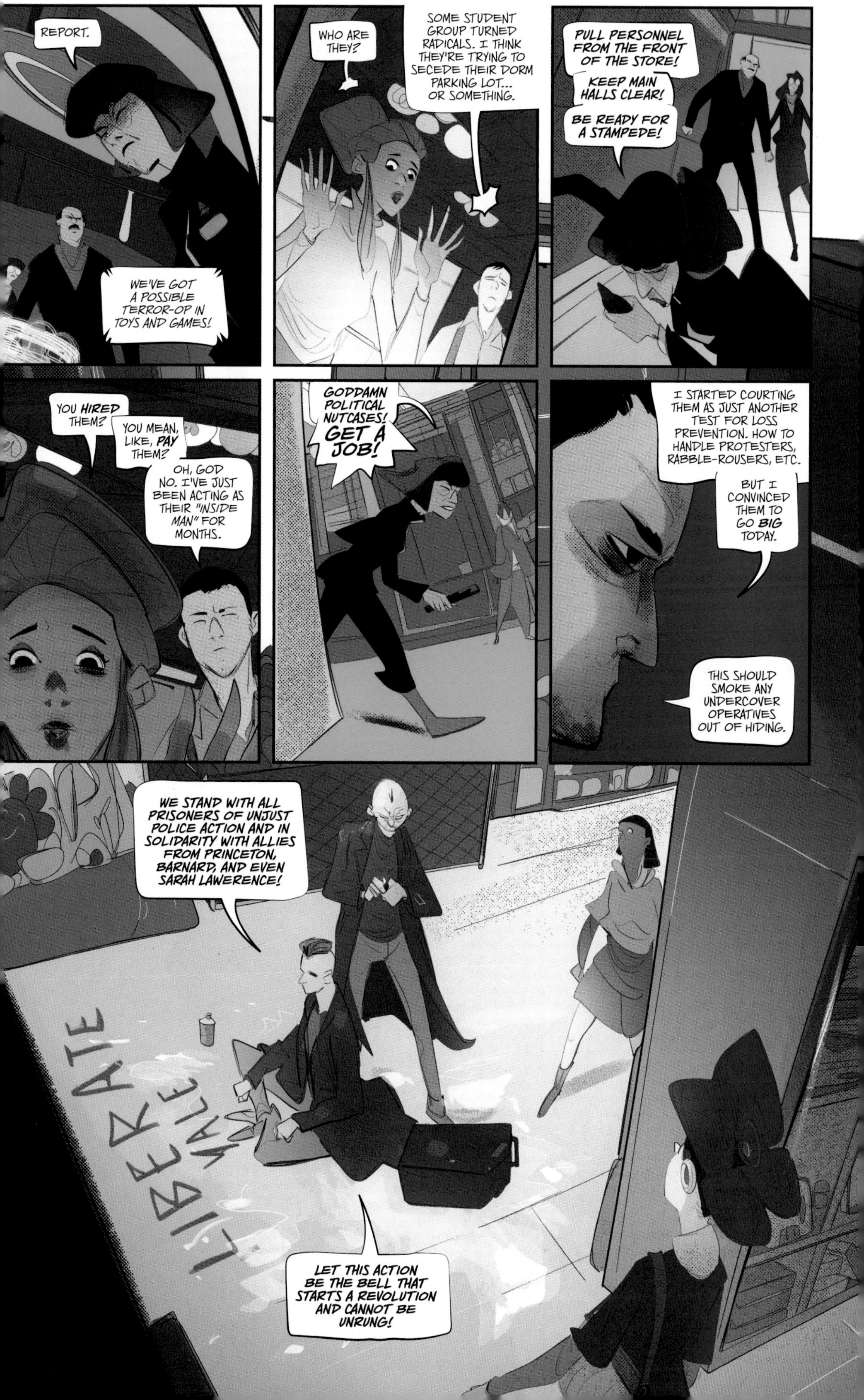
REPORT.
WE'VE GOT A POSSIBLE TERROR-OP IN TOYS AND GAMES!
WHO ARE THEY?
SOME STUDENT GROUP TURNED RADICALS. I THINK THEY'RE TRYING TO SECEDE THEIR DORM PARKING LOT... OR SOMETHING.
PULL PERSONNEL FROM THE FRONT OF THE STORE!
KEEP MAIN HALLS CLEAR!
BE READY FOR A STAMPEDE!
YOU HIRED THEM?
YOU MEAN, LIKE, PAY THEM?
OH, GOD NO. I'VE JUST BEEN ACTING AS THEIR "INSIDE MAN" FOR MONTHS.
GODDAMN POLITICAL NUTCASES! GET A JOB!
I STARTED COURTING THEM AS JUST ANOTHER TEST FOR LOSS PREVENTION. HOW TO HANDLE PROTESTERS, RABBLE-ROUSERS, ETC.
BUT I CONVINCED THEM TO GO BIG TODAY.
THIS SHOULD SMOKE ANY UNDERCOVER OPERATIVES OUT OF HIDING.
WE STAND WITH ALL PRISONERS OF UNJUST POLICE ACTION AND IN SOLIDARITY WITH ALLIES FROM PRINCETON, BARNARD, AND EVEN SARAH LAWERENCE!
LIBERATE MALL
LET THIS ACTION BE THE BELL THAT STARTS A REVOLUTION AND CANNOT BE UNRUNG!

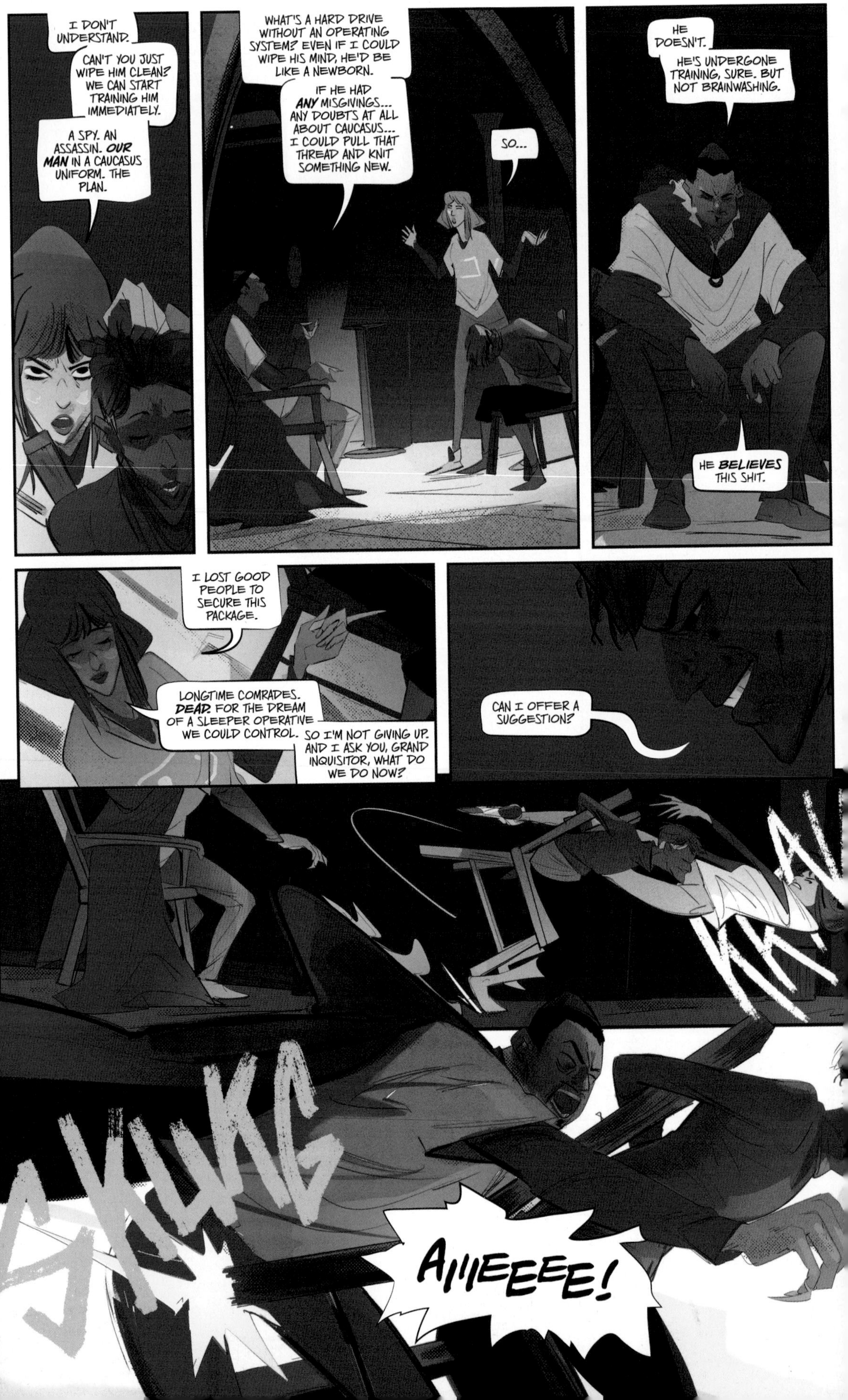
I DON'T UNDERSTAND.
CAN'T YOU JUST WIPE HIM CLEAN? WE CAN START TRAINING HIM IMMEDIATELY.
A SPY. AN ASSASSIN. ***OUR MAN*** IN A CAUCASUS UNIFORM. THE PLAN.
WHAT'S A HARD DRIVE WITHOUT AN OPERATING SYSTEM? EVEN IF I COULD WIPE HIS MIND, HE'D BE LIKE A NEWBORN.
IF HE HAD ***ANY*** MISGIVINGS... ANY DOUBTS AT ALL ABOUT CAUCASUS... I COULD PULL THAT THREAD AND KNIT SOMETHING NEW.
SO...
HE DOESN'T.
HE'S ***UNDERGONE*** TRAINING, SURE. BUT NOT BRAINWASHING.
HE ***BELIEVES*** THIS SHIT.
I LOST GOOD PEOPLE TO SECURE THIS PACKAGE.
LONGTIME COMRADES. ***DEAD.*** FOR THE DREAM OF A SLEEPER OPERATIVE WE COULD CONTROL.
SO I'M NOT GIVING UP. AND I ASK YOU, GRAND INQUISITOR, WHAT DO WE DO NOW?
CAN I OFFER A SUGGESTION?
SHUKG
AIIIEEEEE!

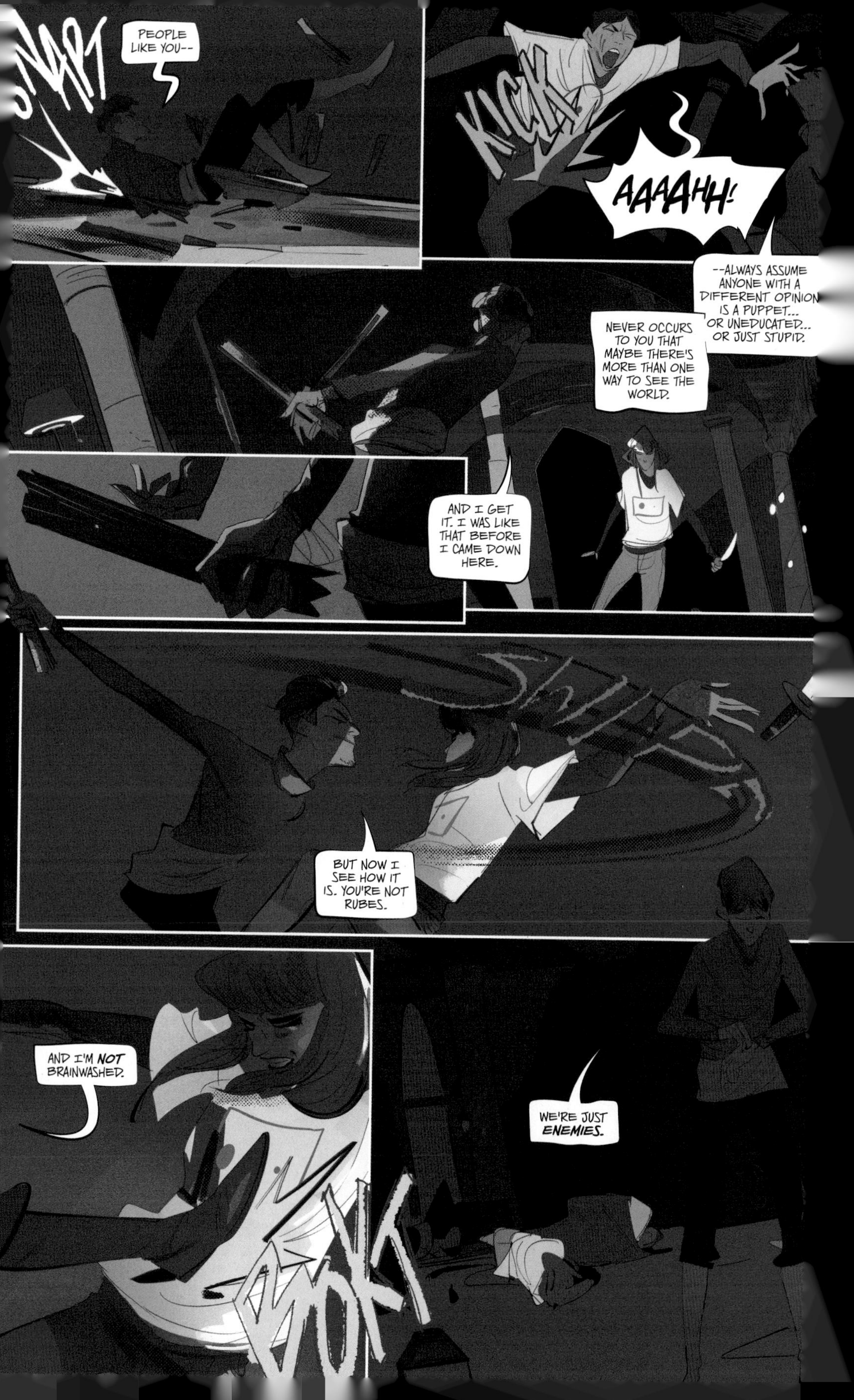

SNAP!
PEOPLE LIKE YOU--
KICK
AAAAHH!
--ALWAYS ASSUME ANYONE WITH A DIFFERENT OPINION IS A PUPPET... OR UNEDUCATED... OR JUST STUPID.
NEVER OCCURS TO YOU THAT MAYBE THERE'S MORE THAN ONE WAY TO SEE THE WORLD.
AND I GET IT. I WAS LIKE THAT BEFORE I CAME DOWN HERE.
BUT NOW I SEE HOW IT IS. YOU'RE NOT RUBES.
AND I'M **NOT** BRAINWASHED.
WE'RE JUST **ENEMIES.**

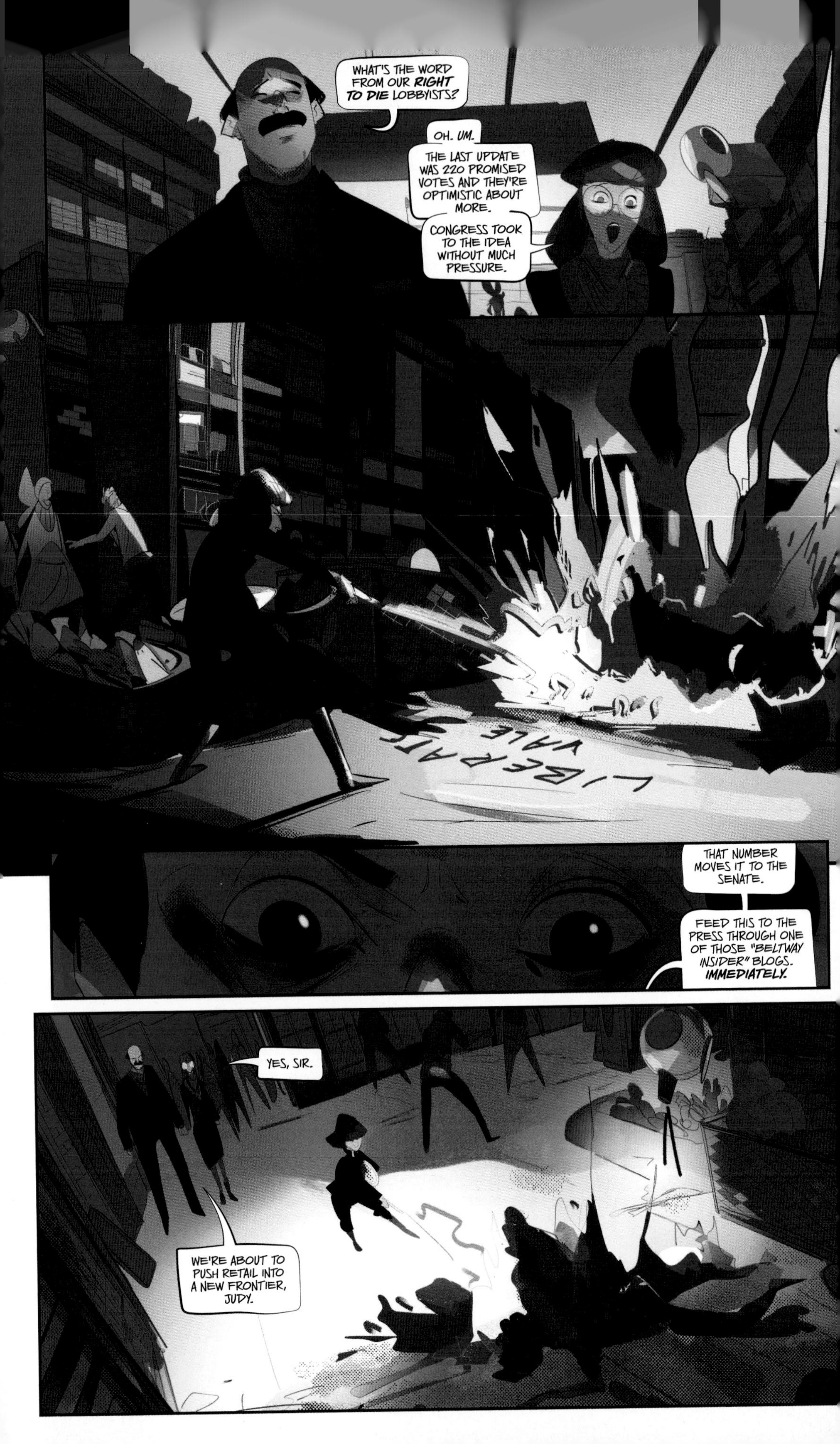
WHAT'S THE WORD FROM OUR RIGHT TO DIE LOBBYISTS?
OH. UM.
THE LAST UPDATE WAS 220 PROMISED VOTES AND THEY'RE OPTIMISTIC ABOUT MORE.
CONGRESS TOOK TO THE IDEA WITHOUT MUCH PRESSURE.
LIBERATE YALE
THAT NUMBER MOVES IT TO THE SENATE.
FEED THIS TO THE PRESS THROUGH ONE OF THOSE "BELTWAY INSIDER" BLOGS. IMMEDIATELY.
YES, SIR.
WE'RE ABOUT TO PUSH RETAIL INTO A NEW FRONTIER, JUDY.

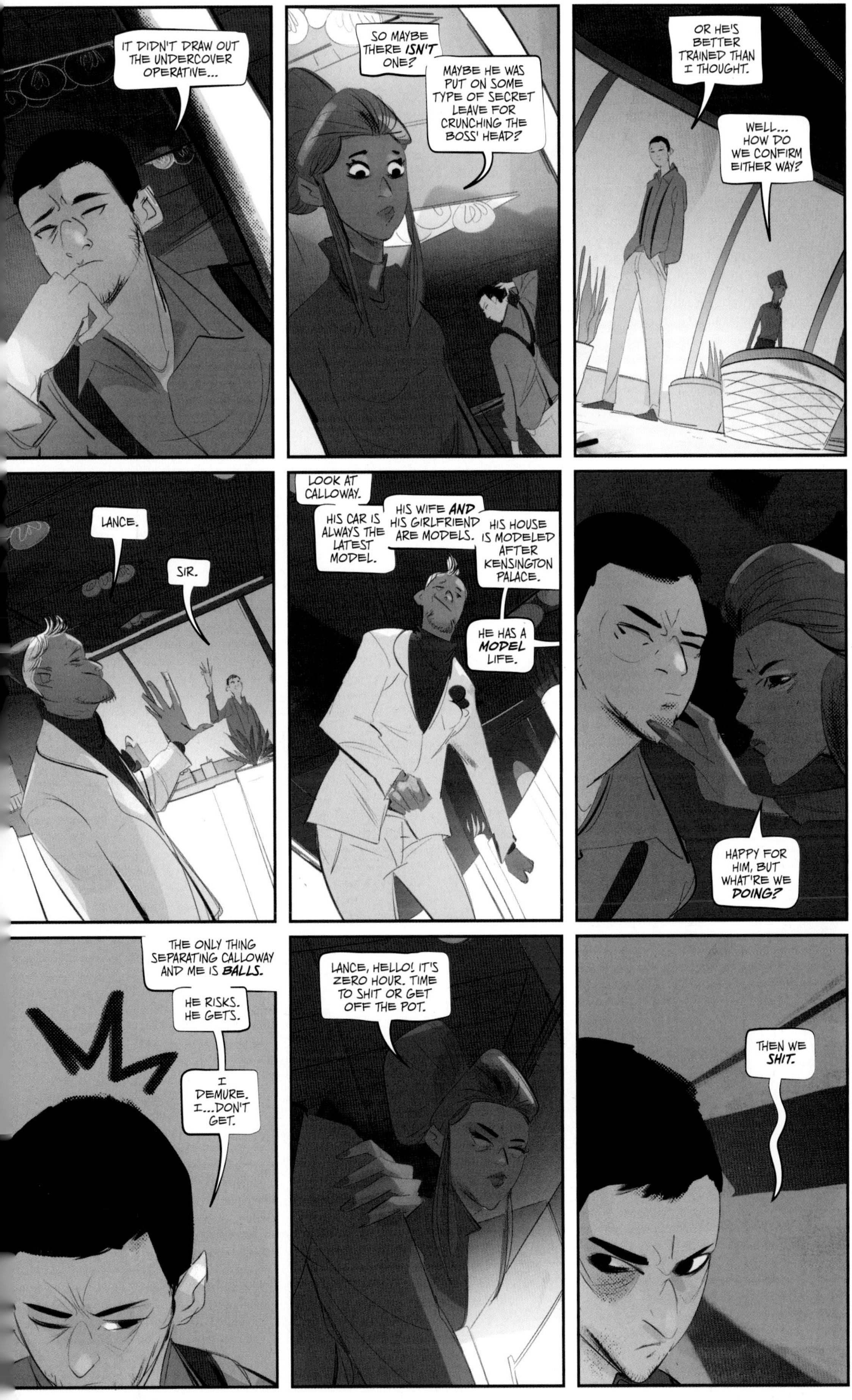

IT DIDN'T DRAW OUT THE UNDERCOVER OPERATIVE...
SO MAYBE THERE ISN'T ONE?
MAYBE HE WAS PUT ON SOME TYPE OF SECRET LEAVE FOR CRUNCHING THE BOSS' HEAD?
OR HE'S BETTER TRAINED THAN I THOUGHT.
WELL... HOW DO WE CONFIRM EITHER WAY?
LANCE.
SIR.
LOOK AT CALLOWAY.
HIS CAR IS ALWAYS THE LATEST MODEL.
HIS WIFE AND HIS GIRLFRIEND ARE MODELS.
HIS HOUSE IS MODELED AFTER KENSINGTON PALACE.
HE HAS A MODEL LIFE.
HAPPY FOR HIM, BUT WHAT'RE WE DOING?
THE ONLY THING SEPARATING CALLOWAY AND ME IS BALLS.
HE RISKS. HE GETS.
I DEMURE. I...DON'T GET.
LANCE, HELLO! IT'S ZERO HOUR. TIME TO SHIT OR GET OFF THE POT.
THEN WE SHIT.

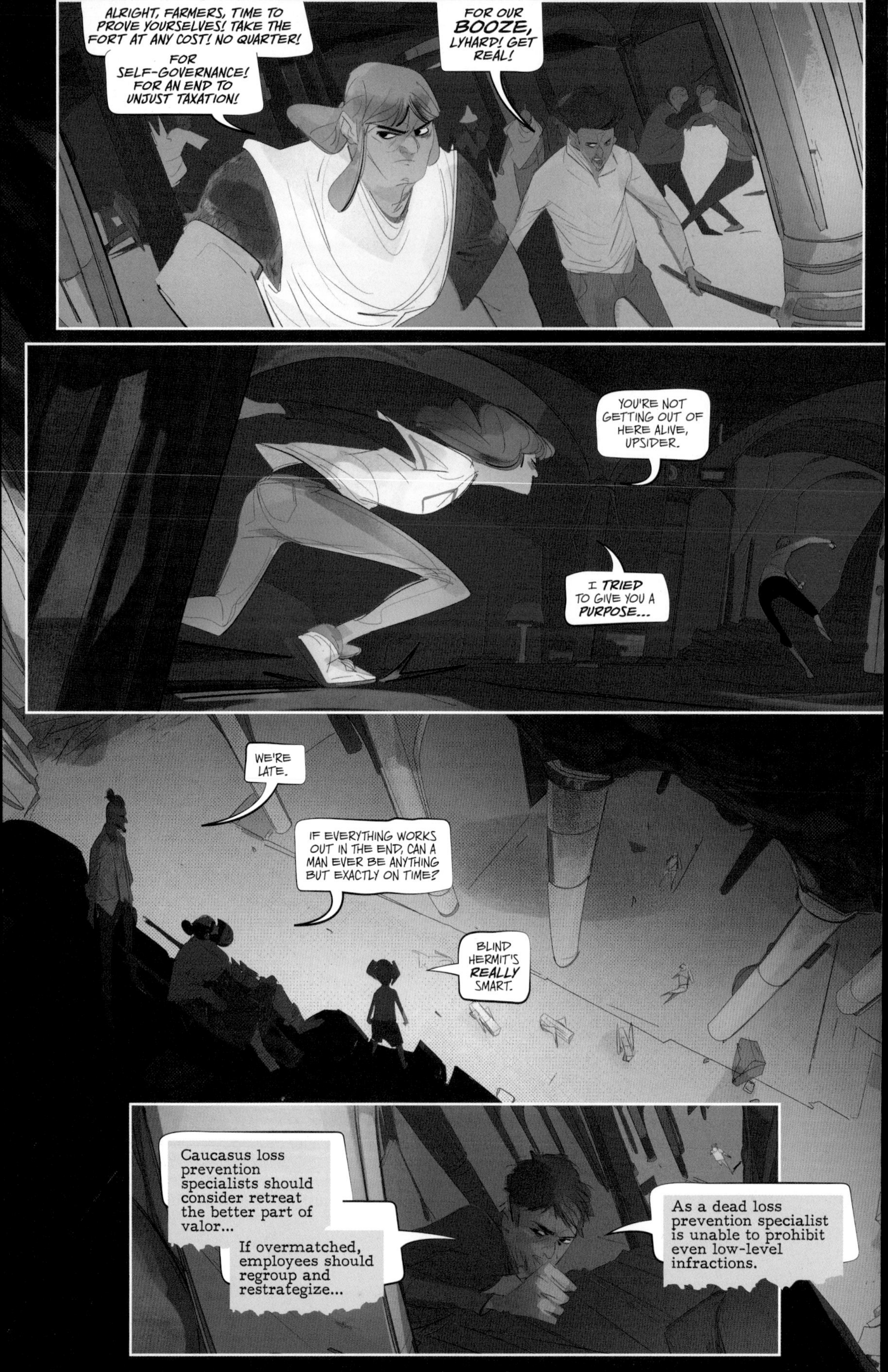
ALRIGHT, FARMERS, TIME TO PROVE YOURSELVES! TAKE THE FORT AT ANY COST! NO QUARTER!
FOR SELF-GOVERNANCE! FOR AN END TO UNJUST TAXATION!
FOR OUR BOOZE, LYHARD! GET REAL!
YOU'RE NOT GETTING OUT OF HERE ALIVE, UPSIDER.
I TRIED TO GIVE YOU A PURPOSE...
WE'RE LATE.
IF EVERYTHING WORKS OUT IN THE END, CAN A MAN EVER BE ANYTHING BUT EXACTLY ON TIME?
BLIND HERMIT'S REALLY SMART.
Caucasus loss prevention specialists should consider retreat the better part of valor...
If overmatched, employees should regroup and restrategize...
As a dead loss prevention specialist is unable to prohibit even low-level infractions.

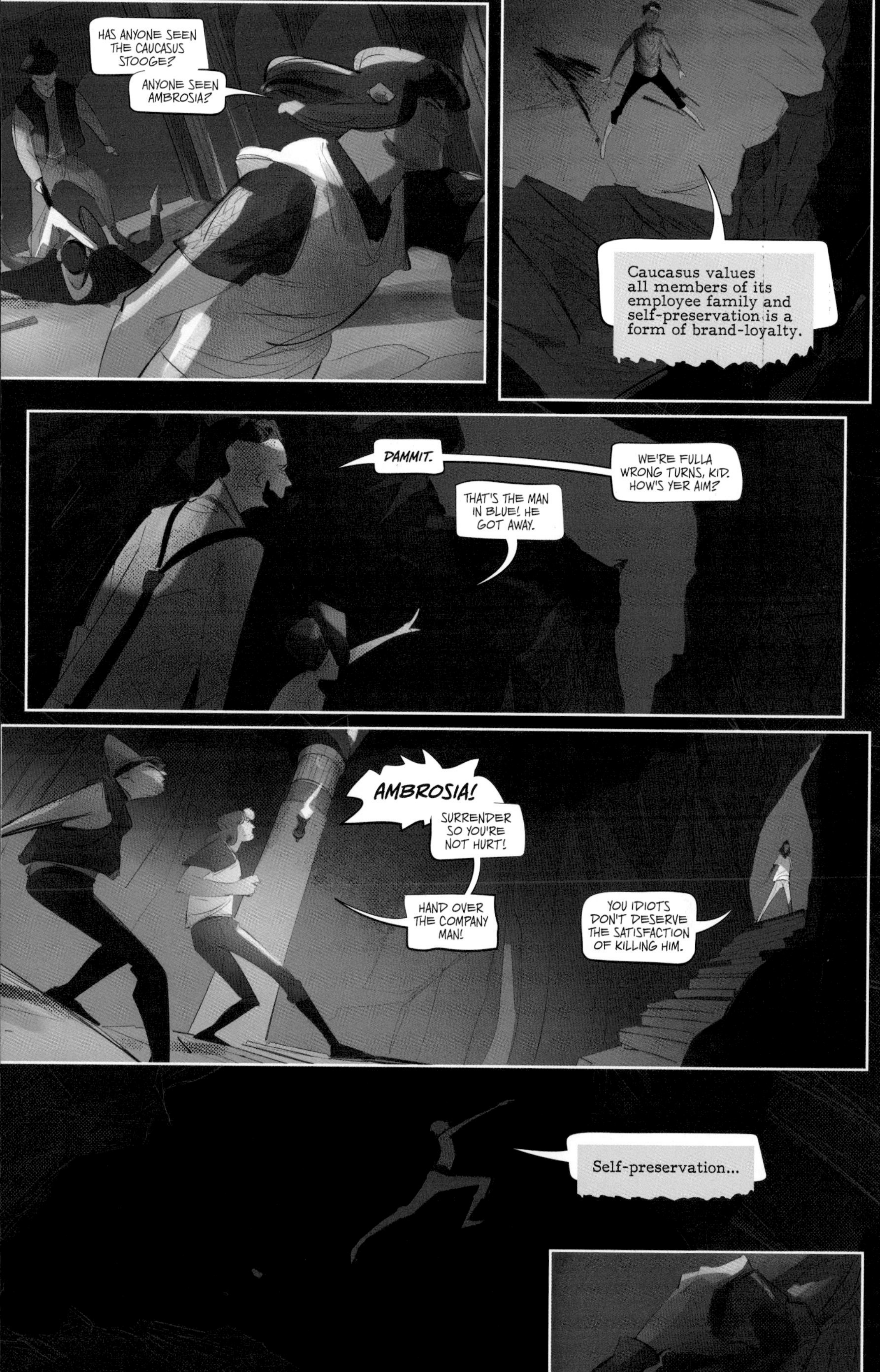

HAS ANYONE SEEN THE CAUCASUS STOOGE?
ANYONE SEEN AMBROSIA?
Caucasus values all members of its employee family and self-preservation is a form of brand-loyalty.
DAMMIT.
WE'RE FULLA WRONG TURNS, KID. HOW'S YER AIM?
THAT'S THE MAN IN BLUE! HE GOT AWAY.
AMBROSIA!
SURRENDER SO YOU'RE NOT HURT!
HAND OVER THE COMPANY MAN!
YOU IDIOTS DON'T DESERVE THE SATISFACTION OF KILLING HIM.
Self-preservation...

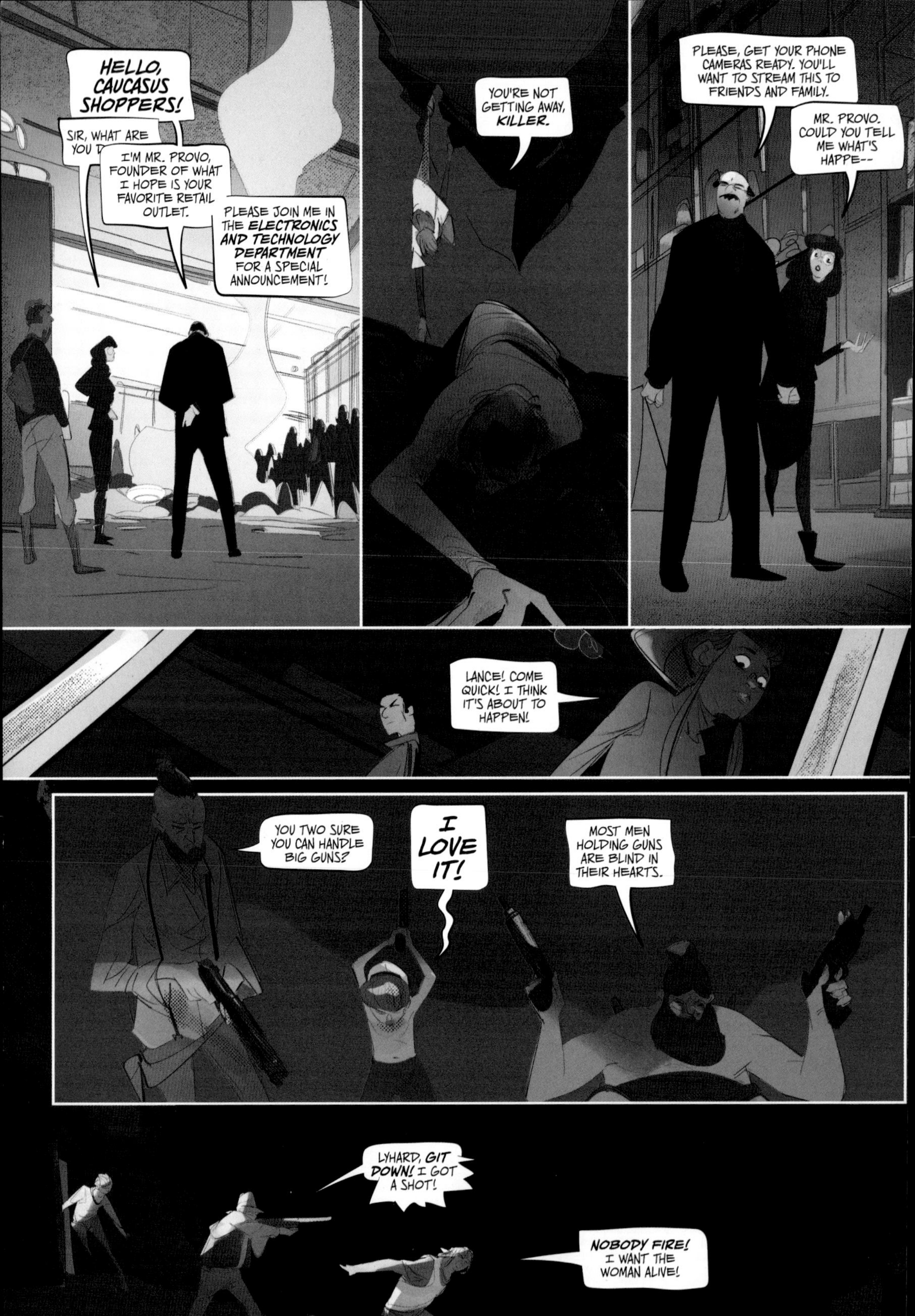
HELLO, CAUCASUS SHOPPERS!
SIR, WHAT ARE YOU D--
I'M MR. PROVO, FOUNDER OF WHAT I HOPE IS YOUR FAVORITE RETAIL OUTLET.
PLEASE JOIN ME IN THE ELECTRONICS AND TECHNOLOGY DEPARTMENT FOR A SPECIAL ANNOUNCEMENT!
YOU'RE NOT GETTING AWAY, KILLER.
PLEASE, GET YOUR PHONE CAMERAS READY. YOU'LL WANT TO STREAM THIS TO FRIENDS AND FAMILY.
MR. PROVO. COULD YOU TELL ME WHAT'S HAPPE--
LANCE! COME QUICK! I THINK IT'S ABOUT TO HAPPEN!
YOU TWO SURE YOU CAN HANDLE BIG GUNS?
I LOVE IT!
MOST MEN HOLDING GUNS ARE BLIND IN THEIR HEARTS.
LYHARD, GIT DOWN! I GOT A SHOT!
NOBODY FIRE! I WANT THE WOMAN ALIVE!

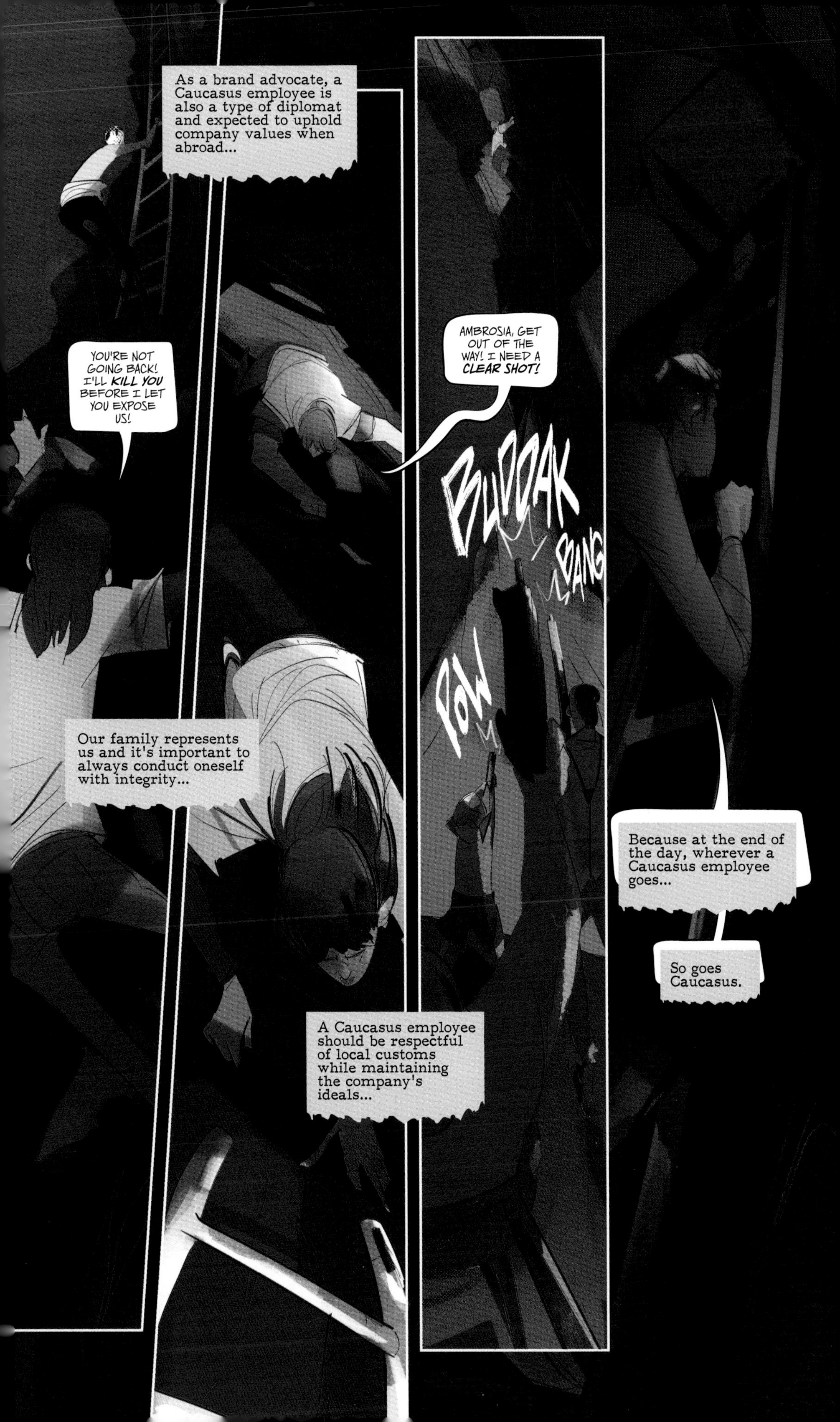

As a brand advocate, a Caucasus employee is also a type of diplomat and expected to uphold company values when abroad...
YOU'RE NOT GOING BACK! I'LL KILL YOU BEFORE I LET YOU EXPOSE US!
Our family represents us and it's important to always conduct oneself with integrity...
AMBROSIA, GET OUT OF THE WAY! I NEED A CLEAR SHOT!
A Caucasus employee should be respectful of local customs while maintaining the company's ideals...
BUDDAK
BANG
POW
Because at the end of the day, wherever a Caucasus employee goes...
So goes Caucasus.

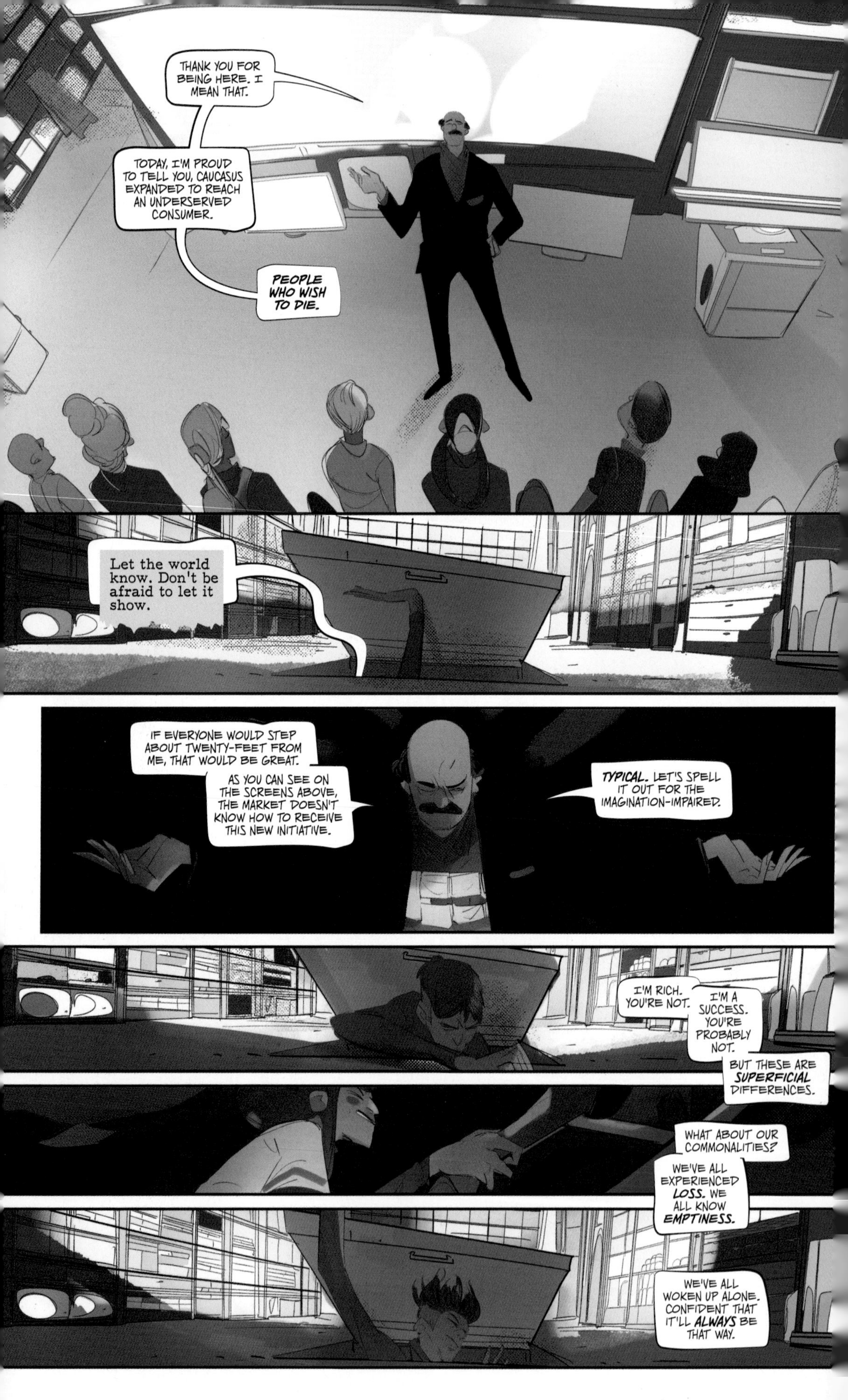
THANK YOU FOR BEING HERE. I MEAN THAT.
TODAY, I'M PROUD TO TELL YOU, CAUCASUS EXPANDED TO REACH AN UNDERSERVED CONSUMER.
PEOPLE WHO WISH TO DIE.
Let the world know. Don't be afraid to let it show.
IF EVERYONE WOULD STEP ABOUT TWENTY-FEET FROM ME, THAT WOULD BE GREAT.
AS YOU CAN SEE ON THE SCREENS ABOVE, THE MARKET DOESN'T KNOW HOW TO RECEIVE THIS NEW INITIATIVE.
TYPICAL. LET'S SPELL IT OUT FOR THE IMAGINATION-IMPAIRED.
I'M RICH. YOU'RE NOT.
I'M A SUCCESS. YOU'RE PROBABLY NOT.
BUT THESE ARE SUPERFICIAL DIFFERENCES.
WHAT ABOUT OUR COMMONALITIES?
WE'VE ALL EXPERIENCED LOSS. WE ALL KNOW EMPTINESS.
WE'VE ALL WOKEN UP ALONE. CONFIDENT THAT IT'LL ALWAYS BE THAT WAY.

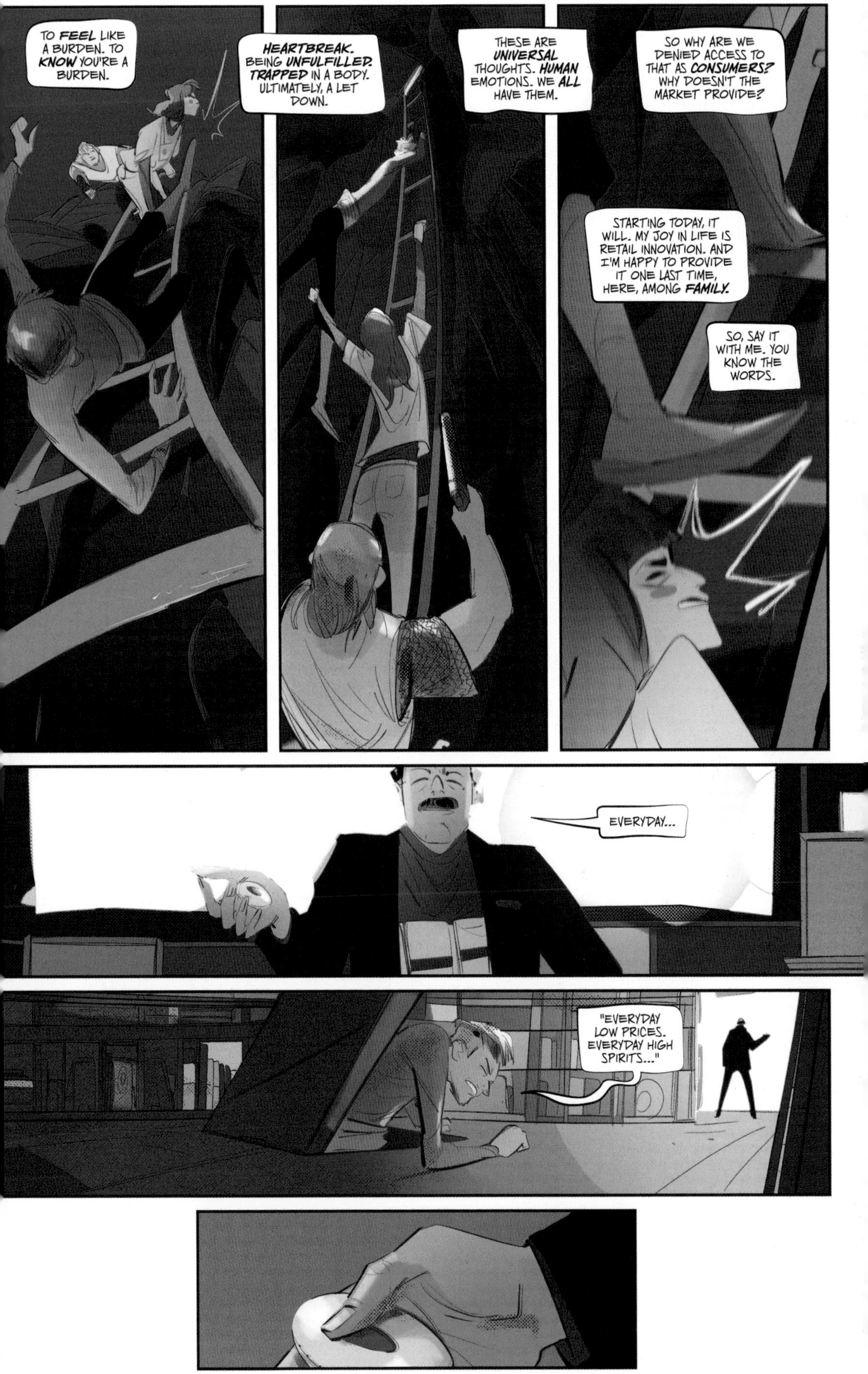
TO FEEL LIKE A BURDEN. TO KNOW YOU'RE A BURDEN.
HEARTBREAK. BEING UNFULFILLED. TRAPPED IN A BODY. ULTIMATELY, A LET DOWN.
THESE ARE UNIVERSAL THOUGHTS. HUMAN EMOTIONS. WE ALL HAVE THEM.
SO WHY ARE WE DENIED ACCESS TO THAT AS CONSUMERS? WHY DOESN'T THE MARKET PROVIDE?
STARTING TODAY, IT WILL. MY JOY IN LIFE IS RETAIL INNOVATION. AND I'M HAPPY TO PROVIDE IT ONE LAST TIME, HERE, AMONG FAMILY.
SO, SAY IT WITH ME. YOU KNOW THE WORDS.
EVERYDAY...
"EVERYDAY LOW PRICES. EVERYDAY HIGH SPIRITS..."

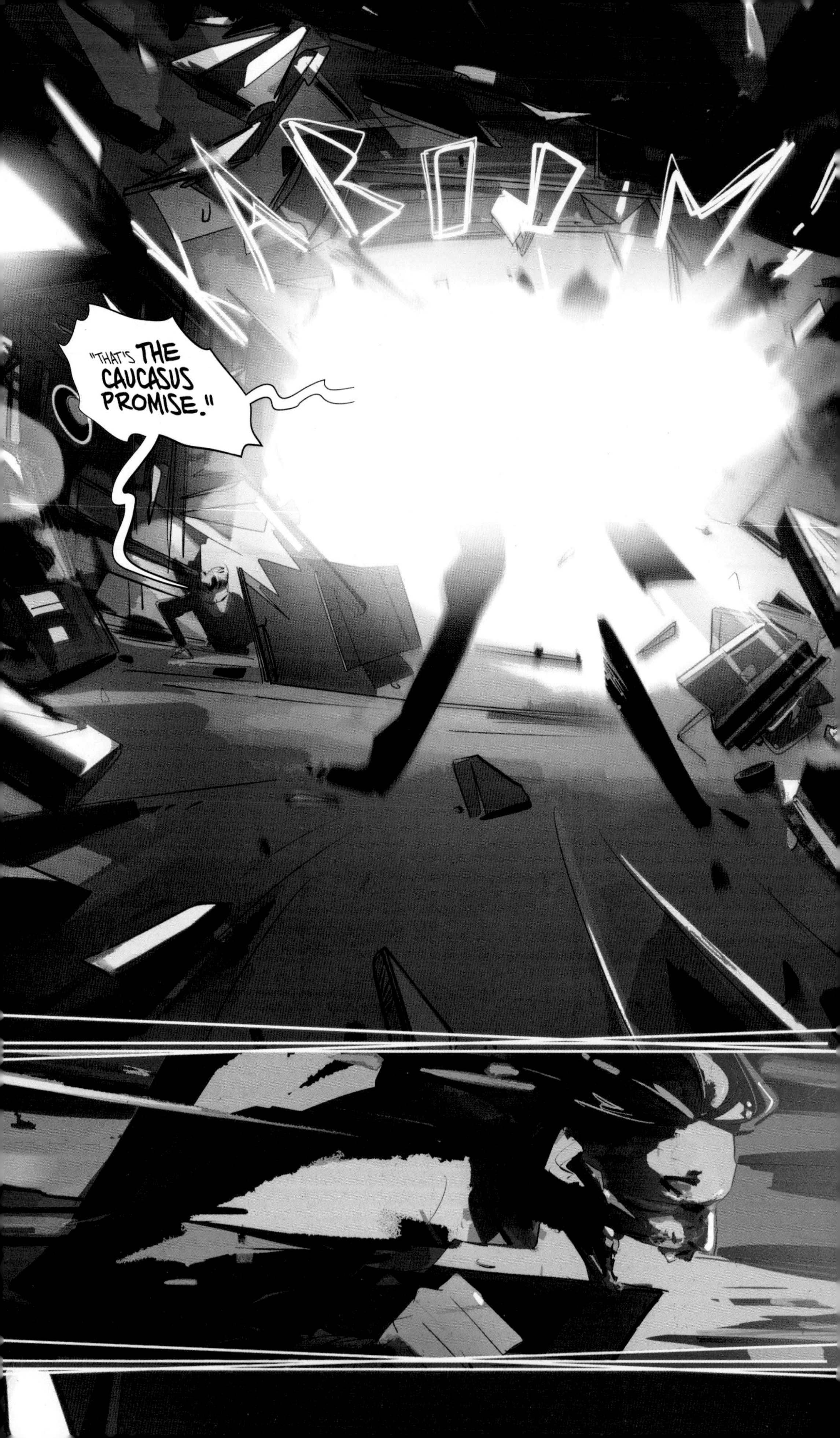
KABOOM!
"THAT'S THE CAUCASUS PROMISE."

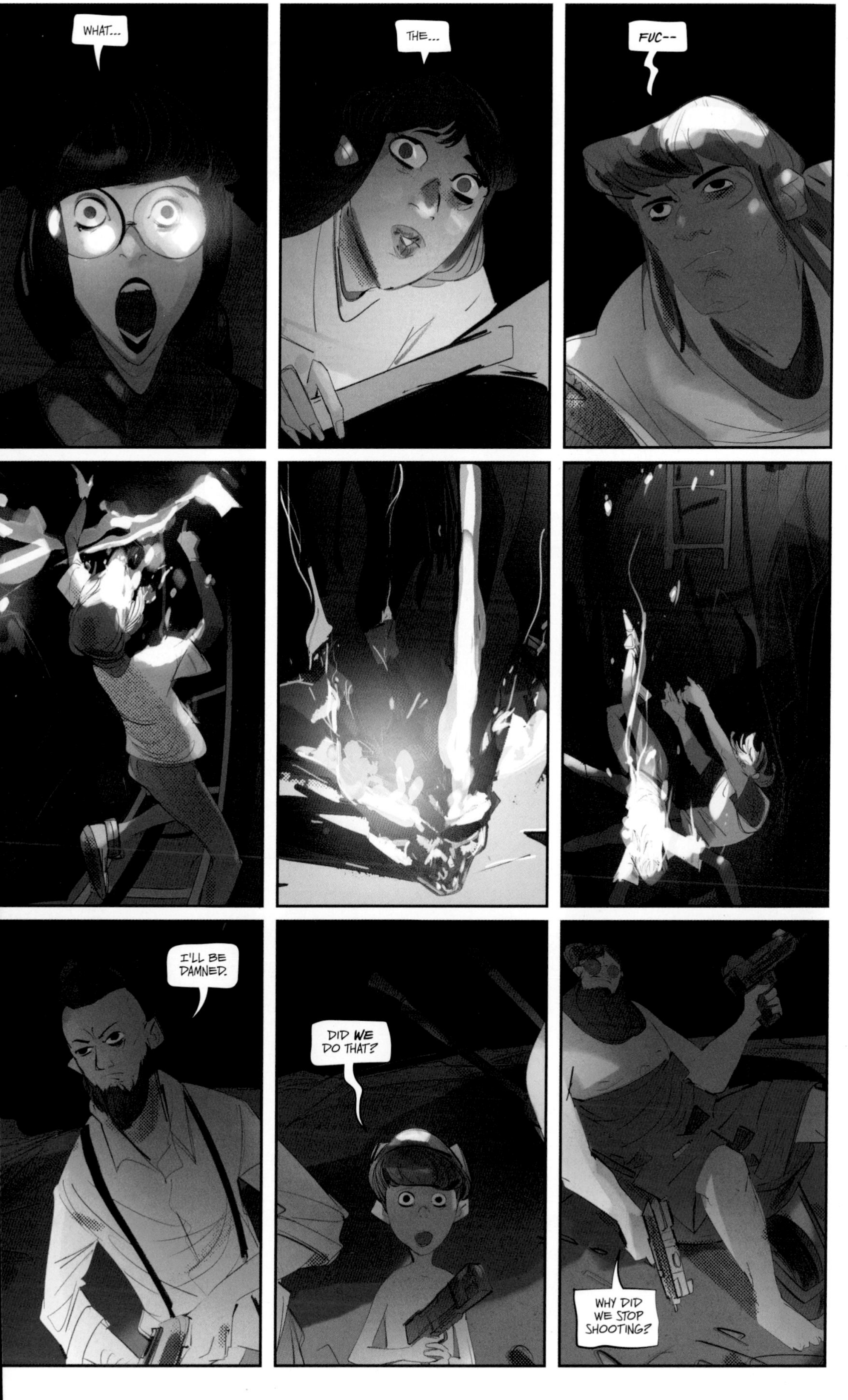
WHAT...
THE...
FUC--
I'LL BE DAMNED.
DID WE DO THAT?
WHY DID WE STOP SHOOTING?

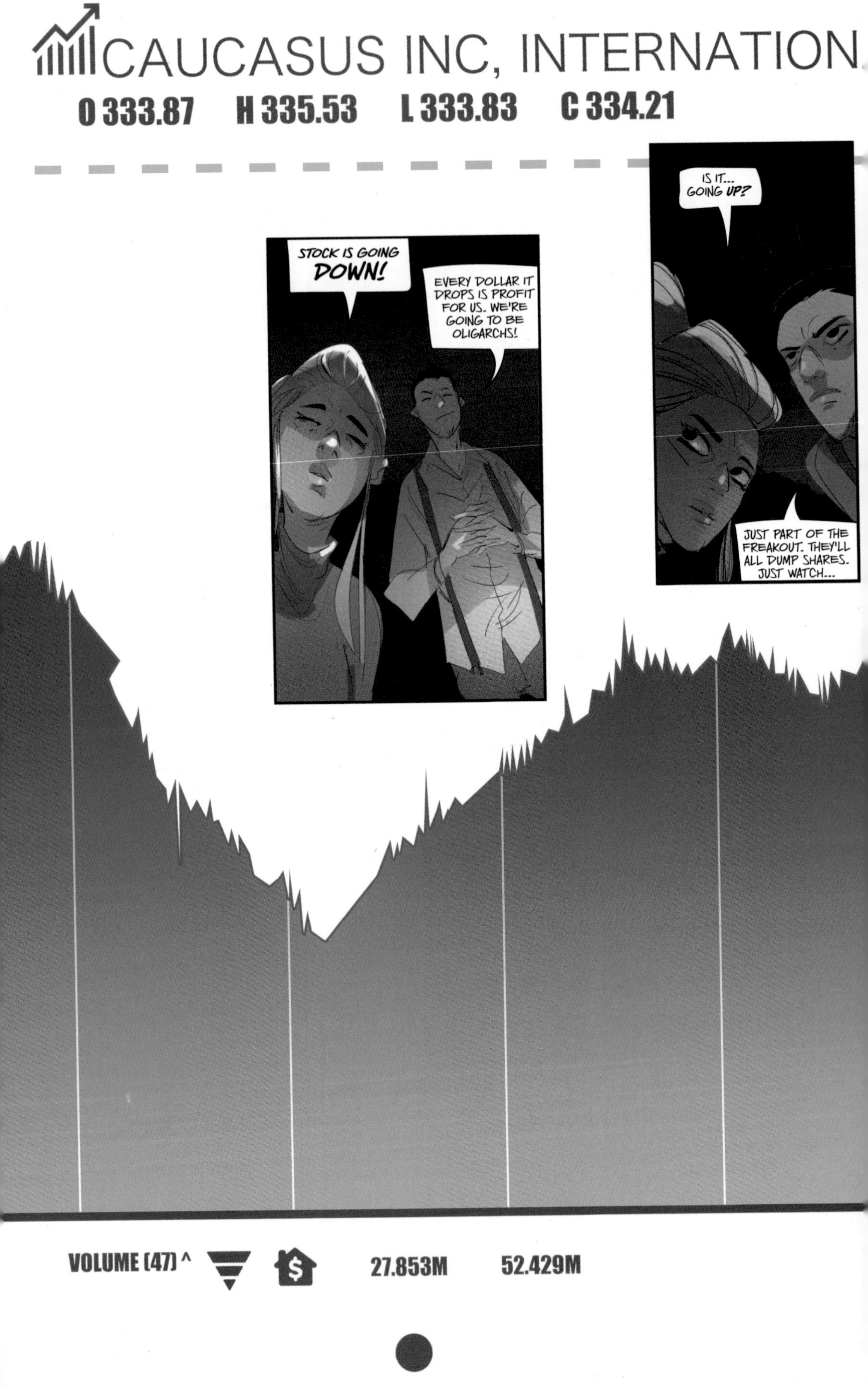
CAUCASUS INC, INTERNATION
O 333.87
H 335.53
L 333.83
C 334.21
STOCK IS GOING DOWN!
EVERY DOLLAR IT DROPS IS PROFIT FOR US. WE'RE GOING TO BE OLIGARCHS!
IS IT... GOING UP?
JUST PART OF THE FREAKOUT. THEY'LL ALL DUMP SHARES. JUST WATCH...
VOLUME (47) ^
27.853M
52.429M

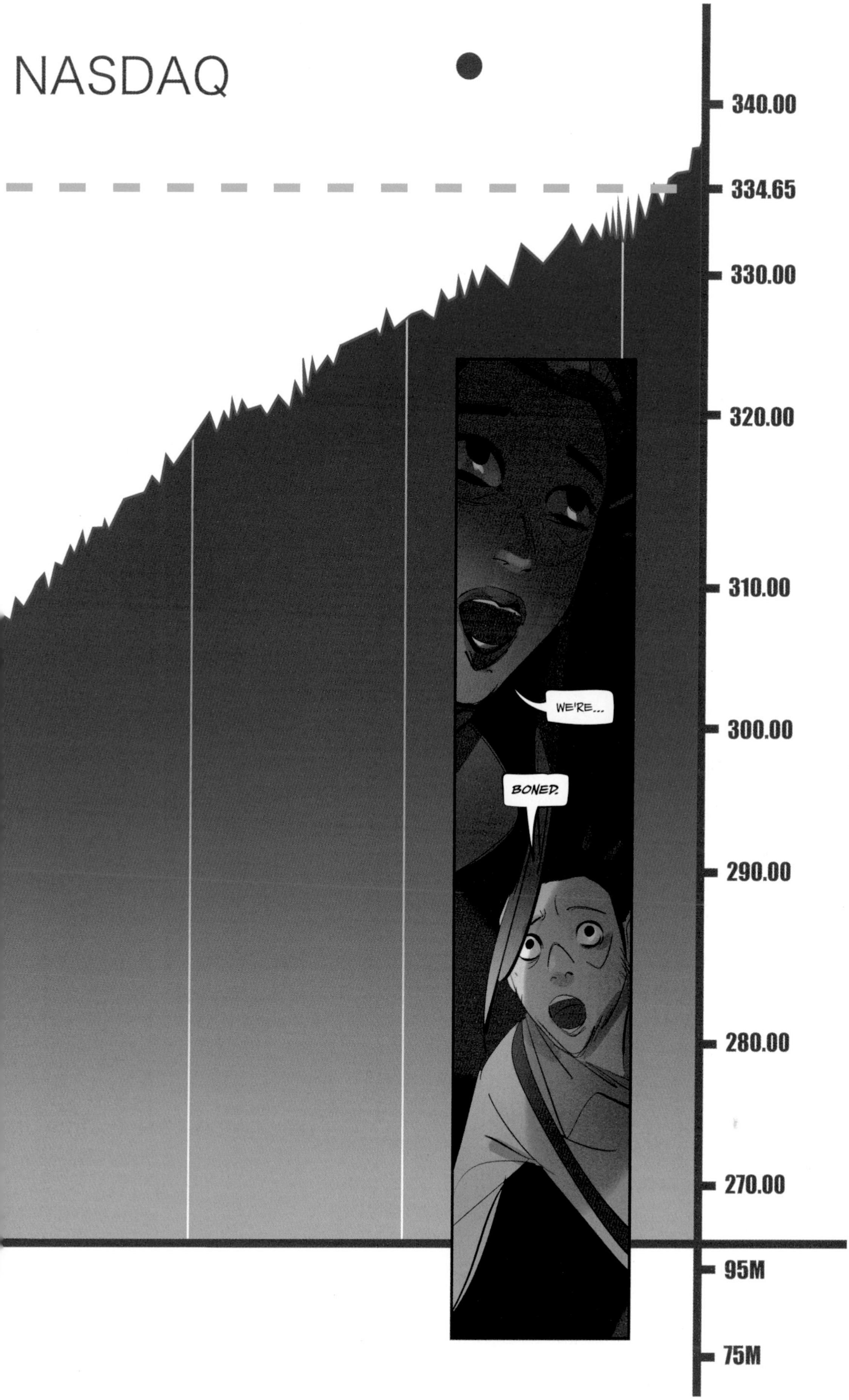
NASDAQ
340.00
334.65
330.00
320.00
310.00
300.00
290.00
280.00
270.00
95M
75M
WE'RE...
BONED.

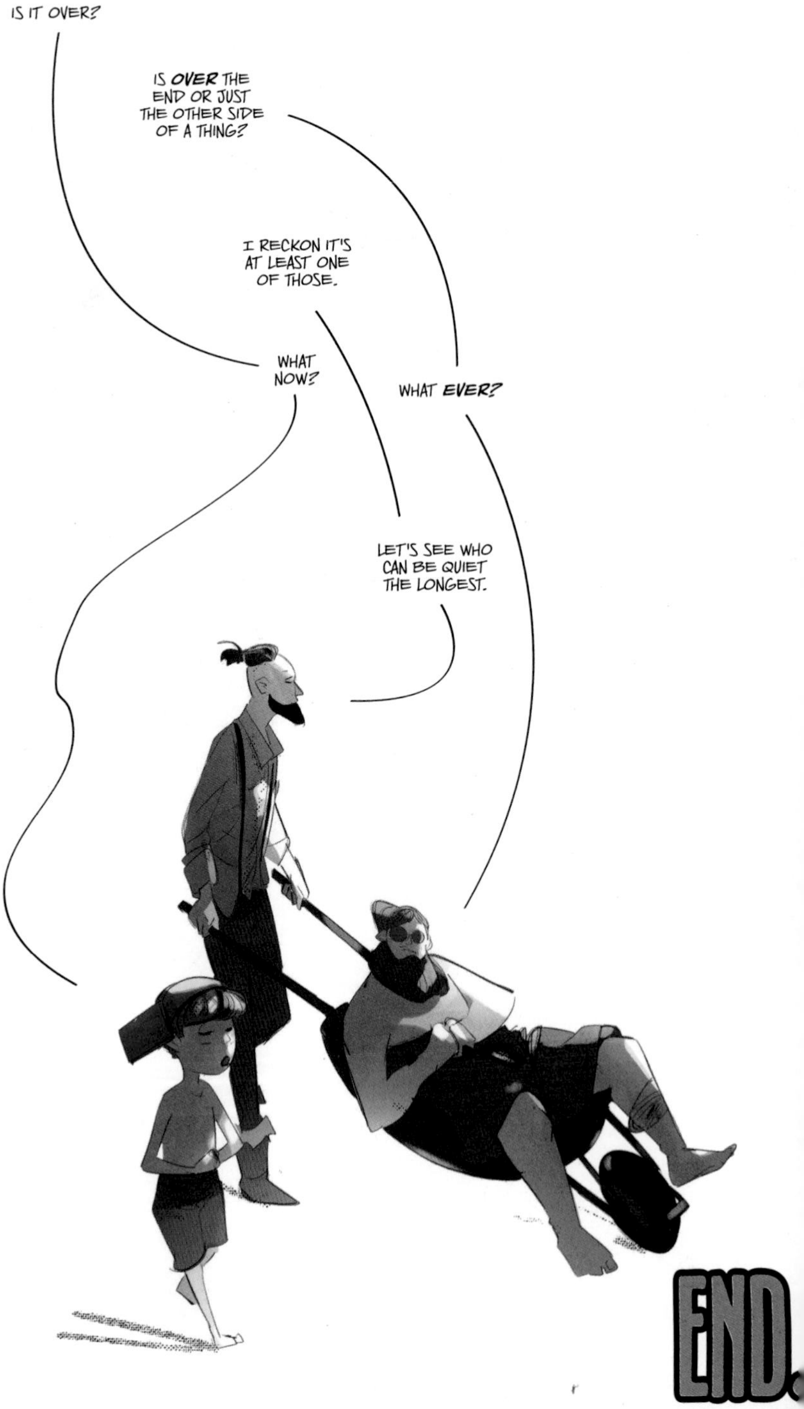
IS IT OVER?
IS **OVER** THE END OR JUST THE OTHER SIDE OF A THING?
I RECKON IT'S AT LEAST ONE OF THOSE.
WHAT NOW?
WHAT **EVER?**
LET'S SEE WHO CAN BE QUIET THE LONGEST.
END.

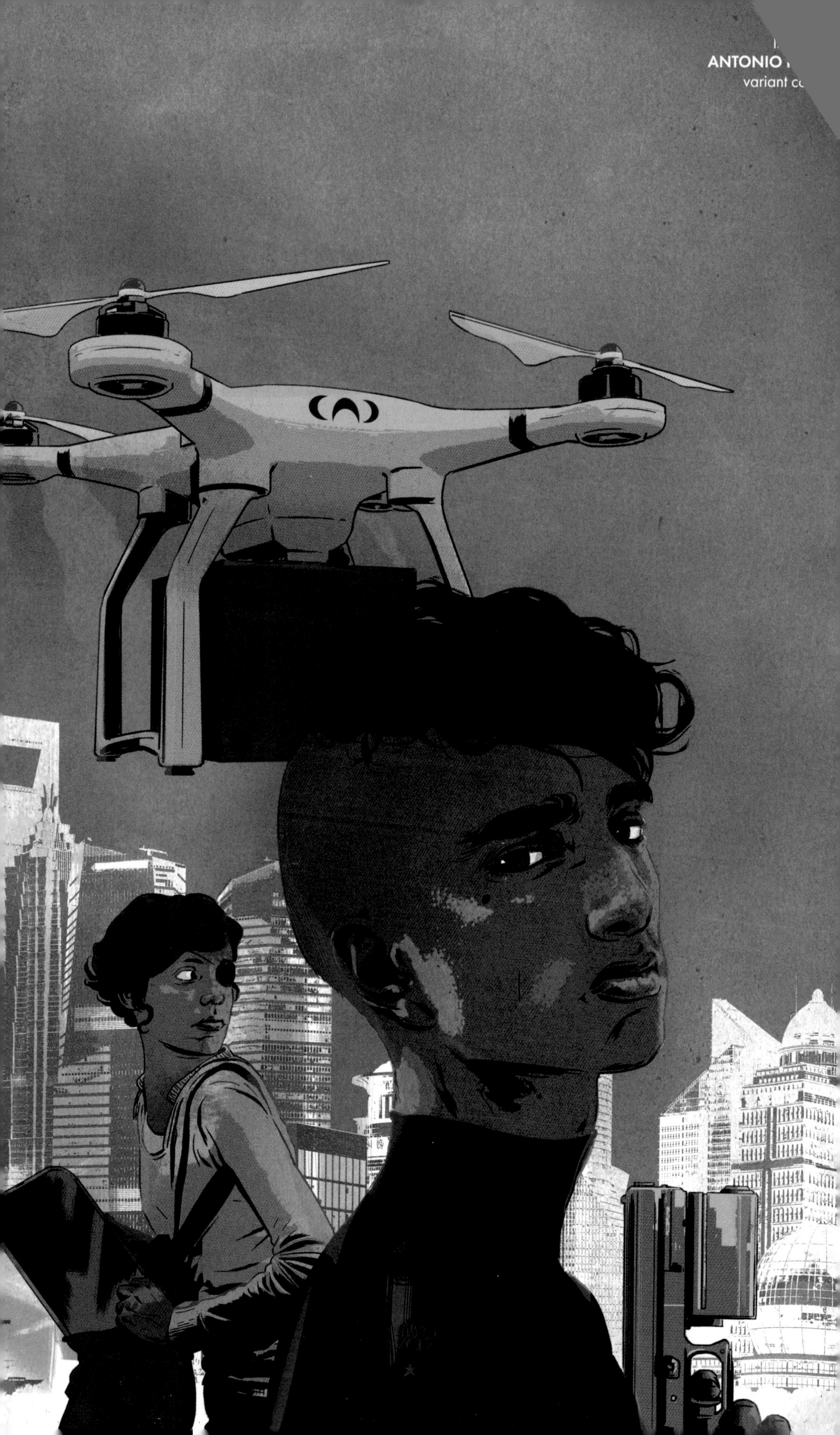
ANTONIO
variant

PLIFTERS WILL BE LIQUIDATED

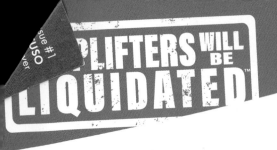

An interview with artist
STEFANO SIMEONE

ELASTIC HOLSTER
GUN
TORCH
TASER
NUSSBAUM

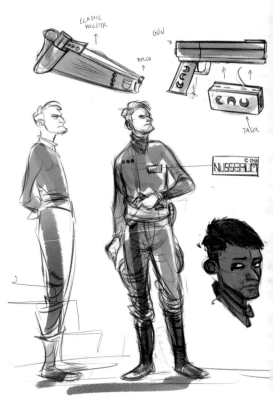

AfterShock Comics: **How do you approach character design usually? Did you do anything different for SHOPLIFTERS?**

Stefano Simeone: Usually, first of all, I try to know more about the story we're going to tell. I think in comics the visual style must serve the narration, so I try to understand the general mood, the atmosphere, the role of each character and how they act with others.

All this previous work helps me a lot in the development. I always use colors in my sketches from the very first time, so in the meantime I start studying the palette. In SHOPLIFTERS, the main challenge for me was that we had a lot of characters--everyone very different--and they had to act together and fit in two totally different worlds.

So, I made Nussbaum funny. He's tired and determined, not the handsome guy we expect, but someone who can make us feel safe. I also wanted to add some kind of nostalgic filter. In SHOPLIFTERS, I started sketching random people, some evil guys, then the main characters. This approach helped me to define the direction we want to keep.

ASC: **How do you approach sequential storytelling?**

S.S: Ah, that's a question that would deserve a long answer.

Let's just say for me the center must be the storytelling. If you draw something just to show you can do a correct anatomy or perspective, but this don't serve what the story needs, you're not doing comics.

When I get a script, first of all, I try to understand the proper shots of this kind of story, so I try to focus on what are the most difficult transitions and how to "resolve" them.

Patrick has been very helpful in this; we had ***a lot*** of characters and environments, but the cuts between the pages made all this very fluid, so most of the times I did exactly what was written.

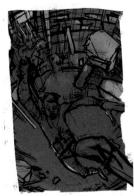

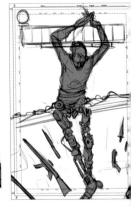

Then, I start layouts. My layouts are quite defined, even in colors. In this way, I can study directly perspectives, shots and most of all the poses of the characters (that usually takes me so much time, so I learned to have the job done first). I look at the layout of the pages and try to not make them too similar, so sometimes, when a scene fits, I do vertical panels, or for example in an action page something crooked.

Anyway, I try to keep a regular layout most of the time, because I usually put a lot of perspective in the panels, so I think having both would not help the reader.

ASC: **Does your work as a colorist impact when you start thinking about colors as a storytelling device?**

S.S: I think in colors, even if I'm only doing black and white art. I just can't think in another way, ahah!
I think I've recently understood how to color my art properly,

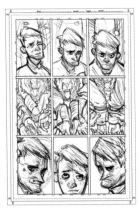

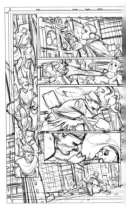

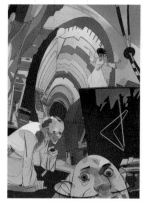

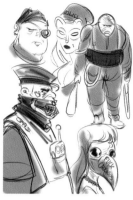

at color style fits, how I must ink and what I can add directly in ors. Most of the times I do this kind of work at the same time. a matter of equilibrium, you know, if you put too much in the s, the color will not be so relevant, but if you draw something h poor ink lines, the color will be weird on it!

main difference between coloring another artist is that in that se, I try to respect his work, so every line he made is still com-tely visible in colors. When I work on my pages, I cover a lot of es in order to give more atmosphere, or I make very dark colors sually use few blacks when inking) so my blacks and shadows in colors.

C: What were some of your inspirations for developing the rld of SHOPLIFTERS?

: I always try to put in a new project the things I like to draw. he case of SHOPLIFTERS, that was perfect, because I like a lot work on dirty environments, post-apocalyptic cities, landfills. you can see, the underground of SHOPLIFTERS was perfect for se kinds of environments.

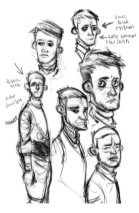

lso love a clear design. If you ask me to draw some soldier, I'll bably give to you something unexpected, rather than some-ng stereotypical. And, in SHOPLIFTERS, that was Caucasus, so most fun for me was to see how these two things I like would together.

LEFT HANDED
LOW MOUTH

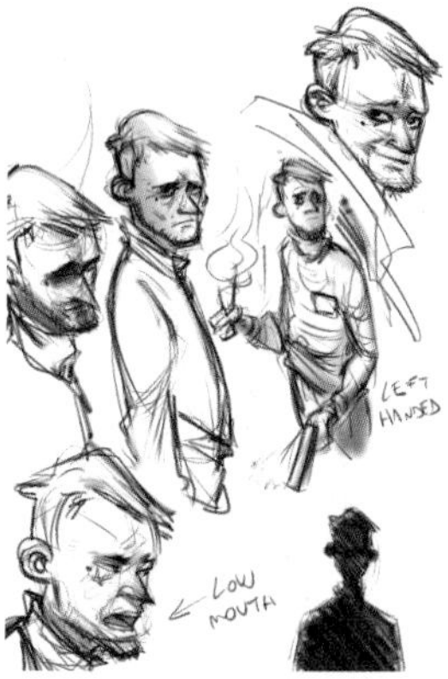

C: The "upstairs" of the store and the "downstairs" of city beneath are two very different locations—how did u approach designing them so they felt different, but still longed to the same world?

: I made two kind of worlds that I like, but the action between se so different environments made me think a lot. I "solved" problem with the colors. So, I made a restricted palette, with rm colors only in a dangerous situation or somewhere in the wnstairs.

C: What was your favorite scene to draw? Why?

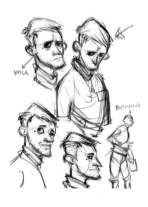

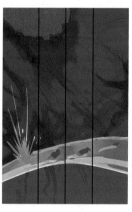

: I think one of my favorite sequences is when, in issue four, ymond and the kid jump off in the water. Those pages gave me opportunity to play in my own way with the panels, and I tried make the water "act" like a character with the same importance Raymond and the kid.

MOLE

C: Any scenes or pages where you wanted to yell at Pat-for making you draw?

: :P

rick, are you really telling me you didn't hear me when I was ing at you while drawing the very final sequence? When Nuss-um tries to reach the surface, followed by a lot of characters? t was very hard, Patrick, you should have heard, even if I live Rome!

C: Who is your favorite character? Why?

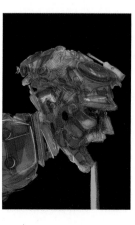

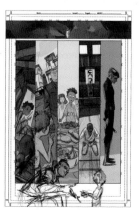

: Every SHOPLIFTERS character is so real, and acts with under-ndable feelings. Patrick is so good in this kind of work on the racters, so my first answer is everyone. Even the characters that in two pages are complicated! One of my favorites is Bryce--I k she's a real bad and complex character, she has feelings doubts but, for whatever reason, she often makes the wrong ice.

ABOUT THE CREATORS OF

SHOPLIFTERS WILL BE LIQUIDATED™

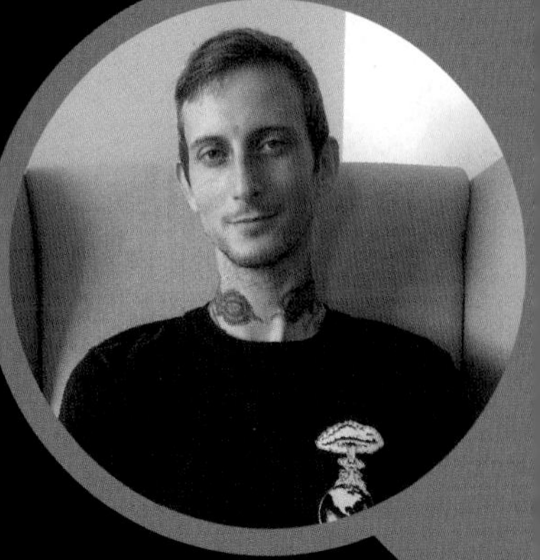

PATRICK KINDLON

writer

@PatrickKindlon

Patrick Kindlon slithered into comics with self-published work before breaking through with the teenage fugitive series *We Can Never Go Home*. Co-written with Matthew Rosenberg and published by Black Mask, it led to further opportunities including the well-regarded horror series *There's Nothing There*, and the post-apocalyptic action/adventure title *Survival Fetish*. Kindlon's chief influences are British guys who knew how to tell stories in 8 pages, and Sergio Aragonés. He's drawn to edgy, dislikable characters, probably because he feels some kinship.

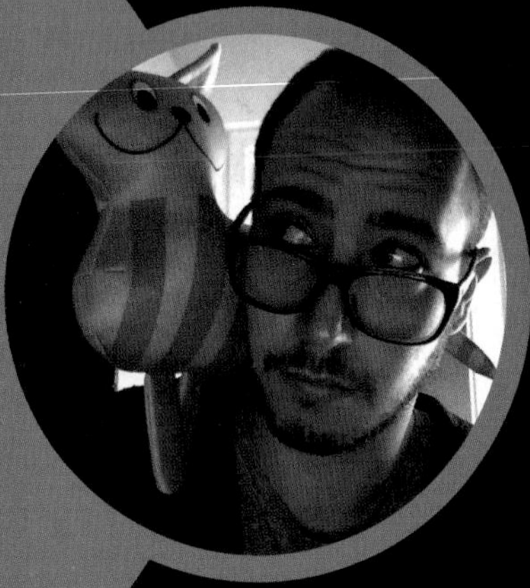

STEFANO SIMEONE

artist

@stefano_simeone

An Italian-born comic book artist and illustrator, Stefano has published four award-winning graphic novels in Italy for Tunué and Bao Publishing. He has also drawn *Cars 3*, *Rogue One: A Star Wars Story*, and *Star Wars: The Last Jedi* comics for Disney and LucasFilm. Stefano has also worked for a number of comic book publishers, including IDW, Image Comics, Boom! Studios and Archaia.

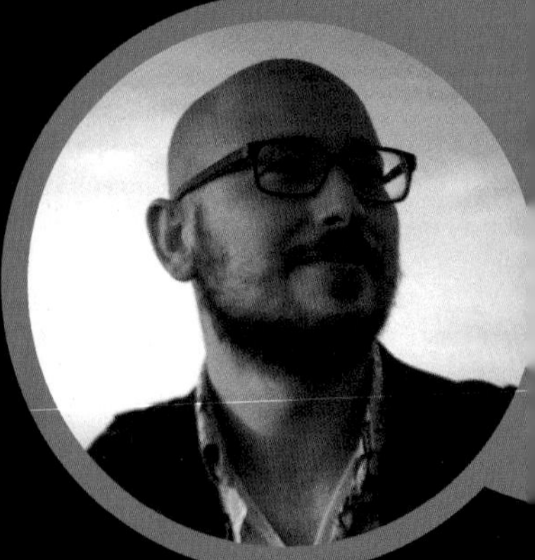

HASSAN OTSMANE-ELHAOU

letterer

@HassanOE

Hassan Otsmane-Elhaou is a writer, editor and letterer. He's lettered comics like *Shanghai Red, Peter Cannon, Red Sonja, Lone Ranger* and more. He's also the editor behind the Eisner-winning publication, *PanelxPanel*, and is the host of the Strip Panel Naked YouTube series. You can usually find him explaining that comics are totally a real job to his parents.